The Sentence of the Court

FOURTH EDITION

CONTENTS

D0267302

---

[1] Reproduced by kind permission of the Magistrates' Association

The Author and Editor

Michael Watkins is Director of Legal Services and Justices' Clerk for Warwickshire. He has contributed to training programmes for magistrates for the Judicial Studies Board and at the Universities of Birmingham and Cambridge. He is a former member of the Executive Committee of the Magistrates' Training Forum. He is a solicitor, a member of the Justices' Clerks' Society's Criminal Law Network and an original co-author of *Introduction to the Youth Court*. He is a member of the Editorial Board for the *Magistrates Bench Handbook*.

Bryan Gibson is Editor-in Chief at Waterside Press (which he founded in 1989). His own works include *Introduction to the Magistrates' Court* (1989, 1995, 1999, 2002), *Introduction to the Criminal Justice Process* (1995, 2002) (with Paul Cavadino/David Faulkner) and the *Waterside A to Z of Criminal Justice* (2003) (forthcoming). He is a barrister and a former Clerk to the Justices who served on the council of the Justices' Clerks' Society, as legal adviser to the Magistrates' Association Sentencing of Offenders Committee and co-editor of the weekly journal *Justice of the Peace*.

Acknowledgment The author and editor acknowledge the work of Anthony Jeffries and Winston Gordon, co-authors over a number of years of previous editions of this work, together with the assistance of Andy Wesson and other individuals who have contributed with information, advice and materials and are grateful to them for this.

The Sentence of the Court

AN OUTLINE OF THE LAW AND PRACTICE OF
SENTENCING IN MAGISTRATES' COURTS

Michael Watkins

Foreword by
Lord Woolf of Barnes, Lord Chief Justice

Edited by Bryan Gibson

Under the auspices of the Justices' Clerks' Society

FOURTH EDITION

WATERSIDE PRESS
WINCHESTER

The Sentence of the Court
FOURTH EDITION

Published 2003 by
WATERSIDE PRESS
Domum Road
Winchester SO23 9NN

Telephone 01962 855567 **Fax** 01962 855567
E-mail enquiries@watersidepress.co.uk
Website and Online Catalogue www.watersidepress.co.uk

ISBN 1 904380 05 0
First edition (1995) 1 872 870 25 2
Second edition (1998) 1 872 870 64 3
Third edition (2000) 1 872 870 88 0
Third edition revised reprint (2002) 1 904380 01 8

Catalogue-In-Publication Data A catalogue record is available from the British Library

Printing Antony Rowe Ltd, Chippenham

Important preliminary notes

- *Further advice* The information contained in *The Sentence of the Court* cannot replace legal/judicial advice, which should be sought *in all but the most straightforward cases:* see, particularly, *Chapter 12.*

- *The 'helping hand' symbol* Within the text, the helping hand symbol (▢♨) serves to indicate complex areas of law where magistrates should proceed with extra caution and seek further explanation/advice locally.

- *Adult court* The Sentence of the Court deals with *adult* offenders, i.e. those aged 18 years and over. For outline details of the position in relation to people below the age of 18 see *Appendix F.*

Foreword to the Second Edition

I am delighted to have been asked at the start of my term of office to provide this short Foreword. I have always been an enthusiastic supporter of the magistracy; perhaps influenced by the fact that my wife has been a magistrate longer than I have been a judge. However, the manner in which magistrates perform their onerous responsibilities is now more closely scrutinised than ever before. One area where they have been criticised in the past is in relation to sentencing. It is said that there are disturbing inconsistencies.

No two cases are identical and therefore there should be room to take into account the particular circumstances of the offence and the offender when sentencing. There is however a need for guidance and information as to the range of disposals which are available and when they are appropriate. In addition from October 2000 there will be the need to take into account the relevant provisions of the Human Rights Act 1998. In a clear but compact format this handbook provides magistrates with the guidance and information they need. It should be widely available. I commend this new edition to all those who are involved in magistrates' courts.

Woolf CJ

Aims and Objectives

The Sentence of the Court was compiled under the auspices of the Justices' Clerks' Society and takes account of extensive experience in the training of magistrates. The aims are:

- to provide a companion for new magistrates as they undertake their basic training and come new to the task of sentencing

- to assist trainers by allowing them to concentrate on imparting skills necessary for making informed, balanced and structured sentence decisions—in the knowledge that background material can be found in the handbook

- to provide an accessible reference point for magistrates generally

- to inform other court users and students about how sentence decisions are approached in magistrates' courts; and

- to produce a lucid account, avoiding jargon and complexity. Statutory and other references—the province of court legal/judicial advisers and other lawyers—are not reproduced unless particularly significant or where they are in everyday use.

CHAPTER 1

Introduction

Upwards of 1.5 million offenders are sentenced each year by the criminal courts of England and Wales. Virtually all prosecutions start out in the magistrates' court—ranging from those for the simplest of offences to those for the most serious and complex. Over 95 per cent are dealt with to their final conclusion by magistrates, by acquittal or conviction and sentence. Conviction stems from a plea of 'guilty' or a finding of guilt by the court where someone has pleaded 'not guilty'. In this latter instance, there is a trial when the court listens to the witnesses and considers all the evidence before arriving at a verdict. The remaining three per cent or so of offenders are sentenced by the Crown Court after being sent there by the magistrates: for trial by jury; for sentence; or to be dealt with: *Chapter 3*.

JURISDICTION[1]

Maximum sentencing powers are set by Act of Parliament. Jurisdiction to deal with cases and, in many instances, the maximum sentence available depends on the legal status of the offence. There are two main classifications (the first divided into two sub-categories):

Indictable offences

(i) Indictable only
Purely indictable offences can be dealt with only by the Crown Court. Examples are: murder (which carries a mandatory life-sentence), manslaughter, rape, robbery, blackmail and wounding with intent to do grievous bodily harm. These offences are brought before a magistrates' court at the very outset, but must then be sent to the Crown Court to be dealt with by a judge and, if contested, a jury. Indictable only matters are thus sent straight from the magistrates' court to the Crown Court, which deals with all future stages of the case.

(ii) Either way offences
Either way offences can be tried by magistrates ('summarily') or the Crown Court ('on indictment'). Everyday examples of either way offences are: theft, criminal damage, assault occasioning actual bodily harm, lesser drugs offences and burglary (provided this last offence is not 'aggravated', e.g. involves use of a weapon—when it is indictable only).[2]

---

1 The sentencing framework and the structure of the courts have been under review. For an outline of proposals in the Criminal Justice Bill and the Courts Bill (both 2002) see the end of *Chapter 4*.
2 Note also that special rules apply to criminal damage: *Chapter 3*.

The decision about venue for trial and/or sentence is outlined in *Chapter 3*. Where either way cases are heard by magistrates their powers are generally limited to six months imprisonment and/or a fine of £5,000 per offence—plus any ancillary orders that are appropriate (such as compensation or disqualification). Sentences of imprisonment may be ordered to be served concurrently to one another, or—where magistrates sentence to imprisonment in respect of two or more offences and at least two of these are either way offences—it is possible, subject to certain general sentencing considerations, to impose consecutive sentences of up to 12 months in aggregate (even if made up in part from imprisonment for summary matters): see further *Chapter 4* and 📖✍.

The Crown Court usually has power to pass a longer sentence for an either way offence than the magistrates' court does (e.g. theft: up to seven years; criminal damage: up to ten years). Whenever magistrates are in a position to sentence for an either way offence there is power to commit to the Crown Court for sentence if they feel that the greater sentencing powers of the Crown Court should be invoked: *Chapter 3*.

Summary offences

In the normal course of events, summary offences can only be tried, and sentences for them can only be passed, by a magistrates' court. Examples of purely summary offences are: most road traffic offences (*Chapter 8*), the less serious public order offences, having 'no television licence' and contravening local bye-laws. The magistrates deal with the entire case: taking a plea, deciding upon guilt or innocence and—in the event of conviction—the sentence. Only in limited circumstances can summary offences be sent to the Crown Court for trial or sentence (e.g. where, in certain circumstances, the summary matter is interwoven with other matters which can be sent to the Crown Court for trial or sentence).

The maximum sentence for a summary offence is fixed by the statute which creates the offence, usually by reference to one of five levels of maximum fine (*Chapter 4*) and in some instances imprisonment of one, two, three or six months.

BACKGROUND TO CURRENT PRACTICE

The Criminal Justice Act 1991[3] made significant changes to the way in which the sentencing of offenders is approached and the criteria set out in the 1991 Act became the framework for sentencing practice. An underlying aim was to ensure—generally speaking—that sentences are proportionate to the seriousness of the offence or offences of which an offender stands convicted. The 1991 Act used the term 'commensurate' to describe such sentences—which became known as the 'just deserts' or 'proportionate' approach. Principal features of the Act (which has been amended in significant respects since 1991) were:

---

[3] The main sentencing provisions are now consolidated in the Powers of Criminal Courts (Sentencing) Act 2000. Proposals contained in the Criminal Justice Bill (2002) are outlined in *Chapter 4*.

A framework for sentencing

A legal framework within which there are statutory criteria for the use of fines, community sentences and custody. The facts of each case—i.e. information about the individual offence—must be considered alongside these criteria. The framework is fully explained in *Chapter 4*, which identifies four distinct levels of sentence:

- **discharges** (absolute and conditional)
- **fines**
- **community sentences** (of which there are eight kinds); and
- **custody.**

When passing sentence, a court must decide upon:

- the appropriate level of sentence within the framework based on the seriousness of the offence; and
- the extent of the chosen sentence within that level, again normally based on the seriousness of the offence (e.g. the *size* of a fine, the total *number of hours* in a community punishment order, the *length* of a prison sentence).

Seriousness

The 1991 Act made the seriousness of the offence itself the main initial focus of sentence decision-making. Assessing seriousness involves:

- forming a view about the general level of seriousness for offences of the type concerned. To bring about consistency of approach, many benches follow the *Magistrates' Court Sentencing Guidelines*. These are endorsed by the Lord Chancellor and represent the collective suggestions of a number of bodies within the Courts Service (see *Appendix C* of this handbook where they are reproduced).[4] The Crime and Disorder Act 1998 established a Sentencing Advisory Panel (whose work, e.g. featured heavily in the case of *R v. McInerney* (2002) in which the Lord Chief Justice gave advice in December 2002 on sentencing for domestic burglary (see *Chapter 4*)). The panel can liaise with the Court of Appeal (Criminal Division) with respect to any possible sentencing guidelines which that court might issue;
- then looking at the facts of the individual offence and considering
  — aggravating factors relating to and present in the offence itself (i.e. which make the offence more serious than other offences of its type); and, correspondingly,
  — any mitigating factors (which make it less so).

For examples of general seriousness factors see *Chapter 3*. An offence committed while the offender is on bail or which is 'racially aggravated' or involves

---

[4] Current version 2000. The association has also published guidance on fining companies for environmental health and safety offences, *Costing the Earth: Guidance for Sentencers* (2002). The *Magistrates' Courts Sentencing Guidelines* are being revised for publication later in 2003. The revised version will appear at the Magistrates' Association web-site: www.magistrates-association.org.uk

'religious aggravation' *must,* by law, be treated as more serious by virtue of that very fact.

Personal factors and seriousness
The *personal circumstances* of the offender may, on occasions, affect a court's view of the seriousness of the offence, but are more normally taken into account later in the sentencing process or as part of the offender's personal (or 'offender') mitigation (page 37). The normal steps are summarised in *A Step-by-Step Guide to Sentencing* on pages 82-3.

Fines
The 1991 Act introduced a short-lived system of 'unit fines' under which courts related the seriousness of an offence to a number of units then multiplied these by the offender's 'disposable weekly income'. The Criminal Justice Act 1993 substituted a more flexible arrangement within which a fine must reflect the seriousness of the offence and the offender's financial circumstances. A fine can be increased or decreased according to the offender's individual financial circumstances, and the court can order the offender to provide details to the court of his or her finances (a 'financial circumstances order'). Courts must take such information into account when available: see, generally, *Chapter 4*. The *Magistrates' Court Sentencing Guidelines* (see *Appendix C*) suggest a structured method of balancing the seriousness of the offence and the offender's financial circumstances, i.e. by using bands of income.

Community sentences
The description 'community sentence' is an all-embracing term for the eight types of adult community order discussed in *Chapter 4* of this work, i.e.:

- **community rehabilitation order** (either with or without added requirements)[5]
- **community punishment order**[6]
- **community punishment and rehabilitation order**[7]
- **attendance centre order** (under 21 years of age only, although the order can be used for fine default up to and including 24 years)
- **curfew order**
- **drug treatment and testing order**
- **drug abstinence order** (where formally available locally); and
- **exclusion order** (where formally available locally).

All these community orders are *sentences* in their own right whereas before 1991 it was commonplace for the more severe forms of community order to be described as 'alternatives to custody'. Although many people thought the 1991 Act had done away with this idea, it seems it may well have survived, or at least re-emerged, in a slightly different guise. This is because although the court's initial assessment is that the offence itself warrants custody, this may be followed

---

[5] Formerly the probation order.
[6] Formerly the community service order.
[7] Formerly the combination order.

by a decision that there are reasons, based on the offender's personal circumstances, for imposing a community order instead.[8]

The 'serious enough' test

A threshold was created whereby an offence must be 'serious enough' to merit a community sentence before one or more of the available community orders can be used—usually called the 'serious enough' test.

Restriction on liberty

The 1991 Act established a new impetus in favour of community-based sentences, which were intended to restrict the liberty of the offender without resort to a custodial sentence. The restriction on liberty created by a community order must be commensurate with the seriousness of the offence. Thus, e.g. a community rehabilitation order with a requirement that the offender attend at a probation centre and take part in a programme—intended to confront, say, his or her offending behaviour, the reasons behind it and work out strategies for change—restricts liberty to the extent that whilst attending the centre the offender is not free to do other things—whilst the demands of the programme itself (which may involve substantial changes in the offender's lifestyle) cannot be discounted. Even a 'standard' community rehabilitation order will usually have accredited programme content and make considerable demands on the time and energies of the offender. Similarly, a community punishment order restricts liberty whilst the offender is doing unpaid community work.

Suitability

When passing a community sentence, the court must select the order (or orders) that is (or are) most suitable for the particular offender. Suitability thus has to be balanced with the restriction on liberty demanded by the seriousness of the offence.

Cumulative orders

The 1991 Act made it possible, in principle, for community orders to be made cumulatively—i.e. in addition to one another—provided that the seriousness of the offence justifies this. Great care must be exercised in relation to cumulative orders so that the overall sentence does not become *disproportionate*. There may also be technical or practical limitations and magistrates should seek advice if considering this course of action 📖✋. A community rehabilitation order (CRO) and a community punishment order (CPO) can only be combined in a community punishment and rehabilitation order (CPRO): see *Chapter 4*. Opinions differ about whether a fine may also be added to a community order in relation to a single offence 📖✋.

Custody

At the very top of the sentencing framework is custody. For adult offenders, custody means:

---

[8] One effect is that a later decision, on breach of the community order, to re-sentence for the original offence could be based on the initial assessment as to seriousness and not necessarily on 'wilful and persistent' failure to comply: *Chapter 4* 📖✋.

- imprisonment in the case of an offender aged 21 or over
- detention in a young offender institution (YOI) in the case of someone aged 18-20 years inclusive.

The 1991 Act introduced three initial bases for custody. The first of these is, by far, the one most commonly applied in the magistrates' court:

- *The 'so serious' test*
  In practice, custody is reserved primarily for situations where the offence is of such a level of seriousness that all other types of sentence are ruled out. The threshold test for custody requires the court to be of the opinion that the offence is so serious that *only* such a sentence can be justified—usually called the 'so serious' test.

- *The 'protection of the public' test*
  In relation to custodial sentences for certain sexual or violent offences (page 74), the 1991 Act also introduced, alongside the generally applicable so serious test described above, an alternative test based upon the need to protect the public from serious harm from the offender in question. This may justify a custodial sentence irrespective of the seriousness of the offence. It may also justify a longer sentence (within the legal maximum). Where the protection of the public from serious harm *is* in the court's mind, there will often be sound reasons to consider committing to the Crown Court for sentence.

- *Custody on refusal of a community sentence*
  Custody can sometimes be used even though neither the 'so serious' test nor the 'protection of the public' test is satisfied. This is where a community sentence is proposed by the court and the offender refuses to consent to certain specific requirements in it. However, this only applies where consent is a legal pre-requisite. The Crime (Sentences) Act 1997 significantly reduced the circumstances where consent to a community order is required: see, generally, under *Community Sentences* in *Chapter 4* and 📖✋.

Custody can also be used (where the offence itself is imprisonable) on re-sentencing for the original offence on breach of a community sentence where an offender wilfully and persistently fails to comply with that community sentence after it has been made; or where it was imposed as an alternative to custody. The above points are expanded on in *Chapter 4*.

Suspended sentences

Once imprisonment has been decided upon—but not before—it can be suspended for one to two years. There must be 'exceptional circumstances' to justify the suspension: *Chapter 4*. (Note that detention in a young offender institution *cannot* be suspended.)

Reasons for decisions

The 1991 Act (and subsequent legislation)[9] has added to the situations in which magistrates are obliged to announce reasons for sentence-related decisions and these are noted at appropriate points in the following chapters. Judicial decisions must always be based on sound reasons, whether needing to be announced under specific statutory provision or otherwise. This is why a structured approach to decision-making—as recommended in later chapters and by the Judicial Studies Board (see e.g. the *Step-by-Step Approach to Sentencing* at pages 82-3)—is advisable. It ensures that all relevant matters are weighed and considered (and that irrelevant matters are excluded), so that sound reasons should flow directly from the decision-making process. The fair trials provisions of Article 6 of the European Convention On Human Rights (see *Chapter 2* of this handbook) also have the effect of requiring most decisions of magistrates' courts to be accompanied by, to some degree or another, a public statement of the reasons for the decision in question 📖✋.

Early release

The 1991 Act introduced a new scheme of early release from prison (and from detention in a young offender institution)—one purpose being to create greater certainty about the proportion of time actually served under a custodial sentence. These provisions are complex and have been subject to subsequent amendment 📖✋. Magistrates acquired, and to some extent retain, important responsibilities to deal with breaches of licence and to return offenders to prison if they commit a fresh imprisonable offence whilst on release: see *Chapter 10* for further information on these provisions in their altered form.

Enforcement

A feature of the 1991 Act was an improvement in the powers and procedures concerning the enforcement of sentences. The powers have since been further enhanced so that if it is proved that the offender has failed without reasonable excuse to comply with any requirements of a relevant community order, the court may, e.g. fine him or her up to £1,000 or re-sentence for the original offence(s). The court must take into account the extent of any compliance, but if the breach was 'wilful and persistent', the court may impose a custodial sentence. As already indicated, the early release provisions (above) sometimes allow magistrates to send or to return offenders to custody.

'Section 95'

Sentencers have traditionally maintained that a court should not be prevented from passing a given sentence merely because of its cost or the availability of prison places. However this approach appears to have been qualified by modern-day statements of the Lord Chief Justice in the light of prison overcrowding and sentencing for domestic burglary: see *Chapter 4*. Section 95 Criminal Justice Act 1991 places a duty on the Home Secretary to inform sentencers of the 'financial implications of their decisions'. It also requires the Home Secretary to provide information to courts and others about discrimination. Relevant publications are usually available locally via court libraries.

---

[9] Now largely consolidated in the 2000 Act: see footnote 3.

APPEALS AND RE-OPENING DECISIONS

People convicted and sentenced by a magistrates' court can appeal to the Crown Court against their conviction, their sentence, or both—or to the High Court on a point of law or concerning the way in which a lower court has exercised its judicial discretion.

In limited but nevertheless fairly common circumstances magistrates can themselves re-open a matter under section 142 Magistrates' Courts Act 1981, thereby often avoiding the need for a costly and time consuming appeal if matters can be appropriately rectified under this provision 📖✋.

To appeal to the Crown Court (currently the most usual method, especially in sentencing matters), the offender must give written notice within 21 days of the imposition of the sentence, setting out the general grounds of appeal. The Crown Court judge will sit with magistrates to hear the appeal. The case of *R v. Swindon Crown Court, ex parte Murray, The Times*, 24 September 1997, confirmed that when hearing an appeal the Crown Court must approach sentencing afresh and form its own independent view. Often, the Crown Court will have later information and the fact that it may impose a different sentence does not of itself suggest that the magistrates were wrong in principle. The sentence imposed by the Crown Court may be less or more severe—but must be limited to magistrates' maximum powers of punishment (and is usually deemed to have been made by the magistrates' court).

In certain, very limited circumstances the Criminal Cases Review Commission can refer a magistrates' court conviction or sentence to the Crown Court for review as if on appeal.

SOME KEY DEVELOPMENTS

Apart from those already mentioned, there have been a number of key developments since 1991, including:

Associated offences
An original restriction whereby a court could consider *only one* associated offence was removed, thereby permitting *all such offences* to be considered when assessing seriousness. Offences are 'associated' offences (📖✋) if they are offences:

- of which the offender has been convicted in the same proceedings; or
- of which the offender has been convicted in other proceedings (by the same or another court) and which have now been referred to the present court for sentencing; or
- offences to be taken into consideration (TICs).

> All references in this handbook to the seriousness of an offence should be understood to mean the seriousness of that offence and any associated offences which are relevant when assessing seriousness

Previous convictions and responses

All previous convictions and responses to earlier sentences can, if considered relevant, be taken into account when assessing the seriousness of the present offence. However, great care is needed when considering how to apply the governing statutory provision (section 151 Powers of Criminal Courts (Sentencing) Act 2000) 📖✌. This is outlined in *Chapter 7*.

The Crime (Sentences) Act 1997 introduced a requirement to impose, in certain circumstances, a *minimum* sentence—based on similar previous convictions. For instance, a third offence of trafficking in Class A drugs will result in a minimum of seven years' custody. Likewise, a third domestic burglary will attract a minimum of three years. In each case the third offence will, if otherwise an either way offence, become triable *only on indictment* and the judge in the Crown Court will, when sentencing, be able to consider whether it would be 'unjust . . . in all the circumstances' to impose custody and at the minimum length. These provisions are often called 'three strikes and you're out' 📖✌.

Pre-sentence reports and specific sentence reports

The 1991 Act introduced the pre-sentence report or 'PSR'. So far as magistrates' courts are concerned, the underlying rule is that a PSR must be obtained before:

- deciding whether an offence is so serious that only a custodial sentence is justified and how long that sentence should be
- deciding, in the case of a violent or sexual offence, whether a custodial sentence is necessary to protect the public from serious harm from the offender or whether a longer sentence should for that reason be passed than is indicated by the seriousness of the offence; or
- making certain community orders (and, in particular, before considering whether they are suitable for an offender).

Although these obligations to obtain a PSR remain, courts can, if they consider it appropriate, as a result of the Criminal Justice and Public Order Act 1994, now deem such a report to be 'unnecessary'. Pre-sentence reports are governed by a 'National Standard'. Because of their key significance PSRs are the subject matter of *Chapter 9*.

At the end of the 1990s there emerged the concept of the specific sentence report (SSR), a limited form of PSR, usually prepared on the day of hearing. Basically, the SSR is aimed at early consideration of the possibility of a short CPO or short CRO with no additional requirements (other than basic, accredited programmes)—and without the need for an adjournment for a full PSR with the delay and extra work that this connotes: see *Chapter 9*.

Credit for a guilty plea

It had long been the practice in the Crown Court, and in those criminal courts above it, to consider reducing a sentence in appropriate cases where the defendant had entered a timely guilty plea. This practice had started to find its way into magistrates' courts, although the scope for substantial reduction was probably more limited because of the different types of cases dealt with by magistrates. The practice was put on a statutory footing for all criminal courts by the Criminal Justice and Public Order Act 1994. Thus courts are now required to consider the possibility of giving credit for a guilty plea based on both:

- the stage in the proceedings at which the guilty plea occurred; and
- the circumstances in which it was entered.

The pre-1994 case law is still pertinent when considering these statutory provisions. Thus credit will reflect factors such as: true remorse and contrition; saving witnesses the ordeal of giving evidence (especially in sexual cases, although the 'protection of the public' consideration will also apply: see above); assisting the police with their enquiries, and e.g. helping to recover stolen goods; and saving public funds and resources by pleading guilty.

Many courts now, following case law, adopt a graded approach to giving credit for a guilty plea. The *Magistrates' Court Sentencing Guidelines* (see earlier in the chapter) recognise this practice. There might be 'no credit at all' where the offender has been caught red-handed committing a serious offence and has no real option but to plead guilty (a case more often perhaps found in the Crown Court). At the maximum the credit could be as much as one third where the offender has really gone out of his or her way to co-operate and make amends. Most magistrates' courts will give at least some minimum credit for a timely guilty plea just to encourage defendants to reduce the pressures on the criminal justice system.

Where the offence is an either way offence, credit for a guilty plea is one of the factors to be considered when magistrates are deciding whether to sentence an offender themselves or to commit to the Crown Court for sentence: see *Appendix C*.

Where credit *is* given the court must announce that fact. The giving of credit is usually recorded on the court file and in the court register. Many courts now announce the extent of credit actually given or which might have been given had the guilty plea been entered earlier and/or in different circumstances, so as to inform the offender and other people, and also to make matters clearer if there is an appeal.

Credit for a guilty plea is, of itself, unlikely ever to result in the reduction of the level of sentence, e.g. from custody to a community order. Equally, case law suggests that someone who pleads guilty will not usually receive the absolute maximum sentence for that offence. Concerning this entire topic, it wise to take further advice locally 📖✋.

Sex offenders
The Sex Offenders Act 1997 introduced a requirement for offenders convicted of a specified sexual offence to report, e.g. their name (including any alternative names), home address, change of home address and certain absences from home to the local police: see *Chapter 6*.

Harassment
The Protection From Harassment Act 1997 introduced offences of harassment based not directly on intent (the *mens rea* element of an offence) but on the effect of behaviour on the victim—and where that behaviour may not in itself amount to, or even resemble, any criminal offence. The defendant may well in such cases

have to prove the reasonableness of his or her behaviour which, if not having the effect, intentional or otherwise, of harassing someone would not otherwise be questioned by the criminal process. Conviction gives rise to the possibility, in addition to sentence, of a restraining order, breach of which is a criminal offence. The restraining order applies only to criminal harassment cases.[10]

Anti-social behaviour orders

Anti-social behaviour orders (ASBOs) were introduced under the Crime and Disorder Act 1998. As their name suggests, ASBOs are based on anti-social behaviour—which may or may not of itself be criminal. Breach of a civil ASBO is a criminal offence.

Applications for ASBOs are brought by way of a *civil* 'complaint' but, by case law, the criminal standard of proof applies and if the order is later breached they have to be treated as criminal matters due to the potential penalties. Both restraining orders under the 1997 Act (above) and anti-social behaviour orders could be styled 'preventive measures', i.e. they can be used even where no other substantive criminal offence is anticipated. Human rights issues arise, such as Article 6 ('fair trial') and Article 10 ('freedom of expression'): see *Chapter 2*. Applications for civil ASBOs may be increasing as the government has encouraged their use. Care needs to be exercised concerning orders involving a mix of civil and criminal strands 📖✍. Note also that this type of ASBO, i.e. the *civil* version, should be distinguished from what have been termed CRASBOs (or 'criminal ASBOs'), i.e. anti-social behaviour orders made—under yet more recently enacted powers—in criminal proceedings themselves and ancillary to the main sentence: see *Chapter 6, Other Orders of the Court*.

Parenting orders: a note[11]

Parenting orders were introduced by the Crime and Disorder Act 1998 and are designed to encourage parents (or guardians) to accept greater responsibility for their children's behaviour. They offer help and training to the parent to help change the offending behaviour of his or her children and contain a requirement that he or she exercise control over them. They can be made in a wide range of circumstances in the youth court or family proceedings court. They will be seen in the adult court only where a parent is convicted under section 444(1) or 444(1A) Education Act 1996 (offences relating to failure to secure regular attendance of school-age children at school). Section 444(1A) is the more serious version of the offence—where a parent/guardian has known of the non-attendance and failed without reasonable justification to remedy it—and carries imprisonment. On conviction of either such offence the court has a discretion to make a parenting order where this is desirable to prevent further similar offending by the parent:

---

10 For a comprehensive account see *Chapter 7* of *Domestic Violence and Occupation of the Family Home*, Chris Bazell and Bryan Gibson, Waterside Press, 1999.

11 Descriptions of the parenting order are contained in *Introduction to Youth Justice*, Waterside Press, 1999 and *Child Law*, Richard Powell, Waterside Press, 2001. Generally, seek advice, including as to the ways in which a parenting order can arise and the specific obligations placed upon the parent in relation to such an order.

- the order lasts for up to 12 months as specified by the court, during which the parent is required to comply with any requirements imposed to prevent similar offending
- during the first part of the order, for a maximum of three months, the parent must usually attend counselling or guidance sessions not more than once a week
- there is no need for a pre-sentence report (PSR) (*Chapter 9*) (although with the section 444(1A) offence there may often be one in any event) but it is usually necessary to enquire into the effect of any such order on the parent and family as well as on religious beliefs or work or educational commitments
- there is provision for review applications.

Failure to comply with a parenting order is itself a summary offence carrying a maximum fine up to Level 3 on the standard scale (currently £1,000).

Fixed penalties for certain criminal (i.e. 'non-road traffic') offences
The Criminal Justice and Police Act 2001 introduced the ability for the police (including British Transport Police) to issue fixed penalty notices for certain criminal (as opposed to road traffic) offences (as to which see *Chapter 8*). There are presently 12 offences covered by the scheme, ranging from being drunk and disorderly and creating minor public disorder to wasting police time although in 2003 the government signified its intention of further extending this approach to other kinds of 'anti-social behaviour'.[12] The penalty is either £40 or £80 depending on the offence. Payment is made to the court for the area in which the notice was issued, or the individual can ask for a court hearing.

Failure to pay a fixed penalty or ask for a hearing results in the penalty being registered in the offender's home court area with a 50 per cent uplift. On enforcement there are some novel and potentially difficult provisions 📖✋. The provisions were piloted in Essex, Croydon, Rhyl, Llandudno and the West Midlands (where British Transport Police were involved). Courts will need to decide how the level of fixed penalty (which is, of course, not related to the offender's financial circumstances) might bear on the level of fine imposed.

DEVELOPMENTS IN CRIMINAL JUSTICE OVERALL

There have been a number of further important developments in criminal justice as a whole. These include:

- an overriding emphasis on crime prevention and crime reduction
- the creation of a National Probation Service for England and Wales (and the simultaneous renaming of certain community sentences: above and see *Chapter 4*)

---

[12] Alongside a widening of those who issue fixed penalties (although a plan to allow headteachers to do so re parents who fail to secure their children's attendance at school was abandoned).

- greater reliance on electronic monitoring of offenders under court orders and on release from prison under home detention curfew
- stricter enforcement of community orders
- widescale drug testing of people passing through the criminal justice process; and
- a general 'tightening' of the process as a whole through reforms to and within the criminal justice agencies so that prosecutions are brought and sentences implemented in a more structured and accountable way, often involving partnerships between the agencies concerned with service delivery. There is, e.g. a joint Correctional Services Board and Correctional Services Accreditation Panel in relation to prison and probation service work with offenders (and a general move to nationally accredited programmes) and joint police/CPS Criminal Justice Units (CJUs) to deal with prosecutions
- an increasing awareness of the need and responsibility to confront racial and religious intolerance, with consequent new sentencing powers
- a renewed emphasis on reparation and compensating victims of crime. In order to ensure that the victim's voice is heard in court the criminal process now allows a victim personal statement which gives the victim a formal opportunity to say how a crime has affected him or her: *Chapter 5.*

In terms of the language of sentencing, the idea that this occurs within what has been called a 'punishment envelope' was reinforced by alterations to the names of certain community sentences: above and *Chapter 4.*

Justice For All and the Criminal Justice Bill (2002)

The courts are not immune from such changes. Following proposals in the White Paper *Justice For All* (2000) there is currently a Criminal Justice Bill that is well advanced before Parliament. The Bill, when enacted, will make significant changes to the current sentencing arrangements. There is also a Courts Bill (2002) that is likely to make alterations to jurisdiction including the maximum powers of magistrates and certain key procedures. It is likely that these changes will be implemented over a period of time—from 2004 to 2005 (it is anticipated). A note of the main proposals appears at the end of *Chapter 4.*

SENTENCING IN CONTEXT

The following chapters place sentencing as a whole into context including *Chapter 2* which deals, in outline, with *Human Rights and Sentencing. Chapter 3* deals with procedural considerations and general factors which affect all sentencing decisions; whilst *Chapter 4* looks in greater detail at the sentencing framework and the entire range of sentences available. The remaining chapters focus on key aspects of sentencing that are essential to a basic understanding of the topic.

CHAPTER 2

Human Rights and Sentencing

All judicial decision-making—including sentencing—is affected by the Human Rights Act 1998 (HRA) and the European Convention On Human Rights and Fundamental Freedoms ('the Convention'), the latter having been incorporated into English law by the former.[1]

GENERAL DUTIES PLACED ON THE COURT

All 'public authorities' (widely defined and clearly including the court and other criminal justice agencies) must act in accordance with Convention rights (below) and take positive action to promote them. The following are examples of how the Convention impacts:

- there is an obligation, as far as possible, to read and give effect to all UK primary legislation (i.e. Acts of Parliament) in a way which is *compatible* with the Convention and its rights. This may require courts to 'read down' the basic words of legislation to reflect human rights concepts—as occurred in *Sheldrake v. Director of Public Prosecutions* (2003), *The Times*, February 25 where the High Court ruled that the statutory reverse onus of proof placed on a driver alleged to have been in charge of a motor vehicle when over the drink driving limit (i.e. to show that there was no likelihood of his or her driving whilst still over the limit) was not compatible with the Convention. To comply with the Convention the *prosecutor* had to prove that there was such a likelihood, once the defendant claimed there was not. Thus, courts may sometimes need to 'qualify' the apparent language of legislation 📖✥.

- there is a similar obligation to read and give effect to UK secondary legislation (i.e. statutory instruments/delegated legislation which, e.g. create rules and regulations for court procedures or the operation of particular sentencing disposals, and bye-laws) in the same way. There is also here an additional feature. Unlike the position in relation to primary legislation, the court has the ability, if necessary, to decide that Convention rights must take priority over the apparent requirements of the secondary legislation if this cannot otherwise be read so as to give effect to such rights. In effect, courts may have some controlled obligation to disregard secondary legislation if that is the only way to give proper effect to the Convention.[2]

---

[1] For a fuller treatment see *Human Rights and the Courts*, Paul Ashworth *et al*, Waterside Press, 1999.

[2] It is doubly important to seek legal advice as certain secondary legislation, known as 'dependent secondary legislation', can only be 'qualified' on the same basis as primary legislation (as to which see the *Sheldrake* case mentioned in the text): 📖✥.

- new Bills (including sentencing Bills) introduced into Parliament are accompanied by a ministerial statement that they are believed to be compatible with the Convention. Acts passed before the 1998 Act may not be read in this way so readily, but every effort still needs to be made
- there is a specific obligation, under Article 14 of the Convention, not to discriminate in the application of *any* Convention rights. There is as yet, under the Convention, no free-standing right not to suffer discrimination, although all basic rights themselves must be applied in a non-discriminatory manner.
- a defendant who feels that his or her Convention rights have not been protected (or promoted) in the court process will have a relevant judicial remedy. If it is the action (or failure to act) of a court which is called into question then this must be dealt with by way of appeal proceedings. In other cases, there will be an accessible form of potential remedy within existing UK systems
- where a defendant suffers arrest or detention in breach of Convention rights there will always be a specific right of redress even if the court acted in good faith. In the instance of 'good faith' breaches the Crown will usually be ordered to pay any appropriate compensation.

CONVENTION RIGHTS AND SENTENCING

Individual Convention rights are contained in the Articles and Protocols[3] of the Convention.[4] Individual rights may be *absolute* (i.e. they can never be departed from), *limited* (i.e. there are limitations on their extent) or *qualified* (i.e. they can be interfered with in certain circumstances). Sentencers need to be aware of the differing implications of the three types of right 📖✋. The main articles relevant to courts on a day-to-day basis are as follows:

- **Article 3** *Prohibition of torture or inhuman or degrading treatment or punishment* (An absolute right). This could, e.g. extend to the improper handcuffing of even convicted and sentenced defendants (📖✋), or to a recommendation for deportation on sentencing which, if carried out, might expose the defendant in the country of deportation to treatment or punishment excluded by the Convention.

- **Article 4** *Prohibition of slavery or forced or compulsory labour* (A mixture of absolute and limited rights). Sentencers also need to be mindful of the exceptions to this right which include work required to be done in 'the ordinary course of detention' (which appears to have been taken as legitimising both work in prison and work under a community punishment order).

- **Article 5** *Right to liberty and security* (A limited right). This may prove to be of importance when considering both community sentences—where some

---

3 Rights added to the original terms of the Convention.
4 *Chapter 3* of *Human Rights and the Courts* mentioned in footnote 1 looks at each in detail.

degree of restriction of liberty is, by definition, always involved—and custodial sentences. There is a list of exceptions to this right, set out in Article 5 itself.

- **Article 6** *Right to a fair trial* (A mixture of *absolute* and *limited* rights). The concept of a 'fair trial' is wider than simple fairness in assessing guilt or innocence. It pervades the criminal process from the investigation of an offence by the police right through to sentence and release (*Chapter 10*). It is the application and interpretation of this article, in particular, which can 'transpose' civil proceedings into criminal ones. This ensures that rights provided in the Convention—such as the presumption of innocence and to legal representation, legal aid and an interpreter—are not lost by varying applications of 'civil' and 'criminal' definitions across Convention countries insofar as legal proceedings involving penalties are concerned. This issue was considered by the High Court in the case of *R (McCann) v. Crown Court at Manchester* (2001) where it was decided that an application for an anti-social behaviour order is a matter subject to a civil application but the criminal standard of proof.

  Article 6 and reasons for decisions A further result of Article 6 is that reasons need to be given for most decisions of a court (with corresponding explanations at appropriate points), including when sentencing, so that both the defendant and other people may know how and why the court arrived at a particular decision or outcome.

- **Article 7** *No punishment without law* (An *absolute* right). This article guarantees, e.g. that there can be no action without clear legal authority and no retrospective criminality or retrospectively increased penalty.

- **Article 8** *Right to respect for private and family life* (A *qualified* right). Although this right might appear to have no immediate relevance to sentencing, it might for instance need to be borne in mind when drafting requirements in community rehabilitation orders which affect the offender's interaction with his or her family—as it will when making, e.g. curfew orders or enforcing financial orders or when considering bail conditions.

- **Article 9** *Freedom of thought, conscience and religion* (A mixture of *absolute, limited* and *qualified* rights. The right to hold a religious belief is *absolute* whereas the right to manifest it is *limited*). This Article might well be engaged, for instance, in relation to those sentencing outcomes that could interfere with an offender's religious beliefs, irrespective of whether or not the matter is already covered by UK legislation.

- **Article 10** *Freedom of expression* (A *qualified* right). This, again, might well be relevant when, for instance, drafting requirements in community rehabilitation orders or anti-social behaviour orders. A defence to a criminal charge might itself be based on this right, and might or might not succeed: in which latter case the right might affect the way a court viewed the offender's mitigation.

- **Article 11** *Freedom of assembly and association* (A *qualified* right). This right, again, might well be relevant in similar circumstances to those mentioned in relation to Article 10.

- **Article 14** *Prohibition of discrimination in the application of Convention rights* (An *absolute* right). This article has already been noted above. The Judicial Oath taken by all judges and magistrates is explicitly against any form of discrimination.

- **First protocol** *Protection of property* (A *qualified* right). Given that sentencing orders such as fines and forfeiture clearly engage this right, there will often be a balancing exercise between the offender's *prima facie* rights and the public interest in dealing with offences and offenders. There may well also be property issues further down the enforcement process where, e.g. it is sought to enforce fines by the issue of distress warrants to seize the defendant's possessions (which might also impact on private or family life: Article 8 above).

KEY CONCEPTS AND TERMINOLOGY

In applying the various Articles and Protocols it is important to be familiar with other Convention concepts and terms such as:

- *Purposive approach* A need to look at what the Convention is trying to achieve in broad terms, not just the face value of its words.

- *Living instrument* A requirement that the Convention be read as adjusting to contemporary society and not stuck in its original 1950s a time warp.

- *Margin of appreciation* Where *prima facie* rights under the Convention are limited or *qualified* by reference to concepts such as 'public interest' or the needs of a 'democratic society' each Convention country is, in effect, given certain latitude to interpret these terms in accordance with its own culture and democratic development. Rights may manifest themselves in different ways in different Convention countries. Whereas section 2 HRA requires United Kingdom courts to 'take into account', e.g. decisions of the European Court of Human Rights, such decisions will not necessarily provide a precedent for similar fact cases.[5]

- *Proportionality* Where rights are *qualified* there will usually still be a need to apply the qualification in a way which is proportional to the merits of the case. For instance, would it be appropriate to make a curfew order (*prima*

---

[5] This applies even if the 'living instrument' concept does not affect the issue involved.

facie an interference with the right to respect for private and family life under Article 8) where a particular type of offence is by UK law not deemed to warrant imprisonment? Equally, how will it affect the rights of other members of the household?

- *Positive obligation* As noted, not only must public authorities not act in a way which is incompatible with the Convention but an omission to act compatibly where human rights issues are engaged is also prohibited. Sentencers may, on occasion, find themselves having actively to promote Convention rights.

- *Horizontality* Although the immediate effect of the Convention is to control the way in which the state treats those affected by its actions (or failures to act), the concept, e.g. of 'positive obligation' may require courts to consider the possibly conflicting rights of two people such as the offender and the victim, i.e. to work 'horizontally' and not just 'vertically'.

- *Declaration of incompatibility* As noted earlier, all courts, including magistrates' courts, have an obligation as far as possible to read and give effect to UK legislation in a way which is compatible with the Convention. Where this is not possible, primary (but generally not secondary) legislation must be complied with although the High Court and House of Lords in particular may issue a formal 'declaration of incompatibility', which could well invoke a form of fast-track review by the United Kingdom Parliament of the 'offending' primary legislation. Magistrates will at some stage have to face the possibility of sentencing offenders where guilt is based on what appears to be incompatible primary legislation. The dilemma which arises is whether to give say an absolute discharge or whether to sentence as if the incompatibility did not exist.

- *Equality of arms* This will ensure that a defendant is not placed at a procedural disadvantage as against the prosecutor. Although this will more frequently arise in the earlier stages of the case—and in any contested hearing, in particular—there may well be arguments, e.g. that the prosecutor should be ready to disclose anything which will potentially assist the defendant at the sentencing stage.

AN EXTRA NEED FOR LEGAL ADVICE

Issues relating to human rights may often be complex yet everything must be 'in order'. This may involve looking at a record of what an earlier bench decided, so proper records are essential. The need to take advice from the justices' clerk/court legal adviser has never been more important. The manner in which such advice is sought and received is, in itself, a human rights issue under Article 6 ('right to a fair trial'): see *Chapter 12, Judicial Advice*.

CHAPTER 3

General Considerations and Procedures

As outlined in *Chapter 1*, sentencing decisions are made within a statutory framework—the central rule being that a sentence should be commensurate with the seriousness of the offence. The framework, which is currently under review, consists of:

- Four levels of sentence (each explained in *Chapter 4*)
- Statutory criteria whereby, for the greater part, the *seriousness of the offence* determines the level within which the sentence should be fixed—and the extent of the sentence within that level
- Special considerations which attach to most sexual or violent offences, and which may lead to a custodial sentence—or a longer custodial sentence than would be justified simply by the seriousness of the offence—if necessary to *protect the public from serious harm* from the offender; and
- Provisions which require courts to consider relevant information (including, when appropriate, a pre-sentence report (PSR) or specific sentence report (SSR)) and to adopt other procedures when passing sentence.

These items must be set against a wider background to sentencing law and practice that has developed over the years—and within which there are certain 'general objects of sentencing'.

GENERAL OBJECTS OF SENTENCING

There are certain traditionally recognised objects of sentencing for courts to try to achieve:

- punishment/retribution
- reparation (including financial compensation to a victim)
- the protection of the public
- deterrence
- reflecting proper public concern
- rehabilitation; and
- reducing crime and preventing offending and re-offending.

There is also the question of 'disposal': each offence requires a sentence. On occasion, a minor sentence (a nominal fine or absolute discharge) may be appropriate simply to dispose of a matter. Also, the (non-statutory) practice of announcing 'no separate penalty' (NSP) allows a court to deal with lesser matters without increasing the total sentence beyond that appropriate for the most serious offences.

When 'proportionate', 'commensurate' and 'just deserts' principles were invoked by the Criminal Justice Act 1991 (*Chapter 1*) there was uncertainty about whether—or to what extent—traditional sentencing objects had survived. Lord Bingham, the then Lord Chief Justice, made the following points:[1]

Punishment/retribution
It is fundamental to the idea of 'just deserts' that sentences contain an appropriate, i.e. a commensurate, level of punishment.

Reparation
Making reparation, i.e. 'putting something back' by way of actions to benefit the victim or the community is an underlying rationale of community sentences, particularly community punishment orders. The fact, e.g. that an offender has made voluntary reparation may indicate remorse or contrition and thereby, depending on the circumstances, justify some reduction of sentence (see also *Credit for a guilty* plea in *Chapter 1* and below). Compensation is one aspect of reparation and a constant sentencing consideration: see *Chapter 5*.

Protection of the public
Lord Bingham also called this aspect 'incapacitation', i.e. while serving a custodial sentence the offender is unable for the period in question to inflict more offending on the public. Protection of the public has emerged in a clearer, more defined way in the special custody provisions affecting most sexual or violent offences: see *Chapter 4*. In relation to other types of offence, the need to protect the public may be a relevant consideration but will not permit any sentence in excess of what is commensurate with the seriousness of the offence.

Deterrence
In one of the first cases to come before the Court of Appeal following the 1991 Act, the then Lord Chief Justice, Lord Taylor, sought to clarify whether deterrent sentences were consistent with proportionality in sentencing. His conclusions can be summarised as follows:

- custodial sentences in particular are meant to punish *and* deter
- the deterrence will affect both the offender and other people; and
- such a sentence—in having to be commensurate with the seriousness of the offence—had to be commensurate with the punishment and deterrence which the seriousness of the offence required. (*R v Cunningham* (1993) 14 Cr. App. R. (S.) 386)

However, the Court of Appeal made it clear that *increasing* a sentence beyond the length which by those criteria is commensurate with seriousness to make an example of the defendant (often called an 'exemplary sentence') offends the principle of proportionality.

---

[1] In a speech to the Police Foundation: see *Justice of the Peace and Local Government Law*, 150 JPN 700.

Rehabilitation

Rehabilitation is a statutory purpose of a community punishment order (CRO): *Chapter 4*. It is also an underlying rationale of the early release scheme and post-custody supervision (*Chapter 10*).

Reducing crime and preventing offending and re-offending

Considerable emphasis is now being placed on crime reduction and the prevention of offending and re-offending, within prison regimes and community programmes. There are, e.g. nationally accredited CRO programmes (and rapidly developing accreditation in relation to community punishment orders (CPOs) and HM Prison Service programmes). This aspect features prominently in the White Paper, *Justice For All* (2002) and Criminal Justice Bill (2002). Such objectives are a key focus for the Correctional Services Board and Correctional Services Accreditation Panel mentioned towards the end of *Chapter 1*.

THE TOTALITY PRINCIPLE

Where there are several offences, the sentences, in combination, should not be out of all proportion to the nature of the overall offending. This means that when imposing a number of sentences on the same individual at the same time—particularly if they concern the same events—magistrates should review the overall effect and make such downward adjustments as may be appropriate. The principle will often be relevant where someone is charged with large numbers of motoring offences.

STRUCTURED DECISION-MAKING

The Judicial Studies Board (JSB) has encouraged courts to make decisions by reference to a structure represented by way of a chart or sequence of questions. Central to this idea in relation to sentencing is an assessment of the seriousness of the offence—to ensure sentence relates primarily to the offence itself and is proportionate to it. This involves deciding:

- how serious it is in general terms. Some offences (e.g. burglary) are inherently more serious than others (e.g. straightforward theft). This gives a starting point within the sentencing framework; and
- what other, more particular and offence-based factors in the present case, affect the initial assessment of the level of seriousness for this type of offence—often called 'aggravating' and 'mitigating' factors.

A main task for the court is to weigh these latter factors to see whether, and to what extent, the offence is more or less serious than the general run of comparable cases. The *Magistrates' Court Sentencing Guidelines* (see *Appendix C*) begin by asking whether a particular level of sentence is appropriate. They then list specific ingredients which might make the offence more or less serious. The main purpose of guidelines is to encourage consistency of approach. The following is a general list of the kind of *offence* based factors which may fall to be taken into account:

—type of offence
—use or threat of violence
—use of or carrying a weapon
—value of any property stolen or damaged
—extent of any injuries
—presence of racial or religious motive (mandatory aggravating factors: below)
—vulnerability of victim
—offence against public servant acting as such
—abuse of trust or power
—premeditated as opposed to 'spur of the moment'
—prime mover as opposed to minor participant
—adult using children in commission of the offence
—time and place of the offence
—involvement of drink or drugs
—offence on bail (a mandatory aggravating factor: below)
—immediate remorse or concern for the victim such as might be shown immediately at the time of the offence (e.g. by calling an ambulance after an assault)
—offence of need as opposed to greed; and
—provocation.

It is sometimes argued that certain personal or *offender* based factors may affect the court's view of the seriousness of the offence, such as age, maturity, intelligence and health. However, these kinds of factors—along with an early guilty plea or the offender's own attitude to the offence (either of which may indicate remorse or contrition), efforts aimed at reparation to the victim, or co-operation with the police—are more typically viewed as *personal* mitigation: see *Sentencing Information* below. A defendant's earlier convictions/responses to sentences can affect the seriousness of the current offence—but great care is needed when applying this rule: see *Chapter 7* which deals with *Previous Convictions and Responses*.

Offences committed while on bail
By law, a court is obliged to treat an offence committed while on bail as more serious *by virtue of that fact*. The relevant statutory provision reads:

> In considering the seriousness of any offence committed while the offender was on bail, the court shall treat the fact that it was committed in those circumstances as an aggravating factor.

Despite the apparent strictness of this requirement, during the relevant Parliamentary debate a spokesman indicated that:

> The Government do not intend that an offence committed on bail will always lead to a longer sentence. That would be absurd where the two offences are totally unconnected, or the second offence is a trivial one . . .

Racially aggravated offences and religious aggravation

The Crime and Disorder Act 1998 (as amended) created four broad types of offence which can be specifically charged in an aggravated form based upon racial or religious aggravation:

- certain assaults
- criminal damage
- certain public order offences
- harassment.

Racial and religious aggravation is defined as follows:

An offence is racially or religiously aggravated . . . if—

(a) at the time of committing the offence, or immediately before or after doing so, the offender demonstrated towards the victim of the offence hostility based on the victim's membership (or presumed membership) of a racial or religious group; or

(b) the offence is motivated (wholly or partly) by hostility towards members of a racial or religious group based on their membership of that group.

All four forms of offence are either way matters (whether or not their 'basic' versions are) and carry correspondingly higher maximum penalties. Such offences will often be referred to the Crown Court for trial or sentence given their very nature. The Powers of Criminal Courts Sentencing Act 2000 provides that *all other offences* apart from those in the four categories mentioned above must be treated as being more serious than they would otherwise have been where racial or religious aggravation is disclosed. The magistrates must state in open court that the offence was so aggravated.

It is thus clear that, as a general rule, the law intends that a court should normally increase sentence if a crime is racially or religiously motivated. However, another general legal rule is that a court can sentence only for the offence before it and not for some other offence (especially a more serious version of that charged) which it might think was disclosed by the facts. Thus, if a specific racially/religiously aggravated version of a basic offence exists under the law (as in the case of assault, criminal damage, public order and harassment, above) but only the basic version is before the court, it is not possible to increase sentence for the basic version on racial or religious grounds.

Prevalence of offences

The fact that an offence is prevalent may make it more serious. This may be within in a particular locality. A distinction must be drawn between the fact that an offence occurs frequently (the usual starting point for sentencing should already reflect this) and what might be termed 'a real outburst' of a particular type of offence and one that is perhaps gaining momentum. Court of Appeal guidance gives examples of ways in which the prevalence of an offence can increase its seriousness: e.g. a spate of sexual attacks on women can increase fear among women generally in an area and limit their freedom of movement. The decision as to what effect prevalence has is ultimately for the court *in all the circumstances*.

THE SENTENCING PROCESS OUTLINED

The trial and sentencing process depends on the status of the offence. The different offence categories ('indictable only', 'either way' and 'summary') are explained in *Chapter 1*.

Indictable only offences
Since implementation of the relevant provisions of the Crime and Disorder Act 1998 indictable only offences are sent forthwith to the Crown Court. Following an initial appearance of the accused person before the magistrates' court the case proceeds to the Crown Court and thereafter that court deals with all matters related to trial and sentence.

Summary offences
In summary cases the magistrates proceed directly to the question of guilt or innocence by asking the defendant, as soon as possible, whether he or she pleads 'guilty' or 'not guilty'. Following a guilty plea or, alternatively, if the defendant is convicted after the court has heard the evidence, the magistrates proceed to sentence the offender. They thus deal with the entire process (exceptionally, summary matters can accompany other classes of offence to the Crown Court: 📖✋).

Either way offences—'Plea before venue'
Section 49 Criminal Procedure and Investigations Act 1996 (together with certain provisions of the Crime (Sentences) Act 1997) radically altered the procedure for processing, and if needs be sentencing, in relation to either way offences (including 'small value' criminal damage charges) 📖✋. Section 17A Magistrates' Courts Act 1980 confronts

- the cost and delay of sending either way offences to the Crown Court for trial when they merely result in a guilty plea; and
- the fact that, historically, a large proportion of either way offences committed to the Crown Court for trial are sentenced within the powers available to magistrates

and places increased emphasis on encouraging defendants to seek sentencing credit for a timely guilty plea: *Chapter 1*. The procedure—generally known as 'plea before venue' (PBV)—is simple in concept but not without problems of interpretation 📖✋. When a defendant appears in respect of an either way offence:

- he or she should be invited to indicate as soon as possible what plea would be entered if the matter were to come to trial (be that before the magistrates or before the Crown Court)
- if a *guilty plea* is indicated, the magistrates, in essence, deem there to have been a formal guilty plea on summary trial and move directly to consider the appropriate sentence
- the magistrates then either:
  —sentence the offender themselves; or

—commit the offender to the Crown Court for sentence (on bail or in custody): see page 40 *et seq.*

- if a *not guilty* plea is indicated or the defendant refuses or fails to indicate any plea then the standard 'mode of trial' procedures outlined below must be followed.

It can be readily appreciated that a range of issues arise in relation to the 'plea before venue' procedure, e.g.:

- the Crown prosecutor (or other prosecutor) will need a sufficiently detailed and full file at the first hearing, so that, e.g. the charges can be finalised ready for the procedure to take place
- the defendant will need to be able to seek legal advice as soon as possible and will, in any event, need to have the procedure explained simply but carefully by the court
- he or she is clearly being encouraged to seek maximum credit through an early guilty plea. An indication of guilt without waiting to see or test the full strength of the prosecution case might be viewed as being 'straight from the heart': true remorse[2]
- magistrates need to be clear as to when custody is appropriate, and how long a custodial sentence should be
- following the Proceeds of Crime Act 2002 where magistrates consider that a confiscation order should be made by the Crown Court they will need to specify whether the committal is for greater sentence generally or simply on the basis that they consider that a confiscation order may be appropriate: see further under *Committal for Sentence* later in this chapter.

Appendix B, Considerations affecting Decisions Whether or Not to Commit to the Crown Court for Sentence contains guidance about the use/length of custody.

Either way offences—'Mode of Trial'
Where the defendant—following an invitation to indicate his or her plea—says that this is 'not guilty', or refuses or fails to indicate a plea then the standard 'mode of trial' procedure must be followed. This means that the magistrates must consider:

- the nature of the case
- whether the circumstances make it one of a serious character
- whether their own sentencing powers are likely to be adequate (usually up to six months' imprisonment and/or a fine of up to £5,000 per offence; with the possibility of an aggregate period of imprisonment of 12 months[3]: *Chapter 4*); and

---

2 However, whilst previously the defendant might forego a right to disclosure of the prosecution case before making a decision, any pressure to do so could lead to this aspect being reconsidered as a result of the fair trial provisions of Article 6 of the European Convention On Human Rights and Fundamental Freedoms 📖✋.

3 The maximum sentencing powers of magistrates' courts would be affected by forthcoming legislation and this aspect could possibly be effective as early as 2004: see *Chapter 4*.

- any other circumstances which appear to make trial at the Crown Court or the magistrates' court more appropriate.

The magistrates must then decide whether they are prepared, subject to the defendant's consent, to hear the case themselves—or whether to commit him or her to the Crown Court for trial. In order for the magistrates' court to arrive at this decision:

- the prosecutor's version of the facts has—for the time being—to be taken as correct (i.e. a 'worst case sentencing scenario')
- the prosecutor and then the defendant will make representations as to the venue for trial; and
- the court should make full enquiry as to the circumstances of the allegations. Traditionally, the court has disregarded the defendant's previous convictions (if any) at this stage, as well as mitigation and personal circumstances. The case of *R v. McInerney* which is noted in relation to the offence of burglary in *Chapter 4* may require the previous convictions aspect of this approach to be reviewed 📖✍.

The court may then direct trial at the Crown Court or declare the matter more suitable for summary trial (i.e. before magistrates). If summary trial *is* found by the magistrates to be appropriate then they must still obtain the defendant's free and informed consent before they can proceed to deal with the case themselves. The defendant must also be informed that if he or she *does* agree to summary trial and pleads guilty or is found guilty then the magistrates can still commit to the Crown Court for sentence: page 40. If consent *is* then given the magistrates proceed to take the defendant's plea. If consent is *not* forthcoming the case will proceed with a view to committal for trial in the Crown Court.

The *National Mode of Trial Guidelines* are reproduced in *Appendix A*. These were issued in 1995 (and have not been amended to reflect the section 17A Magistrates' Courts Act 1980 (PBV) provisions). They should be referred to in all either way cases where mode of trial falls to be determined by magistrates; and may also be relevant as background to *Considerations Affecting Decisions to Commit to the Crown Court for Sentence:* see the commentary to *Appendix B* 📖✍.

SENTENCING BY MAGISTRATES

Sentencing by magistrates only starts when one of the following events occurs:

- the defendant enters an unequivocal plea of guilty to a summary offence or is convicted following a contested hearing

- the defendant indicates an unequivocal plea of guilty to an either way offence under the section 17A Magistrates' Courts Act 1980 procedure described above (i.e. PBV)
- following the mode of trial procedure for an either way offence, the magistrates accept summary jurisdiction, the defendant consents thereto and then enters an unequivocal plea of guilty or is convicted following a contested hearing.

Any question whether the defendant's plea, or indication of plea, is equivocal (i.e. not really clear whether it is a true plea of guilty or not) must be addressed straightaway. If a difficulty remains or the court has residual doubts, the defendant should be invited to take legal advice. If necessary, the plea should be treated as one of not guilty 📖✌.

The facts of the case
The court must sentence on the agreed or proved facts and any other relevant information such as the contents of a pre-sentence report (PSR) (*Chapter 9*) and plea in mitigation. Problems can occur in the following circumstances:

- *Guilty plea—but where the facts are contested* The defendant pleads 'guilty' but then suggests that the facts—though supporting the allegation—are substantially different to those alleged by the prosecutor, e.g. in an assault case both punching and kicking are alleged whereas the defendant may strongly deny using his or her feet. Unless the prosecutor invites the court to proceed on the basis of the defendant's version of events, the court must hold a 'Newton hearing' (named after *R v. Newton* (1983) Cr. App. Rep. 13). The court must make a determination on the disputed facts, and should announce and record its finding. The case can then proceed on the basis of the facts found 📖✌.

- *Conviction on a different basis* Following a 'not guilty' plea, the court finds the case proved but not on the precise basis alleged by the prosecutor (e.g. the court may find that the defendant stole three items and not ten as alleged). Here, the court will convict on the basis of three items and announce and record this. There are also cases, mainly in respect of road traffic matters, where a court hearing a not guilty plea is empowered, of its own volition, to convict of a different and lesser charge (e.g. dangerous driving can be reduced to driving without due care and attention). Again, an announcement should be made so that the basis for sentencing is clear.

- *Self-defence* There are cases of assault where the defence is self-defence and where it is for the prosecutor to disprove matters once properly raised by the defendant. If the case is nonetheless found proved it is essential for the court to announce, on convicting the defendant, whether it totally discounts any suggestion of self-defence or whether it accepts that there was a need for some force but feels the defendant over-reacted.

Credit for a guilty plea
The basic principles affecting credit for a guilty plea were outlined in *Chapter 1* (see page 15). Courts must be clear as to when credit for a guilty plea will be

given—or, indeed, will not be given (including in plea before venue (PBV) situations pursuant to section 17A Magistrates' Courts Act 1980 as outlined above). It is important to know *what credit* will be given and *what announcement* will be made. Courts should never add a 'sentencing premium' so as to *increase* sentence because of a not guilty plea (or late plea of guilty). Rather, it is a question of whether credit should be lost. Where there has been a Newton hearing (see above under *Guilty plea—but where the facts are contested*) the discount may be reduced but not withheld totally (*R v. Hassall, The Times*, 30 April 1999).

Informants

Occasionally an offender will, when pleading guilty and trying to show remorse, seek to obtain sentencing credit by reference to help given to the police as an informer. Although giving offenders credit for doing what might be regarded as their public duty may seem unpalatable, the Court of Appeal has recognised the reality that much serious crime is prevented or detected only with the help of informants. Indeed, informants may have received cash incentives from the police, or have been involved in criminal activity themselves. The submission of such items to the court is a delicate matter and usually involves the receipt by the court of a confidential note, commonly called a 'text'. Such matters, which also raise human rights issues, require careful consideration and legal/judicial advice is essential. The Justices' Clerks' Society issued advice on texts in *JCS News Sheet* No. 97/45 of 1997. 📖✋

Positive good character

The Court of Appeal (*R v. Clark, The Times*, 27 January 1999) has confirmed that a defendant who produces evidence of positive good character may be extended extra leniency. In that case, the defendant produced evidence of substantial voluntary work in a number of local community and charitable activities. Her sentence at the Crown Court of six months' imprisonment for fraud committed over six years and involving a total of £18,000 was reduced to seven days' imprisonment. Her voluntary activities, combined with the absence of any previous convictions, merited a lower sentence than that originally imposed.

SENTENCING INFORMATION

The prosecutor will present the facts fairly and objectively, and will not enter the sentencing arena save in limited ways e.g. by:

- providing details of any criminal record and 'antecedents' (explained below)
- challenging defence information which conflicts with that on the prosecution file
- where the court has a duty to order endorsement or disqualification, by reminding it of this or countering defence suggestions that it should refrain from making such orders (see, e.g. the discussion of 'special reasons' in *Chapter 8*)

- submitting guideline sentencing law in appropriate cases, especially in relation to plea before venue (PBV)/committal for sentence and mode of trial proceedings
- contributing to discussions in court if there are doubts about whether or not the court has certain powers—but without seeking to influence the sentencing decision
- making specific applications, e.g. for forfeiture of weapons or drugs (*Chapter 6*); and
- reminding the court of relevant ancillary powers (including 'criminal' anti-social behaviour orders (CRASBOs)) (*Chapter 6*).

The Pre-Sentence Report (Prescription of Prosecutors) Order 1998 requires certain prosecutors to be shown pre-sentence reports (PSRs) and specific sentence reports (SSRs) on which they may comment. Such comment will presumably be to challenge aspects of a PSR/SSR which do not accord with the prosecutor's view of events, or to comment from the victim's perspective: see *Chapter 5* concerning victims generally.

Once the basic facts of an offence are established, a further information gathering process starts—and may involve questions from the bench. The aim of the court should be to have before it as much relevant information as is appropriate and the extent of that information will depend on the nature of the case. Other things being equal, the more serious the offence—and thus the more severe the likely outcome—the greater the need to explore further avenues of information. Sentencing information might include:

Previous convictions
The prosecutor will provide a list of any previous convictions (courts should be alert to the fact that recent convictions may not appear on such lists). Defence advocates may have difficulty if they know that the list is incomplete. Whereas they are officers of the court, they also owe a duty to their client which would prevent their disclosing omissions without express consent. When defence solicitors are asked to confirm the list they may properly invite the court to put that question direct to the offender.

The list should be in chronological order and will often be submitted for speed and convenience by way of a computer printout.

Under the Rehabilitation of Offenders Act 1974 certain convictions can become 'spent' by the passage of time, i.e. the offender may (subject to exceptions) lawfully deny their existence if asked about them. The time within which convictions become 'spent' depends on factors such as the type and length of sentence originally imposed and the offender's age at the time. Conviction of a further offence during what is known as the 'rehabilitation period' can also extend the original period so that it expires later.

The operation of the 1974 Act is, therefore, less than straightforward, and lists of previous convictions may not always accurately reflect which offences are really 'spent'. When sentencing, courts are, in any event, entitled to receive details of *all* previous convictions, including any which are spent (but which should still be marked as such) and to accord them such relevance as appears appropriate 📖✋.

The potential effect of previous convictions and responses to sentences imposed for them is further outlined in *Chapter 7*.

Antecedents

Previous convictions are sometimes called 'antecedents'. The term antecedents has a wider meaning than 'previous convictions', and encompasses, e.g. information about family, employment, financial commitments and so on. Such details may be provided, if known, subject to local practice.

Cautions

The practice of issuing a caution (a formal police warning) rather than prosecuting is totally non-statutory in the case of adults (unlike reprimands and warnings for youths, see below) and operates at the discretion of the local chief constable although Home Office circulars seek to produce consistency. Normally, the decision to caution will have been made before a prosecution is launched, but the High Court has indicated that the Crown prosecutor must, when reviewing a case, consider whether a caution is preferable to continuing to prosecute. In trying to set informal national standards, the Home Office has advised that cautions should be cited to the court at the sentencing stage by the prosecutor *only where relevant to the offence under consideration* and by way of a list separate from the list of previous convictions (see generally Home Office Circulars 59/1990; 18/1994). It is for courts to decide what relevance to attach to a caution. The offence will have been admitted, but without the protection afforded by a court of law. It will have been accepted as an alternative to prosecution. But a caution will always indicate that an offender has been warned about previous misbehaviour, which may possibly be of a similar kind to that now charged, and this may cancel out mitigation which relies on ignorance, mistake etc.

A special statutory system of reprimands and warnings now exists for juvenile offenders. The chief feature which may affect the adult court is that a warning acts as a bar to a conditional discharge within two years unless the court finds that there are exceptional circumstances: see further under *Discharges* in *Chapter 4*.

Driving licences and DVLA printouts

It is essential for a court to see either the driving licence or a DVLA printout where a road traffic offence is endorsable or attracts disqualification from driving: *Chapter 8*.

TICs

The practice of defendants asking for outstanding offences—for which they have *not* been prosecuted—to be taken into consideration (known as 'TICs') is a non-statutory means of encouraging offenders to 'make a clean breast' of matters. It disposes of possible further allegations easily and quickly. The sentence should reflect any TICs and the court should make an appropriate announcement and keep a record of the relevant offences. The maximum sentence remains that for the offence *charged* (or the maximum aggregate sentence where applicable: *Chapter 4*).

An application should normally only be allowed where the substantive offences and the TICs are either way offences (see *Chapter 1*) and of a similar nature. Endorsable offences should not generally be allowed as TICs, since the offender might escape 'totting-up' or a mandatory disqualification (*Chapter 8*). Usually, the prosecutor prepares a written list of the TICs for adoption by the defendant at the hearing. If the defendant decides not to accept the list, or rejects part of it, the court must disregard that list or part (which may lead to defence claims for a fresh bench under the 'fair trial' provisions of Article 6: see, generally, *Chapter 2*). The prosecutor then has to decide whether or not to bring formal charges instead.

Mitigation
A defendant will often put forward information in support a request for leniency—called 'mitigation'. A poor record may reduce the scope for this. Mitigation may relate to:

- the *offence* (when it should be considered along with other seriousness factors in arriving at the correct sentence level); or
- the *offender*—also called 'personal mitigation' or 'offender mitigation'. This can serve to reduce a sentence below that which the seriousness of the offence itself would merit. Personal mitigation might include, e.g. a character reference, a supportive letter from an employer, details of unusually difficult financial circumstances, ill-health or domestic difficulties.

As always, the court must consider each case on its merits and decide what factors are relevant—as well as the extent to which these ought to be taken into account. It should be clear in the court's mind what kind of mitigation is under consideration, and its effect, if any, on the decision.

A legal representative mitigates 'on instructions' from his or her client and will not usually know whether the information supplied by the client is correct. He or she cannot (and should not be expected to) guarantee its validity—but must never knowingly mislead the court. Courts can call for verification if necessary (e.g. direct proof, a PSR if appropriate).

Derogatory assertions
Sometimes, in seeking to offer mitigation, the defendant may attempt to 'lay the blame' and will make assertions which impugn the character of other people, including sometimes that of the victim of the offence. The court will need to balance the defendant's right to mitigate with the interests of such other people (who, more often than not, will not be present in court at the time). If there are substantial grounds for believing that an assertion is:

- derogatory of another; *and*
- false or irrelevant to sentence

the court may make certain restrictions on the public reporting of that assertion. Obviously, once a court considers *any* mitigation to be irrelevant it should prohibit that line being pursued. However, the right of a defendant to mitigate must never be improperly constrained. Legal/judicial advice should be taken 📖✍.

Written pleas of guilty—Section 12 Magistrates' Courts Act 1980
Where the prosecutor has adopted the written plea procedure in relation to a summary offence (also known as 'MCA', 'paperwork', 'section 12' and 'guilty by post') all the information will be contained in documents: a prosecution 'statement of facts' or a copy of the written prosecution witness statements; the defendant's written plea and any written mitigation; and occasionally a notice to cite previous convictions and a list of those convictions. The offender may, however, address the court in person if he or she attends. Mitigation can concern the offence or the offender's personal circumstances.

Even where the defendant does not send in a written plea of guilty or attend, the case can be proved against him or her in certain circumstances where written witness statements have been served. This could apply even to the first hearing date—seek advice. ▣✋

Financial circumstances
Where a financial penalty or compensation is in mind, the court can order the defendant to provide a statement of his or her 'financial circumstances', in writing or orally in court (when magistrates should bear in mind the defendant's Article 8 rights to 'respect for private and family life': see, generally, *Chapter 2*). There are criminal penalties for failure to provide the statement, or for giving false information: see *Chapter 4*.

Pre-sentence reports and specific sentence reports
The court may require a probation officer or social worker to complete a written pre-sentence report (PSR) to assist the court '. . . in determining the most suitable method' of dealing with the offender. This will require an adjournment, usually for 15 working days but often for a shorter period if the offender is already 'known to the National Probation Service' and/or is to be remanded in custody. In certain instances, the court is obliged to obtain a PSR—unless it considers this unnecessary. Because of their key importance, PSRs and specific sentence reports (SSRs) are considered in *Chapter 9*.

Medical reports
The court can order a report about the offender's physical or mental condition. Psychiatric reports are discussed in *Chapter 11*.

DEFERMENT OF SENTENCE

Deferment is designed to deal with the situation where—because of what a court has discovered about the offender—it considers that it is proper to postpone the sentencing decision '(a) to have regard . . . to his conduct after conviction (including, where appropriate, the making by him of any reparation for his offence); or (b) to any change in his circumstances' (the words in parenthesis added by section 1 Powers of Criminal Courts (Sentencing) Act 2000. The defendant must consent to the deferment. The maximum period for which sentence can be deferred is six months. There is no power to remand an offender or make him or her subject to any requirements or restrictions during the deferment period and the court, in deferring sentence, cannot make ancillary orders except for an interim driving disqualification or a restitution order. However there is specific power to issue a warrant for subsequent non-attendance at the end of the deferment. It should be noted that:

- deferment may only be used *once* in respect of any offence. There are no restrictions as to the offence
- the court must ensure that the offender understands exactly what is being proposed and to what he or she is being asked to consent. (The general principle is that offenders have a right to know their fate as soon as possible after conviction)
- the interests of the victim must be considered. Postponing sentence may mean postponing formal compensation (but note the new emphasis on reparation in the 2000 Act, above).

The offender must consent to the deferment, and the court must be satisfied, having regard to the nature of the offence and the character and circumstances of the offender, that it would be in the interests of justice to defer sentence. The Court of Appeal has given guidance:

The consent of the defendant must be obtained . . . the court should make it clear . . . what the particular purposes are which the court has in mind and what conduct is expected of [the offender] during the deferment. The deferring court should make a careful note of the purposes for which the sentence is being deferred and what steps, if any, it expects the accused to take during the period of deferment.[4]

A specific object should be in mind. Deferment should *not* be used to avoid the sentencing decision. Again, the Court of Appeal has said that:

The purpose of deferment is to enable the court to take into account the defendant's conduct after conviction or any change in circumstances and then only if it is in the interest of justice to exercise the power . . . the power is not to be used as an easy way out for a court which is unable to make up its mind.

Also, deferment should not be used simply to secure a result which could be achieved by a requirement in a CRO, e.g. continuing with a course of medical treatment; and care must be taken not to allow an offender to 'buy' his or her way out of a prison sentence.

Reasons
Reasons should be given to the offender and recorded by the court about the purposes of the deferment—so that he or she is fully aware of what is expected during the deferment period. The court should also indicate how it wishes to be informed about whether the offender has met its expectations—i.e. usually by way of an updated PSR.

End of the deferment period
It is desirable (though not legally essential) that the magistrates who ordered the deferment should sit to impose sentence. The later bench should consider the

---

4 Care is also needed in view of human rights considerations (e.g. fair trial, no punishment without law and right to family life: see, generally, *Chapter 2*).

reasons for the deferment and the nature of any expectations of the offender, and determine whether he or she has substantially adhered to what was in mind. If he or she has done so, then a custodial sentence ought not generally to be imposed. If the defendant has not complied with the terms of the deferment the court should state in what regard.

Where a further offence is committed during the period of deferment
If the offender commits a fresh offence during this period, the court which convicts him or her of that new offence may deal with the deferred case even though the period has not yet expired. If the court which deferred sentence was the Crown Court, then the offender should be committed back to that court to be dealt with.

COMMITTAL FOR SENTENCE

A magistrates' court can commit an offender to the Crown Court to be sentenced in a variety of situations. The most common of these is where he or she is convicted of an either way offence (formally or following the section 17A Magistrates' Courts Act 1980 plea before venue (PBV) procedure as described earlier in this chapter). The magistrates must be of the opinion that the offence is so serious that greater punishment should be inflicted than magistrates can impose. In the case of a sexual or violent offence (page 74) there is an alternative basis for committal, i.e. that a sentence of imprisonment for a term longer than the magistrates have power to impose is necessary to protect the public from serious harm from the offender. Accordingly, if magistrates are dealing with *one* either way offence, they will need to be of the opinion that it merits a custodial sentence of more than six months before committing for sentence. If dealing with *two such offences or more*, they would be contemplating consecutive custodial sentences longer than 12 months in total: see, generally, *Chapter 4*. Case law suggests consecutive sentences normally arise only where, e.g.:

- offences are of a completely different nature to each other; or
- have been committed on totally separate occasions; or
- have been committed while the offender was on bail.

In practice, committal is usually likely to occur only where magistrates believe that the sentence which the Crown Court would pass is likely to be significantly higher than one that they themselves would give: *Appendix B: Considerations Affecting Decisions Whether or Not to Commit to the Crown Court for Sentence.*

Following a section 17A Magistrates' Courts Act 1980 indication of a guilty plea (plea before venue (PBV)) a magistrates' court must look at all relevant factors and will commit for sentence if, in the final analysis, it feels that its powers are inadequate.

Where the standard 'mode of trial' procedure for an either way offence has been followed, the same factors and powers will need to be considered on the defendant pleading guilty or being found guilty by magistrates. The main considerations are likely to be the seriousness of the offence or offences, previous convictions and whether any custodial sentences should be concurrent or consecutive. The effect of credit for a guilty plea is always highly relevant in borderline cases. 📖 ✋

The council of the Justices' Clerks' Society has advised its members that 'Greatest credit should be given where a guilty plea is entered before the magistrates' court. Credit will continue to be given where a guilty plea is entered for the first time in the Crown Court but that credit will normally be less than where the plea was entered in the magistrates' court where there is power to do so'. (*JCS News Sheet* No. 97/63: December 1997). This advice was confirmed in *R v. Rafferty* (1998), *Criminal Law Review* 443. The ruling reiterates that the PBV stage is the earliest opportunity for recording a guilty plea for sentence discount purposes. It follows that the discount for a guilty plea entered in the Crown Court should, in the absence of good reason for the delay, be less than if the plea had been made at the PBV stage.

Mode of trial decisions (*Chapter 1*) involve the magistrates' court in considering the main seriousness factors *prior* to accepting or rejecting jurisdiction. Good practice suggests that if magistrates do assume jurisdiction to deal with an either way case they should normally only use their power to commit the offender to the Crown Court for sentence where new factors emerge—such as previous convictions (presented *after* a defendant is convicted). But care should be taken that these do in fact affect the seriousness of the offence: *Chapter 7*.

Other new information may emerge from evidence during the hearing of a not guilty plea or because the full facts create a quite different impression to the original outline of the case by the prosecutor. The High Court has confirmed that a magistrates' court may commit for sentence if, on reconsidering the appropriateness of its original decision as to venue *in the light of all the facts which have subsequently emerged,* the seriousness of the offence warrants a sentence in excess of magistrates' own powers.

An offender who is committed for sentence may also be committed to be dealt with by the Crown Court for certain other offences even though the magistrates' sentencing powers for these extra offences would otherwise have been sufficient 📖 ✋. Magistrates also have powers to commit for sentence in certain other situations 📖 ✋:

- someone who is an absconder and who should have appeared in the Crown Court
- on breach of an order or sentence of the Crown Court, e.g. a CPO; or
- where the offender committed the offence during the operational period of a suspended sentence of imprisonment imposed by the Crown Court.

Other circumstances include the situation where a prisoner subject to early release (*Chapter 10*) commits an imprisonable offence during the original period of a custodial sentence and is liable to be returned to prison to serve more than six months.

Once an offender has been committed for sentence, any ancillary orders should be left to the Crown Court—apart, possibly, from an interim driving disqualification (see *Chapter 8*).

Committal for sentence for the purposes of a confiscation order

Section 70 Proceeds of Crime Act 2002 (in force from 24 March 2003) provides—as part of an extensive package of measures aimed at confiscating proceeds of criminal activity in the widest sense—a process concerning the proceeds of crime with regard to offences before magistrates. On conviction, the prosecutor may ask the magistrates' court to commit the defendant to the Crown Court (on bail or in custody) so that the Crown Court may make a criminal confiscation order (a power which magistrates do not themselves have). Once such a request is made, the magistrates *must* commit to the Crown Court for sentence under these provisions.

It is most important that the magistrates indicate the basis of the committal, i.e. whether they are committing for sentence in any event—pursuant to the principles already described above (i.e. for a greater sentence)—or whether they are only committing the case to the Crown Court because they lack any power to make a confiscation order. Without a clear statement that it is for the former more general purpose, the Crown Court will be restricted (other than with respect to making a confiscation order) to magistrates' maximum powers. The provisions are novel, lengthy and complex: 📖✋.

Bail or custody on committal to the Crown Court for sentence?

The general right to bail in the Bail Act 1976 does not extend to a committal for sentence. The conventional wisdom was that it would be incongruous for a court to conclude that a defendant deserves a custodial sentence longer than the court itself can impose but then to release him or her on bail. The following advice of the Justices' Clerks' Society was endorsed by the then Lord Chief Justice:

> There are differing views on whether or not a defendant committed for sentence should normally be committed in custody. The two main lines of argument are that:
>
> 1. A committal for sentence presupposes a decision by the magistrates that a defendant would receive a substantial custodial sentence and therefore committal should be in custody.
> 2. The defendant's status after committal should normally be the same as that before committal, that is a defendant on bail up to committal will normally remain on bail after committal and a defendant in custody will normally remain in custody.
>
> It is the view of the council of the Society that the determining criterion should be the defendant's status before committal. Council considers that the authorities usually relied upon are largely based on the need to prevent a defendant going in and out of custody throughout the course of the proceedings and that there is no need for a defendant on bail up to committal to be committed in custody unless the court has substantial grounds for believing that the defendant will fail to surrender to the court or will commit further offences.
>
> Council advises that courts should proceed on this basis. This advice is endorsed by the Lord Chief Justice and was confirmed in *R v Rafferty* (1998) Criminal Law Review 443. The case clarified that the remand status of a convicted defendant on committal for sentence should normally be the same as that before committal, unless the court has new evidence leading to substantial grounds for believing that the defendant would abscond or commit a further offence. Thus, a defendant on bail up to committal will normally remain on bail after committal, and a defendant in custody will remain in custody. (*JCS News Sheet* No. 63/1997).

CHAPTER 4

The Four Levels of Sentence

As indicated in *Chapter 3*, good practice indicates that sentencers should adopt a structured approach to decision-making. This chapter contains:

- a diagram of the *Sentencing Framework* (*Figure 1* on page 45)
- an explanation of the main elements of each sentencing option
- an example of a decision-making structure: *A Step-by-Step Approach to Sentencing* (*Figure 2* on pages 82-3).

THE SENTENCING FRAMEWORK

Figure 1 contains an outline of the sentencing framework which resulted from the Criminal Justice Act 1991.[1] The level of sentence is affected by mainly statutory 'threshold' criteria:

- **DISCHARGES**: punishment is 'inexpedient'.

- **FINES**: by implication punishment *is* expedient, but more severe punishment is not on the face of things appropriate.[2] The size of a fine must reflect the seriousness of the offence *and* the offender's financial circumstances.

- **COMMUNITY SENTENCES**: the offence is 'serious enough'. The degree of 'restriction of liberty' must be commensurate with the seriousness of the offence *and* the particular order(s) which is (are) suitable for the offender.

- **CUSTODY**:
  — the offence is 'so serious' that *only* such a sentence can be justified; or
  — if the offence is a sexual or violent one (see page 74), 'only such a sentence would be adequate to protect the public from serious harm [from the offender]'; or
  — the offender has refused to consent to one of the few types of community sentence which still require such consent (page 56).
  — on breach of certain community sentences following 'wilful and persistent' failure to comply or where the original order was used as an 'alternative to custody'.

---

1 As explained in *Chapter 1* relevant provisions of the 1991 Act and other sentencing statutes are consolidated in the Powers of Criminal Courts (Sentencing) Act 2000. References have been changed in the text except where they are used in the context of historical background.

2 Note, however, that pursuant to the current alternative to custody ethos the Court of Appeal has said in one particular case that a very heavy fine may be preferable to custody: see later in chapter.

The *length* of a custodial sentence must be commensurate with the seriousness of the offence or, as appropriate, the need to protect the public from serious harm from a sexual or violent offender.

In most cases, the seriousness of the offence determines which of the four levels of sentence should be considered and the extent of any penalty within that level. Any number of associated offences can be taken into account when assessing seriousness: *Chapter 1*. The remainder of this chapter deals in detail with the criteria for individual sentences and provides further guidance where necessary.

As outlined in *Chapter 2*, Article 6 of the European Convention on Human Rights and Fundamental Freedoms places a general obligation on courts to give reasons for their decisions. This applies to magistrates in relation to judicial decisions generally, including when sentencing people. Accordingly, there is a need to explain in public why a particular sentence (discharge, fine, community sentence, custody and, where appropriate, an ancillary order) is deemed appropriate. This applies whether or not there is a specific statutory obligation under domestic law to do so.

DISCHARGES

CRITERION: '. . . having regard to the circumstances including the nature of the offence and the character of the offender . . . it is inexpedient to inflict punishment'.

RESTRICTION ON LIBERTY: none implied or arising.

Absolute discharge
This marks the conviction but no other obligations follow. An absolute discharge may be appropriate when the offence is of a truly minor nature, purely technical, or when there are several offences and a comparatively trivial one requires a residual sentencing disposal (which might equally be achieved by imposing 'no separate penalty': *Chapter 3*).

Conditional discharge
This makes the offender subject to a single condition, i.e. that no further offence is committed within a period of up to three years—as set by the court. Conviction of *any* criminal offence during this 'operational period' renders the offender liable to be re-sentenced for the offence which originally gave rise to the discharge—and in addition to any sentence for the new offence. The court must explain the effects of the conditional discharge to the offender. For this reason it is often argued that a conditional discharge cannot be imposed in the offender's absence, and not on a company. There is no monitoring of the offender's behaviour or supervision during the period of the discharge.

CUSTODY

1. 'So serious'
2. 'Protection of the public (sexual or violent offences[1])
3. Refusal of a community sentence (provided consent a prerequisite[2])
4. Wilful and persistent breach of a community sentence (or where original sentence was used as an 'alternative to custody').

PRISON (21 and over)
YOUNG OFFENDER INSTITUTION
(18 to 20)

COMMUNITY SENTENCE
Serious enough

COMMUNITY REHABILITATION ORDER
COMMUNITY PUNISHMENT ORDER
COMMUNITY PUNISHMENT &
  REHABILITATION ORDER
CURFEW ORDER (with optional monitoring)
ATTENDANCE CENTRE ORDER (18 to 20)
DRUG TREATMENT & TESTING ORDER
DRUG ABSTINENCE ORDER (if available) [3]
EXCLUSION ORDER (when available)

FINE
Punishment appropriate

NOTE THAT COMPENSATION TAKES PRIORITY
OUT OF THE OFFENDER'S AVAILABLE
FINANCIAL RESOURCES

DISCHARGE
Punishment 'inexpedient'

ABSOLUTE DISCHARGE
CONDITIONAL DISCHARGE

NOTE THE LEGAL DUTY TO CONSIDER COMPENSATION

---

[1] See the definitions on page 62.
[2] This is now a somewhat rare requirement: see page 48.
[3] Seek advice locally 📖✋

Some people argue that a conditional discharge can be used at any level of seriousness, even instead of imprisonment on occasion, e.g. to give an offender a fresh start. This depends on how courts interpret the phrase 'punishment is inexpedient' and whether this approach can be reconciled with the fact that, as in the example given, the custody threshold will have been reached (though it is clearly established that personal mitigation relating to the offender can justify a less severe sentence when the seriousness of the offence might have justified a more severe one). Magistrates should check what view is taken locally and seek advice if faced with these or similar arguments 📖✋.

A conditional discharge is also sometimes used for an habitual offender with many convictions for a new offence which on the face of it is not serious, e.g. an offender with many convictions for theft who is accused of further offences.

Where a defendant is subject to a final warning made when he or she was a juvenile and within the past two years, he or she cannot be given a conditional discharge unless there are exceptional circumstances—even in the adult court— where a subsequent offence was committed within two years of the final warning being given.

General procedures and requirements when making a conditional discharge

---

- age limits—*None*
- minimum period—*None*
- maximum period—*Three years*
- consent—*Not required*
- explanation—*At time of sentence; and*
- Human Rights Act implications—*Reasons should be announced.*

Breach of conditional discharge

A 'breach' occurs if a fresh criminal offence is *committed* during the operational period. When the court comes to re-sentence the offender for the original offence, the seriousness of that offence has to be considered anew. Apart from substituting a different disposal, the court has the option of taking no action and allowing the conditional discharge to run if it thinks this is the proper course.

Breach of a conditional discharge imposed by a magistrates' court can be dealt with anywhere in England and Wales (subject to the consent of the original court if in a different place). Magistrates cannot deal with a Crown Court conditional discharge (but must inform that court of the breach if not committing for sentence) unless imposed on appeal from a magistrates' court (where the order made on appeal is deemed to have been made by the magistrates' court).

Human Rights Act considerations apply as much on breach as at the time when the conditional discharge was imposed.

FINES

CRITERION: This is not directly covered by statute. By implication, fines should be used where a discharge is not appropriate, i.e. where punishment *is* expedient—but on the face of things a more severe sentence would not be. See, however, footnote 2 on page 43. The *size* of a fine must reflect the seriousness of the offence *and* the offender's financial circumstances.

RESTRICTION ON LIBERTY: Fines do not affect the physical liberty of the offender, but a loss of spending power deprives the offender of the ability to direct money towards recreation and leisure, or to choose how he or she spends a sum of money equivalent to the amount of the fine.

In magistrates' courts the maximum fine is set by statute, in most instances by reference to one of five standard levels. Values are updated by Parliament from time to time. At the time of writing these levels are:

Level 1	£200
Level 2	£500
Level 3	£1,000
Level 4	£2,500
Level 5	£5,000

Fines for individual either way offences tried summarily are usually restricted to a maximum figure of £5,000 per offence. If no maximum is specified (which is rare) then Level 3 applies. There is no over-arching limit affecting multiple offences (as e.g. there is with imprisonment). The global ceiling is, in effect, determined by the proportionality principle, the totality principle (*Chapter 3*) and the offender's own financial circumstances: below. Maximum fines in the Crown Court are often not subject to any legal limit.

Fixing the amount of the fine
This involves:

- reflecting the seriousness of the offence
- an inquiry into the financial circumstances of the offender
- taking those circumstances into account (so far as they are known or appear)
- taking all other relevant circumstances into account.

Financial circumstances
Courts can *increase* or *decrease* the size of a fine according to an individual offender's financial circumstances. Where there are several fines (and/or compensation or costs) the court must bear in mind the total impact on the

offender's finances and may need to make downwards adjustments and/or extend the time for payment.

The term 'financial circumstances' appears to be wide in scope. It probably covers not only direct income but also, e.g. savings, investments, endowment policies and valuable possessions, as well as permitting a court to consider the position of, say, an offender with no apparent income but who is living a fairly lavish lifestyle, based possibly on a partner's support—which thereby reduces the need for personal expenditure. This last point is yet to be tested on appeal in the higher courts. The former law (which was based on the concept of 'means') was against family income being taken into account.

Financial penalties should usually be set at a level which envisages payment within 12 months (but possibly up to two or even three years in appropriate cases, such as where compensation is involved).

In the case of people on state benefits (some of which are set at subsistence level) the amount of each instalment may well have to be kept to the minimum and the number of instalments reduced to enable payment over a matter of months if not weeks. This principle will obviously apply equally to other people with very limited income. Thus in the important case of *R v. Stockport Justices, ex parte Conlon* (*The Times*, 3 January 1997), Lord Justice Staughton expressed concerns about the amount of fines in respect of defendants with limited means:

> What troubles me about these cases is not the remedies which the magistrates had to choose from as means of enforcement, but the size of the fines which those on income support were expected to pay out of resources that are said to be only sufficient for the necessities of life. I can see that over a short period of time the money provided as income support may be sufficient for paying a small but regular amount towards fines but as everybody knows there are contingencies which occur and will strain a tight budget to breaking point. That, I think, is what the probation officer had in mind when he spoke of regularly fining £10 a fortnight over a period of 52 weeks. The fact that, in an ordinary week, there will be £5 available does not by any means lead to the conclusion that there will be no difficulty in every week of the year. I would prefer a solution where fines on those of limited means were lesser in amount—or at least lesser in total—so that they could be paid in a matter of weeks, and where regular payment was firmly enforced. But that is another story from what we are required to decide today.

Financial circumstances orders

After conviction, defendants can be made subject to a 'financial circumstances order' (or *before* conviction if they have written pleading guilty under relevant procedures: *Chapter 3*). The defendant is then required to provide such a statement of his or her financial circumstances as the court may require. This may be by way of written details or in answer to inquiries in court where he or she is present. Failure to comply is an offence punishable by a Level 3 fine (£1,000). False or incomplete disclosure is a separate offence carrying up to three months imprisonment and/or a Level 4 fine (£2,500).

Health and safety offences

The Court of Appeal gave guidance in *R v. F Howe and Son (Engineers) Ltd, The Times*, 27 November 1998, including that the objective of prosecutions for health and safety offences in the workplace is to achieve a safe environment for those who work there and for other members of the public who might be affected. Where the defendant is a company, any fine needs to be large enough to bring that message home, not only to those who managed it but also to its shareholders:

> Particular aggravating features . . . include: (i) a failure to heed warnings; and (ii) where the defendant had deliberately profited financially from a failure to take necessary health and safety steps or specifically ran a risk to save money . . . Particular mitigating features would include (i) admission of responsibility and a timely plea of guilty; (ii) steps to remedy deficiencies after they were drawn to the defendant's attention; and (iii) a good safety record.
>
> Any fine should reflect not only the gravity of the offence but also the means of the offender. That applied just as much to corporate defendants as to any other . . . The starting point was [the company's] annual accounts . . . Where accounts or other financial information were deliberately not supplied, the court would be entitled to conclude that the company was in a position to pay any financial penalty the court was minded to impose.

The Magistrates' Association has also published guidance on fining companies for environmental health and safety offences, *Costing the Earth: Guidance for Sentencers* (2002).

Combining fines with other sentences

Fines are capable of being imposed in addition to custody for a single offence. A widely held view appears to be that a fine *and* a community sentence cannot be imposed for a single offence, or that this would be inappropriate even if technically permissible 📖✋. The possibility of a fine and a discharge for a single offence can hardly arise given the criterion for discharges (i.e. 'punishment is inexpedient', see *Discharges*, above).

As explained in *Chapter 5*, a compensation order can be made on its own or combined with any other sentence. If both a fine and compensation are considered appropriate and the offender cannot realistically be ordered to pay both in full because of his or her financial circumstances then the compensation order must always be preferred at the expense of the fine (and by implication any prosecution costs).

Other ancillary orders can always be added to a fine: *Chapters 6, 8.*

Excise penalties

Certain convictions result in the imposition of an excise penalty rather than a fine. The most common example is the offence of using or keeping an untaxed motor vehicle ('no vehicle excise licence'), although there are many other Customs and Excise offences leading to similar penalties. In these cases:

- the full amount is payable unless mitigated by the court
- any excise penalties collected by the court will be paid over direct to the Commissioners of Customs and Excise unless they direct otherwise (as they have done, e.g. in respect of untaxed motor vehicles where penalties are paid over to the Lord Chancellor along with ordinary fines)
- excise penalties should not be remitted in enforcement proceedings on account of a 'subsequent change in circumstances' or lack of details (see

below under *Remission and alteration of fines*) although practice seems to vary 📖✋.

Otherwise, generally speaking, such penalties are collected and enforced as fines are.

Payment and collection of fines

Fines, compensation and costs are due and payable forthwith unless the court orders otherwise—and offenders cannot automatically expect 'easy terms'. Payment can be allowed by a fixed date or by instalments if appropriate and can be made in various ways including:

- cash (within the normal limits of legal tender, i.e. large amounts of small currency need not be accepted)
- postal order
- cheque (with or without a guarantee card). The court can refuse to accept a cheque especially if it has doubts whether it will be honoured)
- bank giro credit (standing order or *ad hoc* payments) provided the court operates such a system
- credit card or debit card (provided the local court has such methods in place); and
- paypoint card which is acceptable at certain stores, garages etc. (but only in relation to courts that operate this).

Payments received by the court are applied in the following order:

- compensation (which is then forwarded on to the victim)
- costs
- fine.

If the offender is already subject to a suspended committal order (below) for non-payment of an earlier account, that account will, in practice, be credited first unless the offender specifically requests otherwise.

Remission and alteration of fines

A later court has power to remit a fine, in whole or in part, in the light of any *subsequent* change in circumstances. This will often be in enforcement proceedings. A separate power allows a later court to remit all or part of a fine where it was originally fixed in the offender's absence or without an adequate statement of financial circumstances if information before the later court suggests that, had the original court had that information, it would have fixed a lower fine or no fine at all. However, it is not possible to substitute a different type of penalty if such new information suggests that a fine was not appropriate in the first place (i.e. the court can only vary the amount of the fine and set a new rate of payment). However, in extreme cases, section 142 of the Magistrates' Courts Act 1980 (rectification of decisions) might be used to 'move down' to a discharge.

A compensation order cannot be remitted, but it can be discharged or reduced by a later court in limited circumstances: see *Chapter 5*. If necessary, seek legal advice 📖✋.

Immediate enforcement

The following measures are applicable to all types of financial order:

Power to order search

On making a financial order (or in enforcement proceedings) magistrates can have the offender searched—usually by a police officer or gaoler—and any monies found belonging to the offender applied to meet sums due. Regard must be had to domestic need and human rights considerations.

Immediate custody 📖 ✍

There are three circumstances in which magistrates can order custody in default of payment (immediate or suspended custody as appropriate) at the time of imposing a fine:

- where the offence is imprisonable and the offender appears to have the means to pay forthwith (which might include withdrawing money from a savings account)
- where it appears that the offender is unlikely to remain long enough at a place of abode in the UK to allow enforcement by other means (e.g. a person of no fixed abode or who is about to go abroad indefinitely)
- the offender is, on the same occasion, *sentenced* to immediate custody or is already serving such a *sentence* (i.e. not as a result of *committal* for some other default).

General enforcement powers

In all other circumstances the full enforcement process will need to be applied and a subsequent enquiry must be held into the default. 'Good enforcement begins at the point of imposing a fine', it is often said. If the size of a fine is assessed carefully and an appropriate order made for payment, then there should be a greater chance of the defendant complying with the order and, e.g. there will also be a sound baseline from which to address any default. On imposing financial penalties courts can set a review hearing date when enforcement will be considered if payment has not been made. Alternatively, computerised accounts programmes can respond immediately by prompting a:

- reminder
- informal methods such as a call to a fines surgery or telephone chase-up (if operated)
- summons
- warrant backed for bail
- warrant without bail; *or*
- distress warrant.

Note that there must be a careful check against set and appropriate criteria before the process is formally approved and goes out, and note also human rights issues such as Articles 5 ('liberty and security') and 8 ('respect for private and family life') and Protocol 1 ('protection of property'). Once the enforcement process is in being (*and* subject in most cases to the defaulter being before the court) there are various options:

- to set further terms for payment
- to search the defendant (as described above)
- an attachment of earnings order (i.e. requiring an employer to deduct payments from income)
- a request to the benefits office to deduct the fine from income support or job seekers allowance
- a distress warrant to seize the offender's goods (either immediately or suspended on terms)
- an attendance centre order (which, in relation to fine etc. enforcement, is available for defaulters aged up to 24 years inclusive)
- a money payment supervision order (usually operated by the National Probation Service or the court's own enforcement officer)
- detention in the court precincts or at a police station up until 8 p.m. (but usually until the court rises for the day)
- overnight detention in a police station
- imprisonment (or detention if the offender is below 21 years of age) within a scale which relates maximum periods in custody to amounts outstanding as a proportion of the original sum. Either type of order can be suspended on terms
- application to the High Court or county court for civil remedies
- remission (see under *Remission and alteration of fines*, above).

All other options must be considered or tried before imprisonment can be used. The court must state in open court its reasons in respect of each and cause these to be specified in the warrant of commitment and to be entered in the court register.

Human rights issues need to be kept constantly in mind, e.g. measures such as distress warrants may have to be weighed against the impact on the offender and his or her family, see in particular Articles 5 and 8 mentioned above.

Defaulters below the age of 21
Where magistrates are considering detention for default of an offender below 21 years of age they must (in addition to considering or trying all other available options and giving reasons for not using them or why they were ineffective) be satisfied that it is undesirable or impractical to make a money payment supervision order and any such conclusion must be stated in the warrant.

Need for further advice
This handbook does not deal further with any of the above enforcement powers which can be fraught with technical difficulties. Advice should be taken, especially where custody or human rights issues are in prospect: 📖✋.

COMMUNITY SENTENCES

> **THRESHOLD CRITERION**: '. . . the offence, or the combination of the offence and one or more offences associated with it, [is] 'serious enough' to warrant such a sentence'. This criterion applies to *all* eight community orders below, i.e. the community sentence threshold must be reached *before* a particular order or orders can be selected.

> **RESTRICTION ON LIBERTY**: all community sentences place demands on the offender's time, energies or activities. The extent of the restriction must be ' . . . commensurate with the seriousness of the offence, or the combination of the offence and one or more offences associated with it.'
>
> **SUITABILITY**: There is an extra (sometimes conflicting) consideration in that the community order or orders chosen must be the most suitable for the offender: below.

Associated offences

The meaning of associated offences is outlined in *Chapter 1*.

The eight community orders

A community sentence is '. . . a sentence which consists of or includes one or more community orders'. This enables courts to tailor decisions by selecting one or more orders from the menu of eight community orders available in the adult magistrates' court, even theoretically for a single offence: but see further under the heading *Combining community sentences, below.* The eight adult community orders are:

- **community rehabilitation order** (CRO: with or without added requirements)
- **community punishment order** (CPO)
- **community punishment and rehabilitation order** (CPRO)
- **attendance centre order**: under 21 years of age only (contrast the age limit for fine defaulters, i.e. up to 24 years inclusive: page 52)
- **curfew order**
- **drug treatment and testing order**
- **drug abstinence order** (where formally available locally)
- **exclusion order** (where formally available locally).[3]

---

3 'Supervision orders' and 'action plan orders' are available for people under 18 years of age only, i.e. in the youth court. For further information see *Introduction to Youth Justice*, Winston Gordon, Philip Cuddy and Jonathan Black, Waterside Press, 1999; *Child Law*, Richard Powell, Waterside Press, 2001.

Restriction on liberty and suitability
Once the court is satisfied that the offence or offences are 'serious enough' to warrant a community sentence, two main considerations arise:

- the community order (or orders) must be the 'most suitable for the offender'
- the restriction on liberty arising from the community order (or orders) must be commensurate with the seriousness of the offence or offences.

There is thus a dual responsibility for the sentencer: that of deciding on the appropriate degree of restriction on liberty (as determined by the seriousness of the offence or offences), whilst ensuring that the community order or orders is or are the most suitable for the offender. This balancing exercise is one which makes considerable demands on the sentencer's skills, and requires close attention if fair, appropriate and consistent sentencing practices are to be maintained. The statutory provision which creates these considerations mentions suitability *before* restriction on liberty. This is the only clue as to how any conflict might be resolved, i.e. possibly in favour of suitability (except, of course, where a suitable sentence would involve greater restriction of liberty than can be justified by the seriousness of the offence).

Core issues
To make proper decisions, sentencers need an understanding of certain core matters:

- the factors inherent in each type of offence which are likely to affect seriousness, whether as aggravating or mitigating factors
- any personal and other factors which may be relevant to seriousness (e.g. previous convictions: *Chapter 7,* or in some instances the offender's personal circumstances: see *Chapter 3;* and contrast personal information which falls to be taken into account later in the sentencing process by way of mitigation)
- what value to place on each of these factors so as to ensure a fair and consistent approach—taking account of good sentencing practice and local guidelines
- what each type of community order seeks to achieve and what demands it makes on an offender; and
- the comparative restriction on liberty which each of the eight community orders places on the offender's liberty—and how these restrictions correlate in terms of duration, intensity, frequency and effect on offenders.

Dialogue with the National Probation Service and the move to accredited programmes
There is a need for liaison between sentencers and those who write pre-sentence reports (PSRs) and specific sentence reports (SSRs) and supervise community orders—and an understanding on key matters—what is nowadays known as a 'communications strategy' (see *Chapter 9*). Many local probation areas and courts have entered into such dialogue through sentencer/probation liaison forums and this has been accompanied by a move to nationally accredited programmes with clear and consistent content. The intention, it seems, is that *all* community orders

(but especially, to begin with, community rehabilitation orders: below) will operate to nationally accredited formats under the general auspices of the Correctional Services Accreditation Panel (*Chapter 1*). That panel will also deal with HM Prison Service programmes so as to ensure that there is some kind of nexus between what happens in relation to offenders serving sentences in custody and those subject to punishment in the community—meaning both offenders on community orders and those who remain subject to continuing obligations following early (or temporary) release: *Chapter 10*. The NPS has also developed and published information concerning Enhanced Community Punishment (ECP) (see under *Community Punishment Order* below).

Factors relevant to assessing seriousness

A note of some general factors affecting the assessment of seriousness is contained in *Chapter 2* under *Structured Decision-making* whilst other seriousness factors can be seen in relevant parts of *Appendices A* and *B*.

Some factors relevant to 'suitability'

Bearing in mind that offender based factors can also sometimes affect the seriousness of the offence as mentioned in *Chapter 2*, the following may be particularly relevant to the *suitability* of an order or orders for an individual offender:

—the type of restriction on liberty and effort or input required
—family or work commitments
—health issues
—the age of the offender
—the offender's mobility or lack of mobility
—the perceived cause of offending
—the offender's own needs to enable him or her to turn away from offending
—the offender's general ability and motivation to undertake and complete the order
—the offender's consent or his or her willingness to comply with the order (where relevant: see page 56) or his or her motivation
—any risk of re-offending
—the protection of the public
—the prevention of future offending by the offender
—responses to previous sentences by the offender, especially community orders; and
—religious considerations.

Quite apart from the fair trial provisions of the European Convention On Human Rights (Article 6) which place greater emphasis on explanations to the offender at appropriate stages and reasons for decisions, the Convention also has the effect of requiring a court to bear in mind—over and above domestic law considerations concerning restriction of liberty being commensurate with the seriousness of the offence and the suitability of any community sentence for a particular offender—that the offender also has other basic rights, e.g. in relation to Article 4 (liberty and security) and Article 8 (respect for private and family life). See, generally, *Chapter 2*.

Combining community orders

A community sentence may contain one or more of the eight adult community orders (subject to one limitation and any age restrictions). The limitation is that a CRO and CPO can only be combined by way of a CPRO. Case law confirms that a court has no power to make a CRO and a CPO together, even in relation to separate offences for which sentence has been passed at the same hearing. In constructing a community sentence containing multiple orders the court must consider the overall restriction of liberty and be careful not to arrive at a *disproportionate* sentence. Legal advice may be desirable 📖✋.

Despite the apparent intention of Parliament at the time of the Criminal Justice Act 1991, opinion apparently still remains divided on using both a fine and community sentence for a single offence—although this is a possibility in relation to separate offences. By statute, a CRO cannot be made at the same time as a suspended sentence of imprisonment, even in respect of a separate offence. In practice, a CRO alongside a curfew order or a drug treatment and testing order seems to be fairly commonplace and, indeed, commonly said to be practically desirable as part of an overall community sentence package.

Ancillary orders such as costs, endorsement, disqualification and a CRASBO (see *Chapter 6*) can always be added to a community sentence. Compensation *must* be considered in appropriate cases: *Chapter 5*.

Pre-sentence reports (PSRs) and specific sentence reports (SSRs)

In considering the question of suitability, the court must take into account any information before it about the offender. The court must normally obtain and consider a pre-sentence report (PSR) before deciding on the suitability for the offender of:

- a community rehabilitation order (CRO) with added requirements
- a community punishment order (CPO)
- a community punishment and rehabilitation order (CPRO)
- a drug treatment and testing order.

Failure to comply with this requirement will not, of itself, render the sentence invalid and, indeed, the court can deem a PSR to be 'unnecessary'. Good practice nevertheless suggests that a PSR—or when appropriate a specific sentence report (SSR) (a focused form of PSR which addresses specific community sentences)—should normally be called for when any type of community order is being considered: see, generally, *Chapter 9*.

Consents and/or willingness to comply

The need for offenders to consent to, or express a willingness to comply with, community orders has been dispensed with by statute. Such 'agreement' is now *only* required under domestic law in relation to CROs with additional requirements relating to treatment for a mental condition or alcohol dependency (page 59) and drug treatment and testing orders (page 67). The situations in which custody can be imposed because of unwillingness to undertake a community order are thus correspondingly fewer. In other situations offenders who might at first indicate that they are not willing to undertake, say, a CPO can now, under domestic law, be made subject to such an order nonetheless.

Consent and Human Rights
Article 4(2) of the European Convention On Human Rights states that 'no-one shall be required to perform forced or compulsory labour'. Following the Human Rights Act 1998, there was an initial difference of opinion as to whether the effect of Article 4(2) was to reintroduce the concept of consent in relation to community punishment orders (which involve work in the community: see later in the chapter). The view that consent was being reintroduced is not now widely held. It can also be noted that Article 4(3) excludes work done 'in the ordinary course of detention'. Generally, if such points arise seek advice: 📖✋.

A prudent approach to 'willingness to comply'
It is sound practice for more general reasons to seek from the offender at least an assurance of his or her preparedness to comply with the order if it is to be effective. This is dictated by ordinary prudence and good sentencing practice. Knowing that an offender *will* cooperate helps to make best use of finite resources and avoids the need to bring enforcement proceedings and possibly the need to sentence afresh where breach of the order (see below) appears inevitable from the outset. Similarly, where the defendant indicates clearly that he or she *will not* cooperate, this lack of motivation is bound to influence the court's assessment whether, on reflection, that particular order is the most suitable community sentence for the offender. Magistrates need to proceed with caution: an offender cannot be seen to be dictating his or her terms, nor should the NPS have recalcitrant people on orders.

Legal effect of refusing a community sentence
In those few situations where consent *is* still required by domestic law (see above), a refusal to consent allows the imposition of custody at the outset, again assuming the offence carries imprisonment. This is so even if the particular offence was not deemed 'so serious' in the first place. Custody can be used on breach of the order: page 71. However, the fact that refusal to consent to some community orders can lead to a custodial sentence need not preclude the court from considering other forms of community (or financial) orders to which the offender might consent, or for which consent is not required. Again, care must be taken that the offender is not dictating his or her own terms. It should be noted that any 'consent' generated by good sentencing practice or human rights considerations cannot in itself lead to custody for refusal to consent, but only if domestic law allows this: 📖✋.

Explanations
There is in respect of most community orders an obligation to explain to the offender the effect of the proposed order. This is good practice and a precursor to obtaining full and informed consent or an expression of willingness to comply where required. This aspect is further reinforced as a result of the Human Rights Act 1998.

Breach aspects
'Wilful and persistent' breach of *any* community order (whether or not consent remains necessary at the outset: above) permits custody as an option on re-sentencing provided the original offence carried imprisonment and irrespective

of whether the community sentence was made as an alternative to custody: see *Breach of Community Orders* later in this chapter.

COMMUNITY REHABILITATION ORDER (CRO)

A CRO[4] can be made whether or not the maximum sentence for an offence includes imprisonment. The statutory purposes of a CRO are:

- to secure the offender's rehabilitation; or
- to protect the public from harm from the offender; or
- to prevent further offences by the offender.

Effect of a CRO
The offender is placed under the supervision of a probation officer for the area in which he or she resides or will reside. The offender must keep in touch with the supervising officer in accordance with instructions which the latter may give, and notify the officer of any change of address. These are sometimes called 'standard' or 'basic' requirements'.

Duration
A CRO lasts for such period as the court decides—from six months to three years.

Pre-sentence reports (PSRs) and specific sentence reports (SSRs)
Only CROs containing any of the statutorily provided specific additional requirements must be preceded by a PSR (unless on the facts of the case the court declares one to be 'unnecessary'). With the advent of nationally controlled accredited programmes in CROs the more common practice now appears to be to incorporate such programmes through such a specific additional requirement (so as to ensure a clear enforcement/breach route). This can usually be done via the SSR. However, any more particular additional requirements would usually call for a full PSR. See further in *Chapter 9*.

Willingness to comply ▢ ✍
By statute, *only* CROs with requirements relating to treatment for a mental condition or alcohol dependency (both below) require an expression of willingness to comply on the part of the offender. However, the general comments on page 56 concerning good sentencing practice and a prudent approach suggests that an indication of willingness to comply with the order (and any requirements) may serve to confirm 'suitability'.

Additional requirements ▢ ✍
All CROs, even 'basic' orders (above) involve some element of accredited activity. If felt desirable for any of the statutory purposes of a CRO (above) the court may insert one or more extra requirements as follows:

- *a requirement as to residence*. This could be:
  —residence in an approved probation hostel managed by the NPS or a voluntary sector organization

---

4 Formerly called the probation order.

—residence at a non-approved hostel or other institution such as a dependency clinic which may tackle drug or alcohol addictions (often private organizations)

—a requirement to reside where directed by the probation officer. This is likely to be in the offender's home area at a private address considered suitable by a probation officer and the requirement will restrict the offender from moving without first seeking approval from the probation officer.

- *a requirement to attend (i) a probation centre or (ii) other specified activities for up to 60 days*

  —a probation centre is a resource approved by the Secretary of State offering an intensive programme which addresses offending behaviour and its various causes. Offenders are expected to attend for a full day and for as many days as necessary (up to 60 days in all) to complete the programme. Probation centres are usually for those at the top end of the 'serious enough' scale.

  —specified activities are currently approved locally by the area probation board. Offenders can be required to attend a specified activity—e.g. an alcohol education group—for up to 60 days or a range of activities according to their needs (e.g. an offending behaviour group, anger management course, substance misuse group). A 'session' lasting for, say, two hours counts as a day.

  —there is one exception to the 60 day maximum rule and this applies to sex offenders. There is no upper limit on the number of days for which attendance can be required (subject to not exceeding the CRO term), but the court which imposes the requirement must specify the number of days the offender must attend a sex offenders' group (or other facility) when making the order. 'Specified activities' is the usual route where it is felt preferable to have a specific requirement to incorporate accredited programmes.

- *a requirement to receive treatment for a mental condition.* This condition can only be used when the court has an assessment from a 'section 28 Mental Health Act 1983 approved' psychiatrist and treatment is actually available from either a psychiatrist or chartered psychologist. The requirement can be for the length of the CRO or part as specified by the court. (For *Mentally Disordered Offenders* generally, see *Chapter 11*).

- *a requirement to receive treatment for alcohol dependency.* This refers to out-patient or residential facilities—usually for the seriously addicted. There is no restriction on the period of the requirement. It can be for the full duration of the CRO or a specific part of it, as determined by the court.

Other requirements
Courts have a general discretion to construct other requirements to meet special needs within the overall purposes of a CRO. However, this discretion should not be used to circumvent any of the statutory requirements 📖✋.

Enforcement
The general enforcement provisions for community orders are described later in the chapter. Where the offender has been required by the NPS to participate in an

accredited programme it is important at the enforcement stage for the court to be satisfied that the programme is covered by the terms of the order, e.g. by way of a specified activities requirement subject to a degree of leeway where an accredited element is delivered as an integral part of a 'basic' or 'standard' order. Advice is desirable at the enforcement stage during a developing situation 📖✋.

Key procedures and requirements when considering/making a CRO

> - community sentence—*The offence must be 'serious enough'*
> - age limits—*16 or over*[5]
> - minimum period—*Six months*
> - maximum period—*Three years*
> - PSR—*Required unless deemed 'unnecessary'*—*Good practice suggests at least a specific sentence report (SSR)*
> - explanation—*At time of sentence (and any other appropriate stages)*
> - willingness to comply—*Essential for requirements relating to treatment for a mental condition and those for alcohol dependency. Prudent in other situations.*
> - human rights implications—*The defendant must be able to understand clearly what is happening at each stage and be given appropriate opportunities to participate in the proceedings by making representations. Reasons should be announced.*

COMMUNITY PUNISHMENT ORDER (CPO)

Under a CPO[6] the offender must perform unpaid work in the community (a form of reparation) for a fixed number of hours, specified by the court, within a set period. A probation officer or someone employed by the NPS oversees this. At the time of writing, the NPS is developing 'Enhanced Community Punishment' (ECP) and has announced that 'once implemented nationally', all CPOs will be delivered as ECP. ECP is based on 'What Works' principles with the aim of maximising the rehabilitative potential of a CPO but without detracting from its effectiveness and rigour. It seeks to take advantage of the significant amount of NPS contact time with people carrying out such orders when the offender can be encouraged, e.g. to develop pro-social attitudes, employment-related and problem solving skills. The scheme is described in *NPS Briefing*, No.8 of 2002 📖✋. The content of a CPO is also likely to attract accreditation as this approach extends and develops (above).

Duration
The minimum number of hours of work is 40 and maximum 240. This must be performed within 12 months of the order being made, although the order remains in effect until the work is completed. All periods (even those made for

---

[5] If an offender in the adult magistrates' court is under 18 years of age the case will need to be remitted to the youth court where a community sentence is in view 📖✋.

[6] Formerly called the community service order.

breach of a community order) will take effect forthwith (i.e. concurrently) unless specifically ordered to be consecutive to another order, whether made on the same or a separate occasion: advice is desirable 📖✋.

Imprisonable offences and 'alternatives to custody'
A CPO can *only* be made if the maximum sentence for the offence includes imprisonment. Until 1991, community service (the forerunner of the CPO) was often viewed as an 'alternative to custody' (i.e. custody was said to be deserved on the facts but the court would instead impose a direct alternative, on the clear understanding that custody would almost inevitably follow on any breach). The Criminal Justice Act 1991 was seen by many people as abandoning this approach. However, there has apparently survived or re-emerged in some minds the concept of any community sentence, and a CPO in particular, being viewed as such an alternative. This is based on a decision that the offence itself is 'so serious' that custody is appropriate, but (following *R v Cox* [1993], 2 All ER 19) which held that custody does not by law need to follow automatically from such a decision) that a lesser sentence can be imposed, e.g. to reflect personal factors/mitigation. In such cases, the court would announce the basis of its decision (which should be recorded for later reference) and thereafter custody could follow on breach (see later in this chapter), irrespective of whether the breach was 'wilful and persistent' (the usual criteria).

Pre-sentence reports and CPO 'assessment'
A PSR (*Chapter 9*) is required before deciding whether to impose a CPO unless the court deems such a report to be 'unnecessary'. A specific sentence report (SSR) may suffice. There is, in any event, with the CPO a quite separate legal requirement whereby the court must be satisfied that the offender is a suitable person to perform work under such an order and that work is available—often by way of a 'CPO assessment' (which, unlike the PSR itself, can be oral or written: the assessment can, of course, be incorporated in a PSR or SSR). Care must be taken when calling for reports not to pre-empt the eventual decision: *Chapter 9*.

Consent and willingness to comply 📖✋
Since 1997 the offender's consent to a CPO is no longer required under domestic law. However, the general comments on page 56 concerning good sentencing practice and the need for a prudent approach suggests that an indication of willingness to comply with the order should be obtained from the offender.

Key procedures and requirements when considering/making a CPO

- community sentence—*The offence must be 'serious enough'*
- age limits—*16 or over* (see footnote 5, page 60)
- criteria—*Offender suitable person to perform unpaid work; work available*
- minimum period—*40 hours*
- maximum period—*240 hours (performance of work normally within 12 months)*
- Imprisonable offence—*Essential*
- PSR/information—*Required unless deemed 'unnecessary'—Good practice suggests at least a specific sentence report (SSR); CPO assessment essential*
- consent—*Not required, but prudent to ensure willingness to comply*
- explanation— *At time of sentence (and any other appropriate stages)*
- human rights implications—*The defendant must be able to understand clearly what is happening at each stage and be given appropriate opportunities to participate in the proceedings by making representations. Reasons should be announced.*

COMMUNITY PUNISHMENT AND REHABILITATION ORDER (CPRO)

The community punishment and rehabilitation order (CPRO)[7] combines elements of the CRO and the CPO (including 'Enhanced Community Punishment', above). This is the *only* way in which both such sentences can be imposed together for a single offence or on the same sentencing occasion. There are no specific statutory purposes for CPROs themselves, but the fact that the order incorporates elements of a CRO means that the purposes set out in relation to CROs (above) are incorporated into the thinking behind that part of the order—and work must be available with regard to the CPO part.

This is a single order even though the constituent parts are supervised or monitored separately. The offender is subject to the same obligations for each part of the order as he or she would be if each had been made independently and, e.g. restrictions concerning the effect of the CPO part of the order on work, education and religion equally apply.

Requirements can be added to the CRO part of the order (see under *Community Rehabilitation Order* above and where necessary seek advice: 📖✋). However, attention must always be paid to the total restriction on liberty to ensure that this does not become disproportionate to the seriousness of the offence or offences concerned.

---

[7] Formerly called the combination order.

Duration
A combination order involves:

- a CRO element of *at least* 12 months (as opposed to the six months minimum for 'a straight CRO') up to three years

- a CPO element of between 40 and 100 hours (as compared to a maximum of 240 hours for a free-standing CPO).

Restriction of liberty and suitability
The very nature of the CPRO means that care needs to be taken when assessing the extent of restriction on liberty and the suitability of what may be a particularly demanding order for the offender in question—especially if requirements are to be added to the CRO part of the order. The outcome must not be *disproportionate* to the offence.

Imprisonable offences
The maximum sentence for the offence must include imprisonment.

Pre-sentence reports
A PSR is required before considering a CPRO unless the court deems such a report 'unnecessary'. Taking the component parts of a CPRO individually, logic might suggest that a specific sentence report (SSR) might suffice if there are no added requirements to the CRO part of the order and provided there is a CPO assessment. But practice seems to dictate a full PSR due to the overall restriction of liberty involved and that the court is operating at the upper end of the community sentence band. There is a separate requirement whereby the court must be satisfied that the offender is a suitable person to perform work under the CPO part—i.e. for a CPO assessment—and work must be available: see under *Community Punishment Order*, above.

Consent and willingness to comply 📖✋
By statute (and since 1997) the offender *only* needs to consent to a CPRO to the extent that there are requirements in the CRO element which, if inserted in a free-standing CRO, would require that consent: see under *Community Rehabilitation Order* above. However, the general comments on page 56 concerning good sentencing practice and the need for a prudent approach suggests that willingness to comply with both the CRO and the CPO elements of the order should be obtained from the offender.

Key procedures and requirements when considering/making a CPRO

- community sentence—*The offence must be 'serious enough'*
- age limits—*16 or over* (see the comment in footnote 5, page 60)
- minimum period of CRO supervision—*One year*
- maximum period of CRO supervision—*Three years*
- CPO element—*Minimum 40 hours; maximum 100 hours*
- criteria—*As for CRO and CPO respectively (see above)*
- imprisonable offence—*Essential*
- restriction of liberty—*Special attention should be paid to the combined effect of imposing both CRO and CPO elements at the same time*
- PSR/information—*Essential for certain CRO requirements, as per CROs above. Otherwise, required unless deemed 'unnecessary' (SSRs would appear to be insufficient: see page 63); CPO assessment essential re that part*
- explanation—*At time of sentence (and other appropriate stages)*
- consent—*No longer required by law (except for those CRO conditions which do require consent), but it is prudent to ensure willingness to comply*
- human rights implications—*The defendant must be able to understand clearly what is happening at each stage and be given appropriate opportunities to participate in the proceedings by making representations. Reasons should be announced.*

CURFEW ORDER

Under a curfew order the offender is required to remain—for periods specified by the court in the order—at a particular place (usually, but not necessarily, his or her home) or places. Different places may be specified for different periods. The order is monitored by someone selected from a list of people specified for the purpose by the Home Secretary (who may be drawn from the private sector). Restrictions apply comparable to those for community service (above) concerning the effect on work, education and religion. Monitoring is by way of electronic 'tagging' of the offender (see below).

Duration
The order can be for between two and 12 hours a day which may be spread over one or more blocks. It can last for up to six months.

No need for an imprisonable offence
Curfew orders can be made in respect of *any* offence whether or not the maximum sentence for that offence includes imprisonment—although the 'serious enough' test for a community sentence must be satisfied and the court needs to consider, in particular, the extent of restriction of liberty.

Pre-sentence reports
There is no statutory obligation to obtain a PSR. However, the court must obtain information about the place(s) which it is proposed to specify in the order, and the effect that the order will have on people likely to be affected by the offender's presence at that place—pointing to the desirability of a PSR or at least a specific sentence report (SSR).

Willingness to comply 📖✋
Since 1997 the offender's agreement to a curfew order is not required. However, the comments on page 56 concerning good sentencing practice and a prudent approach apply equally here as they do in relation to those community sentences already discussed.

Electronic monitoring of curfew orders
Electronic monitoring of curfew orders is now available to all courts in England and Wales in respect of offenders aged 16 (see footnote 5, page 40) and over.

Key procedures and requirements when considering/making a curfew order

---

- community sentence—*The offence must be 'serious enough'*
- age limits—*16 or over* (see the comment in footnote 5, page 60)
- parameters—*Maximum sentence is six months. The curfew order can specify between one and seven days per week. Length of curfew may be two to 12 hours per day*
- the offence need not be imprisonable
- restriction of liberty—*Special attention should be paid to the effect on the offender*
- PSR/information—*Not required. Good practice suggests at least a specific sentence report (SSR). Must obtain and consider information about proposed curfew address including attitude of others affected by order*
- explanation—*At time of sentence (and any other appropriate stages)*
- consent—*No longer required, but prudent to ensure willingness to comply*
- human rights implications—*The defendant must be able to understand clearly what is happening at each stage and be given appropriate opportunities to participate in the proceedings by making representations. In constructing the order, there may a need to consider the offender's right to private and family life and that of other people who may be affected. If the offence is non-imprisonable, the restriction of liberty involved in a curfew raises issues of proportionality. Reasons should be announced.*

ATTENDANCE CENTRE ORDER (UNDER 21s ONLY)

The occupation and instruction at an attendance centre includes 'a programme of group activities designed to assist offenders to acquire or develop personal responsibility, self-discipline, skills and interest'. Centres operate under the auspices of the police/youth offending teams (YOTs) (regime changes are currently taking place: the plan appears to be to integrate provision with youth justice services). The regime is typically one of discipline, physical training, social awareness and social skills (and currently subject to possible changes). A centre must be accessible to the offender, i.e. within reasonable distance 📖✋.

Duration and prerequisites
Attendance centre orders (ACOs) are available for offenders aged ten to 20 years inclusive, although there are separate junior and senior facilities. In the case of adult offenders (i.e. aged 18 to 20 inclusive) the order may be for between 12 and 36 hours. The court must fix the time of the first attendance but the centre organizer determines the length of individual attendances and further dates. Attendance can be required only once on any one day and for no more than three hours on any one occasion.

Pre-sentence reports
A PSR is not a legal prerequisite but special attention should be paid to the following: the centre must be reasonably accessible to the offender having regard to means of access, age and other relevant circumstances (centres for females, or 'mixed centres' are less common than those for males); as far as practicable, attendance must not interfere with school/work.

Imprisonable offences
The maximum sentence for the offence must include imprisonment.

Consent
The consent of the offender is not required.

Key procedures and requirements when considering/making an attendance centre order

---

- community sentence—*The offence must be 'serious enough'*
- age limits—*Ten* (see footnote 5, page 60) *to under 21 (under 25 when used in respect of fine default)*
- minimum period—*If defendant at least 14* (footnote 5, page 60), *minimum is 12 hours*
- maximum period—*36 hours where defendant aged 16 or over* (see footnote 5, page 60)
- prerequisite—*A reasonably accessible centre must be available*
- imprisonable offence—*Essential*
- PSR—*Not a legal prerequisite.*
- explanation—*At time of sentence (and any other appropriate stages)*
- consent— *Not required.*
- human rights implications—*The defendant must be able to understand clearly what is happening at each stage and be given appropriate opportunities to participate in the proceedings by making representations. Reasons should be announced.*

Attendance centre for fine default
Attendance centre orders can also be used for fine defaulters up to age 24 inclusive.

DRUG TREATMENT AND TESTING ORDER (DTTO)

The Crime and Disorder Act 1998 introduced this form of community sentence which is aimed at people convicted of a crime or crimes to fund their drug habit and who show a willingness to co-operate with treatment. The offender must be dependent on drugs or have a propensity to misuse them and such dependency/propensity must require and be susceptible to treatment. In order to ascertain dependency or propensity the court may, before making a DTTO and provided the offender is willing, require him or her to provide samples for testing. Whilst not specified in legislation, there must presumably be some actual or assumed nexus between drugs and the individual's offending.

The offender must be aged 16 years or over (see footnote 5, page 60) and the order will have effect for between six months and three years. The court can, with the offender's consent, make an order requiring him or her to undergo treatment for a drug problem under a DTTO. This can be and usually is in tandem with another community order (especially a CRO), or can be on its own. Once agreed to, testing is mandatory. The court must be satisfied that arrangements for implementing the order have been made in the relevant area. The offence need not be imprisonable but this *is* a community sentence, so that the offence(s) must pass the 'serious enough' test (above).

Nature of the order
The DTTO must include:

- a treatment requirement stating whether this will be residential or non-residential and the identity of the treatment provider
- a testing requirement with a specified frequency of drug testing
- provisions specifying the petty sessions area where the offender will reside; a minimum frequency for providing samples each month; that for the treatment and testing period, the offender shall be under National Probation Service supervision, and the responsible officer must be informed of the results of tests; and
- the offender is required to attend review hearings which are held at intervals of not less than one month. At these hearings the court might encourage or warn the offender and may amend the order. If the offender fails to express willingness to comply with whatever the court proposes by way of amendment, the court may revoke the order and the offender can be re-sentenced. If this happens, the court should take into account the extent of any compliance with the order. Re-sentencing could involve a custodial sentence provided the original offence is imprisonable.

The offender will have to consent to the order and the treatment provider's assessment will have to accompany/be incorporated into the PSR so that the court can be satisfied that the offender is susceptible to treatment and that there is a place on a treatment programme.

The treatment provider will be the main supervisor of testing and will decide when and where the tests, to be randomly allocated, are taken, subject to the court's testing requirement. Treatment providers may take as many tests as they wish, but they must take the minimum number of tests required by the court and submit the results to the supervising probation officer, who will report them to the court. In addition, the offender must report to a probation officer as required by him or her and notify the probation officer of any change of address.

If the court receives satisfactory reviews, it may decide that subsequent reviews should be without a formal hearing or in the absence of the defendant—when the supervising officer will still make a written report to the court. It can, at any time, reverse this decision.

Explanation to the offender

A court intending to make a DTTO must explain in ordinary language: the effect and meaning of the DTTO's requirements; the consequences of failure to comply; and the powers of the court to review the order. As well as the offender indicating that he or she is willing to comply with the order, copies must also be given to him or her, the treatment provider and the supervising probation officer.

Key procedures and requirements when considering/making drug treatment and testing orders

---

- community sentence—*The offence must be 'serious enough'*
- age limits—*16 plus* (see footnote 5, page 40)
- minimum period—*Six months*
- maximum period—*Three years*
- need not be an imprisonable offence
- prerequisites—*The court must be satisfied arrangements for implementing order have been made in the relevant court area (these should now be available nationwide); offender must be dependent on drugs or have a propensity to misuse them*
- PSR—*Required*
- explanation—*At time of sentence (and any other appropriate stages)*
- consent—*Essential (testing is then mandatory)*
- *the defendant must be able to understand clearly what is happening at each stage and be given appropriate opportunities to participate in the proceedings by making representations. Reasons should be announced.*

DRUG ABSTINENCE ORDER (DAO)

Drug abstinence orders were added as community orders to the Powers of Criminal Courts (Sentencing) Act 2000 by the Criminal Justice and Courts Services Act 2000. Courts cannot use this power until specifically notified by the Secretary of State that arrangements are in place for implementing the order in the court area in which it is to have effect. Basically the order applies as follows:

- the offender must be aged 18 or over at the time of conviction
- he or she must stand convicted of an offence (although *it need not be imprisonable*)
- the offence has, however, to pass the 'serious enough' test for a community order
- the offence also has to be a 'trigger offence' or the misuse of any specified Class A drug must have caused or contributed to its commission
- the offender also has to be dependent on, or have propensity to misuse, specified Class A drugs
- a PSR appears not to be a formal prerequisite but, in practice, is likely to be needed
- the offender is put under the supervision of a 'responsible officer' for a period of between six months and three years
- he or she has to refrain during the order from misusing specified Class A drugs and must provide samples when required by the responsible officer to check for any specified Class A drug
- there are periodic review hearings much as for DTTOs (above)
- the usual community order breach and review provisions apply (see below).

Key procedures and requirements when considering/making a drug abstinence order

> - community sentence—*The offence must be 'serious enough'*
> - age limits—*18 or over at the time of conviction*
> - minimum period—*Six months*
> - maximum period—*Three years*
> - *prerequisites*—A 'trigger' or class A drug misuse offence etc. and for notification by the Secretary of State that formal arrangements are in place in the local area.
> - PSR—*Not a formal prerequisite—Good practice suggests at least a specific sentence report (SSR)*
> - explanation—*At time of sentence (and any other appropriate stages)*
> - willingness to comply—*Prudent.*
> - human rights implications—*The defendant must be able to understand clearly what is happening at each stage and be given appropriate opportunities to participate in the proceedings by making representations. Reasons should be announced.*

EXCLUSION ORDER

Exclusion orders (not to be confused with similarly named, but quite different, orders used to exclude offenders from licensed premises where convicted of an offence of violence on such premises: *Chapter 6*) were added as community orders to the Powers of Criminal Courts (Sentencing) Act 2000 by the Criminal Justice and Courts Services Act 2000. Courts cannot use this power until specifically notified by the Secretary of State that arrangements are in place for implementing the order in the court area in which it is to have effect.

Whereas curfew orders (above) require offenders to be in certain places at certain times, exclusion orders require them *to keep out of* certain places at certain times. Basically the order applies as follows:

- there is no restriction on the age of the offender who can be subject to such an order
- he or she must be convicted of an offence (although *it need not be imprisonable*)
- the offence has, however, to pass the 'serious enough' test for a community order
- the offender is prohibited from entering specified places
- the order lasts for up to two years for offenders aged 18 years or over
- the order can apply on different days and to different periods
- a PSR appears not to be a formal prerequisite but, in practice, is likely to be needed
- care must be taken not to conflict with religious beliefs, work commitments, attendance at school or other educational establishment or with any other community orders
- there will be provisions for monitoring (including electronically)
- the usual community order breach and review provisions apply (see below).

Key procedures and requirements when considering/making an exclusion order

---

- community sentence—*The offence must be 'serious enough'*
- age limits—*None*[8]
- minimum period—*None specified*
- maximum period—*Two years*
- prerequisite—*the need to avoid conflict with work, education and religious beliefs etc and for notification by the Secretary of State that formal arrangements are in place in the local area.*
- PSR—*Not a formal prerequisite—Good practice suggests at least a specific sentence report (SSR)*
- explanation—*At time of sentence (and any other appropriate stages)*
- consent—*Not required.*
- human rights implications—*The defendant must be able to understand clearly what is happening at each stage and be given appropriate opportunities to participate in the proceedings by making representations. Reasons should be announced.*

---

[8]   If an offender in the adult magistrates' court is under 18 years of age the case will need to be remitted to the youth court where a community sentence is in view 📖✋.

BREACH OF COMMUNITY ORDERS

There have been extensive efforts to promote good practice in relation to the breach of community orders. These emphasise the importance of effective enforcement. The range of options is set out below. The National Probation Service (NPS) is expected to apply rigorously the breach provisions. For legal enforcement purposes, each community order is a self-contained disposal. Re-offending during the currency of an order does not, in itself, amount to a breach. Different provisions apply to failures to comply with the requirements of the different types of order.

CROs, CPOs, CPROs, curfews, DTTOs, drug abstinence orders and exclusion orders

Failure 'without reasonable excuse' to comply with a requirement of any of these orders can, on the matter being returned to court, result in one of the following outcomes:[9]

- no action (usually seen as an exceptional course given that the breach will have been 'without reasonable excuse')
- a fine of up to £1,000
- a CPO for up to 60 hours (now known in this context as a 'secondary order'); or
- an attendance centre order (under 21 year olds only).

In each case the original community order continues to run. However, see next heading.

Resentencing and revocation

The court has the option of re-sentencing for the original offence and, if needs be, revoking the original order (if still in force). If it does resentence, there is a legal requirement to give credit to the extent, if any, to which compliance occurred.

'Wilful and persistent' failure to comply with the terms of the order may, *if the original offence carried imprisonment*, result in a custodial sentence on resentencing in breach proceedings. This is a basis for a custodial sentence even if the seriousness of the original offence did not in itself warrant custody: see generally under *Custody*, below. If, however, the original community sentence was made as an alternative to custody (i.e. where the 'so serious test' was, in fact, satisfied but the court imposed a lesser sentence), it is not strictly necessary to find wilful or persistent breach. It is thus important that sentencing courts announce and make a full record of their reasons for imposing a community order since this may be of central relevance in any later breach proceedings.

Community orders made by the Crown Court

If the community order was made by the Crown Court, the breach, once established, must (except where the order was made on appeal against sentence

---

[9] The Child Support, Pensions and Social Security Act 2000, section 62 provides for potential loss of state benefits, at the instance of the Secretary of State, on breach of certain community orders. The method, now being piloted, seems draconian and has human rights implications. See an article in *The Times*, 14 May 2002.

from a magistrates' court) be referred back to the Crown Court if re-sentencing is to be considered. The Crown Court can, on making a community order, reserve determination of any breach to itself. In such cases, magistrates' courts issue the relevant enforcement process but the offender is taken to or appears directly in the Crown Court.

Attendance centre order (ACO)

Failure to attend or comply with the rules of the centre may result in:

- no action: there is no need to prove that breach of an ACO (unlike most other community orders) was 'without reasonable excuse'
- a fine of up to £1,000
- re-sentencing for the original offence and revocation of the original order (or committal to the Crown Court if that court made the original order). There are provisions analogous to those for other community orders whereby credit must be given to the extent that compliance has occurred, and allowing a custodial sentence to be imposed if the failure was 'wilful and persistent'.

Human rights considerations

It should be noted that the human rights considerations outlined in *Chapter 2* apply equally at the breach stage as they do when a community order is first made. Any temptation to lose sympathy with an offender (who might be viewed as having been already allowed his or her chance) should be avoided insofar as this may lead to cutting corners or premature or unsupported conclusions. Explanations will need to be made and valid reasons given even at this stage.

AMENDMENT/REVOCATION OF ORDERS

There are provisions for amending CROs, CPOs, CPROs, curfew orders, drug treatment and testing orders, drug abstinence orders and exclusion orders; and for the offender or supervisor to apply for revocation if there is a change in circumstances. Revocation can be ordered on its own, or coupled with re-sentencing depending on the circumstances. In some instances a subsequent court, on sentencing an offender to an immediate custodial sentence, can revoke an earlier order, but then it has no power to re-sentence for the original offence. Attendance centre orders have their own statutory code for amendment and revocation. Seek further advice as necessary: 📖✋.

CUSTODY 📖🤚

> **THRESHOLD CRITERIA:** There are four bases for custody:
>
> • the offence, or the combination of the offence and one or more offences associated with it, is so serious that *only* such a sentence can be justified (known as the 'so serious' test); or
>
> • the offence is a sexual or violent offence (both widely defined by statute: see page 74 but also seek advice: 📖🤚) and only such a sentence would be adequate to protect the public from serious harm from the offender (known as the 'protection of the public' test); or
>
> • following refusal to consent to a community sentence which requires consent; or
>
> • on breach of a community sentence for 'wilful and persistent' failure to comply with the sentence or where the original order was used as an alternative to custody.

> **RESTRICTION ON LIBERTY:** The restriction resulting from custody is obvious—in that the offender is deprived of his or her physical freedom. However, the offender will normally be released under the scheme described in *Chapter 10* after serving part of his or her sentence.

Meaning of custody

Offenders aged 21 and over are sentenced to *imprisonment*. For those aged 18 to 20 years inclusive the order is for *detention* in a young offender institution (YOI)—when the *minimum* sentence is 21 days.[10] Custodial sentences take effect straight away (and, where there are two or more such sentences, concurrently unless the court has specifically ordered that they take effect consecutively, i.e. one after the other).

Associated offences

This has the meaning outlined in *Chapter 1* (see page 14).

Imprisonable offences

The offence must be imprisonable. The statute which creates the offence will state whether the offence in question attracts imprisonment. Contrast a term of custody for failure to pay a fine (above) that can be ordered regardless of whether the offence itself carries imprisonment and relates solely to the non-payment/default.

---

[10] Changes have been pending for some time that may affect the type of custody for people under 18 and 21 respectively 📖🤚. Note that, unlike imprisonment, detention in a YOI cannot be suspended.

Procedural requirements

Before imposing a custodial sentence, the court must take into account all information:

- available to it regarding the circumstances of the *offence* or *offences*, including aggravating or mitigating factors
- before it about the *offender* where custody or longer custody is being considered to protect the public from serious harm from an offender convicted of a violent or sexual offence.

'Sexual offence' and 'violent offence'—definitions

The 2000 Act lists those sexual offences to which the protection of the public ground for custody applies (the list covers most sexual offences—but not, e.g. indecent exposure). Violent offences are widely defined so as to cover situations where an offence 'leads, or is intended or likely to lead' to death or physical injury (including arson). Protection from 'serious harm' means '. . . protecting the public from death or serious injury, whether physical or psychological'. Court advisers will normally anticipate situations where definition is likely to be a live issue 📖✋.

Legal representation

There is a restriction on imposing custody (including a suspended sentence: below) where the offender is not legally represented after conviction and he or she is:

- under 21 years of age; or
- aged 21 or over and has never served a prison sentence (which does not include, e.g. an unactivated suspended sentence, detention in a young offender institution or committal for contempt or for non-payment of fines).

The court should explain the effect of these provisions to an unrepresented defendant—with a warning to use the opportunity that the court is obliged to offer by way of adjournment to acquire representation (if need be by applying for a grant of legal representation). Failure to obtain representation or to apply for a grant of legal representation will allow a subsequent court, if it considers it appropriate, to impose custody without the defendant being represented. An offender can waive these rights by declaring an unwillingness to consult a solicitor or to apply for a grant of legal representation—although it may be sensible to encourage him or her to consult the duty solicitor or probation officer before proceeding.

Pre-sentence reports (PSRs)

The court must obtain a PSR before deciding that either of the first two criteria for custody above (i.e. the 'so serious' test or the 'protection of the public' test) is made out—unless it deems a PSR to be 'unnecessary'. Such a report is similarly needed in order to assess the appropriate length of the custodial sentence.

The Court of Appeal indicated in *R v Gillette* (1999) that in every case where a court is considering sentencing any offender to imprisonment for the first time *it should be the inevitable practice* for a PSR to be first obtained.

There is no comparable legal requirement for a PSR before deciding on a custodial sentence for failure to consent to a community sentence which requires consent, or for wilful and persistent failure to comply with such a sentence (see above)—although the same considerations apply here as they do to other community sentence breach situations: the same standards of fairness and depth of consideration apply making a PSR prudent and good practice. There will always be a need for evidence of the failure and other relevant circumstances and information. Care must be taken as to what is said when calling for a PSR: see *Chapter 9.*[11]

Criteria for custodial sentences

In 1998, the Court of Appeal in *R v. Craig; R v. Howells and Others* gave guidance to judges and magistrates concerning the custody threshold. The guidance indicates that courts will usually find it helpful to begin by considering the nature and extent of the defendant's criminal intention and the nature and extent of any injury or damage caused to the victim. Other things being equal, an offence which is deliberate and premeditated will usually be more serious than one which is spontaneous and unpremeditated, or which involves an excessive response to provocation; an offence which inflicted personal injury or mental trauma, particularly if permanent, will usually be more serious than one which inflicted financial loss only. In considering the seriousness of any offence, the court might take into account any previous convictions of the offender or any failure to respond to previous sentences—and must treat it as an aggravating factor if the offence was committed whilst the offender was on bail or which involved racial or religious aggravation. The checklist guidance includes the following advice:

- an admission of responsibility for the offence, particularly when combined with a timely guilty plea and genuine remorse shown, e.g. by an expression of regret or an offer of compensation, is mitigation to which the court will have due regard
- previous good character will usually attract some measure of leniency, the more so if there is evidence of positive good character such as a good employment record and the faithful discharge of family responsibilities
- youth and immaturity will often justify a less severe penalty
- where the offence was fuelled by drink or drugs, any practical, genuine and self-motivated efforts by the offender to address his or her addiction will be looked upon favourably
- it will sometimes be appropriate to take into account family responsibilities or physical or mental disability
- courts must be mindful of the importance of maintaining public confidence in the sentencing system; and
- a court would never impose custody unless satisfied this was necessary; there would be yet greater reluctance to impose custody on an offender who had never served such a sentence.

---

[11] Specific sentence reports (SSRs) are not, it seems, appropriate for custody situations.

'Domestic' Burglary after R v. McInerney (2002) (Offenders aged 18 years or over)

Type of domestic burglary	Some typical Circumstances	First such offence	Second such offence	Subsequent offences	Plea before venue (Where applicable)	Mode of trial (Where applicable)
LOW LEVEL	No damage to house and no/low value stolen. Minimal damage to attached garage or vacant property and little/low value stolen.	Probably a community sentence (unless has significant previous convictions). Otherwise under 6 months.	Possibly a community sentence (unless has significant previous convictions). Otherwise up to 6 months.	Compulsory 3 years minimum if within 'three strikes' provisions. Indictable only.	Magistrates will usually retain sentencing jurisdiction.	May be asked to consider previous convictions, especially for domestic burglary. Will usually find suitable for summary trial.
STANDARD	Some damage on break in. Some turmoil. General household, electrical, personal goods stolen. No injury or violence.	Probably a community sentence if effective and practicable in circumstances (unless other previous convictions). Otherwise up to 12 months.	Possibly a community sentence if effective and practicable in circumstances (unless other previous convictions). Otherwise 9 months or more.	Compulsory 3 years minimum if within 'three strikes' provisions. Indictable only.		Magistrates may be asked to consider previous convictions, especially for domestic burglary. Not often suitable for summary trial.
STANDARD WITH MEDIUM RELEVANCE FACTORS	Vulnerable victim (need not have been targeted as such). Victim at home. High value or sentimental value goods stolen.	Possibly a community sentence if effective and practicable in circumstances (unless other previous convictions). Otherwise 12 months or more.	Indictable only.	Compulsory 3 years minimum if within 'three strikes' provisions.	*Usually commit for sentence:* 1. Crown Court to decide all matters thereafter 2. Unable to commit for sentence on breach of community order (*R v Chute* 2003).	*Not often suitable for summary trial.*
STANDARD WITH HIGH RELEVANCE FACTORS	Force, injury, trauma, vandalism, 'professional', racial, religious or targeted vulnerable person.	Possibly 18 months	Possibly up to 3 years	Indictable only.	*Always commit for sentence:* 1. Crown Court to decide all matters thereafter 2. Unable to commit for sentence on breach of community order (*R v Chute* 2003).	Magistrates should never retain sentencing jurisdiction. *Never* suitable for summary trial.
NB Use or threat of violence will make offence indictable only; see below						
SECTION 111 PCC(S) ACT 2000	Intent to commit indictable only offence or use of violence/threats					Indictable only
PARAGRAPH 28 OF SCHEDULE 1 MCA 1980	Third such offence after 30 September 1999 ('three strikes' provision)					Indictable only. Minimum 3 years

Legal advice should be sought in all the situations described above unless the position is clear and straightforward 🛑.

The use of custody post *R v. Kefford* and *R v. McInerney*

In *R v Kefford* (2002) Lord Woolf, Lord Chief Justice, indicated that prison overcrowding is a relevant consideration when deciding whether or not to send someone to custody because it impacts on the ability of HM Prison Service to tackle offending behaviour and reduce reoffending (see also *R v. Mills*, 14 January 2002 in the context of a dramatic increase in the women's prison population). In Lord Woolf's words, courts should heed the principle: 'imprisonment only when necessary and for no longer than necessary'. [12]

There had been a long held view amongst sentencers that, if an offence warranted custody, then courts should be free to make the order, and for the appropriate length of time, regardless of any financial or other resource considerations which might arise. This was first challenged, albeit obliquely, by section 95 of the Criminal Justice Act 1991 which required the Secretary of State to publish annually 'such information as he considers expedient' to inform sentencers and others in the criminal justice system of the 'financial implications of their decisions'.

However, general publicity about the increase in the prison population and about overcrowding in prisons and the escalating cost of running the penal system (said to be around £36,500 per annum per person in prison) cannot have escaped anybody's attention. In *R v. Kefford* (2002) (21 offences of dishonesty as an employee involving over £11,000 by a first offender—where sentence was reduced from 12 months to four months) the Lord Chief Justice recognised the following:

- there was at least a temporary situation in prisons where numbers were becoming unmanageable
- sentencers had to accept the 'realities of the situation'
- sentencers should, therefore, be more prepared than ever to consider 'alternative to custody' community orders wherever possible
- only crimes involving, e.g. violence, intimidation or sexual elements routinely needed (and indeed *prima facie* called for) a custodial sentence; and
- any custodial sentence should be for the shortest possible period.

Other rulings echoed this theme by suggesting, e.g. that custody was not even inevitable for an offence of dishonesty committed in breach of trust, and that a prime carer of a child (especially in the case of a woman) should be sent to custody only if really necessary. Later in 2002, in the case of *R v. McInerney*, the Lord Chief Justice, in a lengthy guideline judgment, took the matter much further in respect of 'domestic burglary' and, by implication at least, in respect of all other types of cases which hitherto had regularly attracted custodial sentences. The general points in that case included:

---

[12] For similar sentiments concerning community as opposed to custodial sentencing see the White Paper, *Justice For All*. In March 2003 the prison population stood at approximately 71,500 (virtually at capacity and well above HM Prison Service's 'uncrowded' figure of 64,000). *R v. Kefford* involved theft and false accounting in breach of trust but with significant personal mitigation.

- a direct consideration of suggestions made by the Sentencing Advisory Panel[13]
- the realities of overcrowding were reinforced
- the issue of cost became a more direct consideration
- community penalties were now seen as being more effective in many cases in preventing re-offending (taking over more strongly from the 1991 Act 'just deserts' approach) than custodial sentences
- an 'acceptance' by HM Prison Service that there is little it can do in practice to turn offenders away from crime unless they are in custody for at least 12 months
- a recognition that many offenders come out of custody fairly quickly in any event on home detention curfew
- a reference to the *British Crime Survey* which suggested that the public are often more in favour of effective community sentences rather than custody as a way of preventing further offending, but coupled with a greater call for custody for repeat offenders; and
- a possible suggestion that some guideline sentences could initially be reduced but then directly increased based on re-offending.

Sentencing for 'domestic burglary'

The case of *R v. McInerney* did not define 'domestic burglary' although there is a definition in section 111 Powers of Criminal Courts Act 2000 (the 'three strikes' provisions) which refers to a burglary 'committed in respect of a building or part of a building which is a dwelling'. Nonetheless, it appears that:

- the guideline starting point for certain domestic burglaries is now a community penalty
- this may be displaced in certain circumstances by factors such as:
  —the possible lack of efficacy of a community sentence in the particular circumstances
  —the existence of previous convictions, especially for domestic burglary.

The chart on page 76 attempts to summarise matters but must be read alongside detailed advice from the court legal adviser 📖✋.

How long should the custodial term be?

The seriousness of the offence (or need to protect the public from serious harm by the perpetrator of a sexual or violent offence) should determine the length of any custodial term within the legal maximum. The protection of the public criterion allows a sentence longer than is justified by 'seriousness' in respect of a sexual or violent offence. Orders which are possible in the magistrates' court are as follows:

- imprisonment may be imposed for any period from five days to the maximum available on summary conviction (this is usually fixed by statute at from one month to six months per offence)
- custodial terms can be ordered to take effect *consecutively* as follows:

---

[13] The first time, perhaps, that the panel's deliberations have truly had a direct impact on magistrates' courts sentencing practices.

— to previous sentences (i.e. those imposed on an earlier occasion)
— to other sentences passed on the same occasion subject to the following
limits:
  (a) six months in aggregate; or
  (b) where magistrates sentence to imprisonment in respect of two or
      more offences and at least two of them are either way offences,
      normally up to 12 months in aggregate (even if made up in part
      from imprisonment for summary matters)
— a suspended sentence (below) which is being activated can (and usually
  should) be made to run consecutively with other sentences passed on the
  same occasion or previously (see *Suspended Sentences*, below).

The above limits also apply to detention in a young offender institution (i.e. to
offenders in the age range 18 to 20 inclusive) but subject to a minimum sentence
of 21 days. This is designed to ensure that young offenders are not sentenced to
custody unless the offence warrants more than a nominal period. If the court
decides upon a custodial sentence, the Court of Appeal has—as already
explained—indicated that a sentence should be no longer than necessary to meet
its purpose (*R v. Kefford* and *R v Mills* (above); *R v. Howells*, [1997] 1 All ER 50).
An oft approved dictum is that of Lord Justice Rose in *R v. Ollerenshaw* (1998),
The Times, May 6:

> When a court is considering imposing a comparatively short period of custody, that is
> about 12 months or less, it should generally ask itself, particularly where the defendant
> had not previously been sentenced to custody, whether an even shorter period might be
> equally effective in protecting the interests of the public, and punishing and deterring
> the criminal. For example, there will be cases where, for these purposes, six months
> may be just as effective as nine, or two . . . as effective as four.

How these principles are applied

The facts of *Howells* and a connected case (*Robson and Howard*) demonstrate how
these principles are applied in practice. Howells pleaded guilty to affray and was
initially sentenced to nine months imprisonment. The affray concerned an
incident that took place outside a public house where Howells had been with two
friends. Initially a row started in the public house with the landlord and a fight
that had commenced inside the public house continued outside. Howells had
initially left but was struck on the back of the head and he retaliated by striking
his assailant a number of blows. His record of convictions and the serious
violence inflicted pointed towards imprisonment. However, his early plea, the
fact that he had not initiated the violence but retaliated, the fact that he had used
no weapons nor was he involved in kicking and that he had never been
sentenced to imprisonment before, were all features which pointed to a short
sentence. The Court of Appeal also considered that he had sole parental
responsibility for a very young child. In the event, that court replaced this
sentence with one of four months' imprisonment to indicate clearly that his
conduct was unacceptable.

Robson and Howard had no previous convictions. They were both under the
age of 21 and pleaded guilty to assault occasioning actual bodily harm which
involved gratuitous violence against a member of the public. This clearly pointed
to custody and each was sentenced to six months' detention in a young offender

institution. The Court of Appeal was impressed that both had exemplary work records and accepted that they were genuinely ashamed of their behaviour. The injury received by the victim (a severe black eye) was of a temporary nature and neither defendant had an alcohol problem albeit the offence itself had arisen from them drinking to excess. A period of two months' detention in a young offender institution was substituted for the original sentence.

Concurrent and consecutive sentences

As indicated above, magistrates can order custodial sentences to be served concurrently to one another or consecutively (within magistrates' maximum powers: above). The decision is a judicial one. The court must state clearly whether sentences are concurrent or consecutive, for even stronger reasons with respect to the latter.

In practice, sentences are usually ordered to take effect concurrently unless there is a specific reason for them to be made consecutive. This will primarily depend on the court's assessment of the combined seriousness of the particular offences under consideration, or as the case may be—in sexual or violent cases—the extent to which there is a need to protect the public from serious harm from the offender. Case law suggests that custodial sentences may be made consecutive where, e.g. the offences are of totally different types and/or are committed in separate incidents or whilst on bail.

Where an imprisonable offence has been committed during the operational period of a suspended sentence (below), the court should sentence for the new offence then decide whether to activate the suspended sentence. If it decides to do so, this will normally be consecutive to any period of imprisonment imposed for the fresh offence.

Committal to the Crown Court for sentence

Where magistrates conclude that their powers are insufficient they can commit to the Crown Court for sentence (see *Chapter 3*).

Short local detention

Where the offence carries imprisonment, the offender may instead be detained within the precincts of the court or at a police station for any period up until 8 p.m. (typically until the court rises). The offender must not be deprived of the opportunity to return home that day. None of the standard criteria, restrictions or prerequisites apply. The power can only be used where the offender is 21 years of age or over,[14] but the usual criteria for custody do not apply. Justices should check on the availability and suitability of local cells.

Explanations

Lord Bingham, a former Lord Chief Justice, indicated that courts should explain to a defendant the effect of a custodial sentence taking account of the early release provisions (*Chapter 9*) 📖✋. Reasons and explanations are reinforced by human rights considerations.

---

[14] Defendants aged 18 years upwards may, however, be placed in short local detention for fine default or contempt of court.

SUSPENDED SENTENCES

Imprisonment (but *not* detention in a young offender institution) may be suspended for between one and two years. The court must first be satisfied that immediate imprisonment is appropriate, i.e. that the 'so serious' threshold has been reached. A suspended sentence should never be viewed as some lesser disposal. There must thereafter be 'exceptional circumstances' to justify suspension. Case law indicates that the following *cannot* be exceptional circumstances: previous good character, provocation, youth, early guilty plea, domestic difficulties, loss of career, long public service, the effect on pension entitlements (factors which should have been taken into account as personal mitigation before custody was settled upon). The Court of Appeal has interpreted the term 'exceptional circumstances' narrowly. An example might be where an offender is in extremely poor health or where there is provocation.

Duty to consider a fine in addition
If the sentence of imprisonment *is* suspended the court *must* consider imposing, in addition, compensation and/or a fine.

Suspended sentences and CROs
A CRO cannot be made at the same time as a suspended sentence of imprisonment, even in relation to a separate offence.

Commission of a further imprisonable offence
Conviction of *any* imprisonable offence *committed* during the operational period of the suspended sentence makes the offender liable to serve the sentence in full. He or she should be warned of this. If so convicted:

- the original period can be implemented for its full length (consecutively or concurrently to any imprisonment for the new offence: see generally *Concurrent and consecutive sentences,* above). Implementation in full is compulsory unless the subsequent court considers that this would be unjust in all the circumstances, including the facts of the subsequent offence; or
- the original sentence can be implemented but reduced in length; or
- the sentence can be further suspended for up to two years; or
- the court can 'take no action'. This *is* a formal response. Courts should not take no action in the erroneous belief that the original court can still deal with the breach, particularly in the case of a Crown Court suspended sentence which magistrates cannot implement. They can either take no action or commit to the Crown Court (on bail or in custody) for it to consider the matter.

A Step-by-Step Approach to Sentencing

To be considered in conjunction with:

- the sentencing criteria in this chapter (and *Figure 1* on page 45)
- the *Magistrates' Court Sentencing Guidelines:* see *Appendix C;* and
- other complementary materials. e.g. Judicial Studies Board structured decision-making charts; reasons forms which may be in use locally: 📖✋.

NB Consideration of **COMPENSATION** pervades the whole sentencing process.

Consider the need for a PSR at appropriate points: *Chapter 9.*

Stage 1

DECIDE GUIDELINE LEVEL for an average offence of the type in question i.e.:

Level 1 Discharge
Level 2 Fine
Level 3 Community sentence
Level 4 Custody/consider committal for sentence

Stage 2

REVIEW in the light of aggravating and mitigating factors affecting the *particular* offence
MAKE ASSESSMENT as to sentence level

Stage 3

Do previous convictions or responses to earlier sentences affect this initial assessment? (see *Chapter 7*)
Was an offence committed whilst on bail?
Is the offence a racially or religiously aggravated offence?
REVISE ASSESSMENT as to level if appropriate.

Stage 4

CONSIDER whether, in certain situations, any matters concerning the particular offender affect the sentence level.
REVISE ASSESSMENT as to level *if appropriate*
Arrive at FINAL decision as to which level applies.

Stage 5

CONSIDER sentence WITHIN the level selected.
Do any of the following serve to reduce sentence *within* the level:
Previous good character?
Other personal mitigation ('offender mitigation')?

Fines: Consider guidelines and the defendant's individual financial circumstances and revise up or down as appropriate.

Community sentence: Consider 'restriction of liberty' and 'suitability'.

Custody: Consider length of sentence (noting the special rules for violent or sexual offences).

Whether or not considered at *Stage 3:*
Do previous convictions or responses to earlier sentences affect the above?
Is there an offence on bail, or is the offence racially or religiously aggravated?

Is any credit due for a timely guilty plea?

Stage 6

MAKE SURE COMPENSATION HAS BEEN ADEQUATELY CONSIDERED

Stage 7

CONSIDER the TOTALITY PRINCIPLE
Is the final sentence still proportionate to the offence or offences?
If you have departed significantly from the guideline level at *Stage 1,*
check your reasons.

Stage 8

Obtain any appropriate consent, agreement or indication of 'willingness'.

ANNOUNCE SENTENCE including any ancillary orders e.g. compensation, disqualification, endorsement, costs, forfeiture, ASBO (where appropriate).
Give reasons including any statutory ones 📖✋
Give appropriate explanations 📖✋
Note: *Always seek judicial advice before making a pronouncement in all but the most straightforward cases:* see, generally, *Chapter 12* 📖✋

Figure 2: A Step-by-Step Approach to Sentencing

Suspended sentence supervision orders

The Crown Court has power to make a suspended sentence supervision order when it suspends *more* than six months' imprisonment for a single offence. Magistrates can in theory commit to the Crown Court for sentence with this possibility in mind (although the Crown Court will, of course, have the option of using immediate custody). The supervisor will be a probation officer but the supervision may be of a nature different from that under a CRO as there will be no accreditation aspects as such (above). Failure to comply with the supervision element may result in a fine but not revocation and re-sentencing, nor activation of the sentence. Only a further conviction can result in this (on the same bases outlined above). Suspended sentence supervision orders never proved attractive to sentencers and have largely fallen into disuse.

Custody and mentally disordered offenders

Where the offender is or appears to be mentally disordered, the court is obliged—in addition to the standard procedures for custody, above—to:

- obtain and consider a medical report from a registered medical practitioner approved for the purposes of the Mental Health Act 1983 unless it considers such a report to be 'unnecessary'
- in any event to consider all information before it relating to the offender's mental condition; and to
- consider what treatment may be available.

Chapter 11 provides further general guidance on mentally disordered offenders.

Reasons for decisions

Whenever magistrates pass a custodial sentence they are *legally required* to state in open court:

- that they are of opinion that either or both of the 'so serious' or 'protection of the public' grounds for custody apply; and
- why they are of that opinion.

They must also explain to the offender in ordinary language why they are passing a custodial sentence. The reasons are specified in the relevant warrant and entered in the court register. There is a duty to give extra reasons where the court passes a sentence for a sexual or violent offence which is longer than is commensurate with the seriousness of the offence. Again, this must also be explained in ordinary language.

Clearly, all such reasons and explanations must be valid in the legal and judicial sense that they are relevant and supportable in law. See also the need to explain the effect of the early release provisions on custodial sentences: *Chapter 10*. Magistrates should, as a matter of good practice—and to assist them in complying with statutory and human rights obligations concerning explanations to the offender—check out their intentions *before* a custodial sentence is announced 📖✋.

EXTENDED SENTENCES

Section 85 Powers of Criminal Courts (Sentencing) Act 2000 deals with extended sentences for *sexual* and *violent* offenders. This amounts to extended periods of post-release supervision. Section 85 allows a court to impose an extended sentence in cases where it considers that the period of supervision which an offender would otherwise receive would not be long enough to prevent the commission of further offences by the offender or to secure the rehabilitation of the offender. An extended sentence must remain within the maximum penalty for the offence. In practice the provisions only apply to magistrates courts (and youth courts) in respect of certain sexual offenders: 📖 ✋. Thus, e.g. magistrates could pass an extended sentence of six months (three months custody and three months extended supervision, making a six months sentence). The court will have decided that a short custodial sentence is appropriate but the assessment of the offender suggests he or she would re-offend and would benefit from a longer period of post-release supervision. If this would extend the sentence beyond six months, the magistrates should commit to the Crown Court. Advice is highly desirable (📖 ✋) as is relevant information in a PSR.

THE CRIMINAL JUSTICE AND COURTS BILLS

As this handbook goes to press, two Bills are before Parliament that will significantly affect the overall sentencing and administrative arrangements for criminal courts in England and Wales. These are the Criminal Justice Bill (2002) and the Courts Bill (2002), respectively. The Bills flow from two key reports: *Making Punishments Work: Report of a Review of the Sentencing Framework for England and Wales* (2001);[15] and *Review of the Criminal Courts* (2001).[16] They are also based upon the subsequent White Paper, *Justice for All* (2002). A central theme of the White Paper is what is described as 'rebalancing the criminal justice system', i.e. in favour of victims of crime and with a renewed emphasis on restorative elements—but consistent with the fair treatment of suspects and offenders. A further aim is 'tough action on anti-social behaviour, hard drugs and violent crime'.

Impending changes
Under the Courts Bill, magistrates' overall jurisdiction would be increased to 12 months' imprisonment per offence[17] and magistrates' courts would themselves come under a new 'seamless' and centralised administration alongside the Crown Court. One practical effect would be to facilitate the transfer of cases between different levels of court involving, in the context of this handbook, a

---

[15] Home Office. 'The Halliday report' (after John Halliday, the senior official involved).

[16] Home Office. 'The Auld report' (after Sir Robin Auld, Lord Justice of Appeal).

[17] Assuming it is enacted, this increase was rumoured to be coming into force ahead of other main provisions, possibly in 2004. Once the whole of the new legislation is in force, the 12 months may not involve actual incarceration throughout that period but only for part of it under one of the new forms of custody described under the heading *Impending changes*, i.e. with an overall 'control' period of 12 months.

fundamental revision of existing concepts of mode of trial and committal for sentence (*Chapter 3*).

The Criminal Justice Bill lays fresh emphasis on sentences being served in the community, adopts a yet more rigorous approach to community sentences and places greater reliance on the use of electronic monitoring in relation to community sentences generally (as currently provided for under section 36B Powers of Criminal Courts (Sentencing) Act 2000: see earlier in the chapter under *Community Sentences*) and post-custody supervision. It also proposes a number of new sentences:

- intermittent custody: 'weekend gaol' or 'evening gaol' whereby a low risk offender is in custody part-time and can be allowed to retain his or her links with the community
- custody minus: perhaps best understood as a form of 'suspended' sentence conditional on completion of punishment in the community, but backed by automatic custody if an offender fails to comply with the conditions of his or her sentence; and
- custody plus: whereby a larger proportion of a custodial sentence is spent in the community so as to ensure that short sentence prisoners are properly supervised and supported following their release.

All forms of sentence will be accompanied by fresh and 'less compartmentalised' sentencing criteria than those that go to make up the current sentencing framework described earlier in this chapter—what, in relation to community sentences, has been described as a 'generic' approach. There will also be new sentencing guidelines and greater uniformity and consistency of approach would be encouraged through a new Sentencing Guidelines Council. The use of custody itself would then focus more on dangerous, serious and persistent offenders and those who repeatedly breach community sentences—with dangerous violent and sexual offenders being kept in custody for as long as they are believed to represent a risk to the public.

The wider picture
Naturally, this is a simplistic account of what are extensive and in some instances fundamental changes to existing jurisdiction, sentencing powers and accompanying procedures. These changes are in turn part of a widescale current programme of reforms which are already affecting the criminal process as a whole and which, in broad terms, are geared towards crime reduction, the prevention of offences (including re-offending) and more effective, proven and (increasingly) accredited ways of punishing offenders and tackling their offending. The innovations are part of what the Home Office describes as a 'coherent long-term strategy to modernise the criminal justice system from end-to-end—from the detection to the rehabilitation of offenders—with a clear focus on fighting and reducing crime' (*Justice For All*).[18]

---

[18] For an overview of developments across the agencies, see *Introduction to the Criminal Justice Process*, Bryan Gibson and Paul Cavadino (with assistance from David Faulkner), Waterside Press, 2002.

CHAPTER 5

Compensation for Victims

In 2001, Lord Woolf, Lord Chief Justice issued a *Practice Direction: Victim Personal Impact Statement* outlining a scheme to give a victim a more formal opportunity to say how a crime affected him or her. Under the scheme, the victim makes an initial statement to the police at the time of the investigation into the offence and then, if he or she wishes, updates this—e.g. by setting out any longer term effects or ongoing fears—in a further statement, closer in time to the court hearing. If a court is presented with such a statement it and any evidence in support must be considered and taken into account. Evidence of the effects on a victim must be in the form of a witness statement or expert report, served on the defence prior to sentence.[1] The *Practice Direction* further states:

> Except where inferences can properly be drawn from the nature or circumstances surrounding the offence, a sentencer must not make assumptions unsupported by evidence about the effects of an offence on the victim . . . The court must pass what it judges to be the appropriate sentence having regard to the circumstances of the offence and of the offender, taking account, so far as the court considers it appropriate, the consequences to the victim. The opinions of the victim or the victim's close relatives as to what the sentence should be are not relevant, unlike the consequence of the offence on them. If, despite this advice, opinions as to sentence are included in a statement, the court should pay no attention to them . . . The court should consider whether it is desirable in its sentencing remarks to refer to the evidence provided on behalf of the victim.

Priority

As noted in *Chapter 3*, reparation—of which compensation is an important aspect—is one of the general objects of sentencing. In practice, magistrates are required and encouraged to award compensation whenever possible. Two factors are important:

- sensitivity to the interests of victims (hence the direction above); and
- the extent of the financial information about the offender.

Where both a fine and compensation *are* considered appropriate, but the offender's financial circumstances are not adequate to pay both in full, courts are required to give preference to a compensation order. It would thus be wrong to reduce the amount of compensation because of the defendant's financial circumstances and then to impose a fine as well. Where compensation and a fine cannot both be imposed due to lack of finances and no additional form of sentence is felt necessary, compensation may be used as a sentence *in its own*

---

1 Relevant information may also be contained in a PSR: which should deal among other things with the offender's attitude towards the victim: *Chapter 9*. Various developments proposed in a Victims Bill (2003) have been 'shelved', but possibly only temporarily: see end of chapter.

right. Whenever coupled with another sentence compensation is described as an 'ancillary order'.

Personal injury, loss or damage

Where an offence results in personal injury, loss or damage the court is *obliged by law* to consider whether the offender should pay compensation. Financial loss resulting, say, from theft or criminal damage may be relatively easy to deal with provided evidence of the amount of the loss (or agreement by the defendant as to the value involved) is forthcoming. Personal injuries are less straightforward. Medical evidence and legal/judicial advice may be needed 📖❦. Personal injury includes physical or mental injury, so that, e.g. an award can be made for terror or distress caused by the offence. In *Bond v. Chief Constable of Kent* (1982) 4 Cr. App. Rep. (S.) 324, the High Court held that distress or anxiety directly arising from an offence could constitute 'personal injury' or 'damage'. Other rulings have established, e.g. that assault can be committed without the use of direct physical force and that this includes psychiatric injury (*R v. Burstow, The Times*, 30 July 1996); which can be committed by telephone (*R v. Ireland, The Times*, 22 May 1996). The Protection From Harassment Act 1997 is principally designed to address non-physical injury. Again, the 2001 *Practice Direction* (above) emphasises the need for supporting evidence.

Maximum amount of compensation (subject to means: see below)

The magistrates' court limit is £5,000 per offence. But the court can order compensation for loss etc. caused by offences taken into consideration (TICs: *Chapter 3*), as well as those of which it has convicted the defendant. The total is limited to the maximum the court could order for offences of which the offender stands convicted. Thus for two convictions and seven TICs the maximum that can be ordered is £10,000 (i.e. 2 x £5,000).

Application

No application is needed (although prosecutors often make one for the victim). The court can *always* make an award—on the basis of proper information. The procedure noted at the start of the chapter involving a victim personal statement may assist here.

Reasons

The court must give reasons if it decides *not* to make an order for compensation where there has been loss, damage or personal injury. These must be announced in open court and be recorded in the court register. Human rights obligations suggest that a sufficient and appropriate explanation and reasons should be given whether compensation is awarded or not.

Straightforward cases

Magistrates should order compensation in straightforward cases where the amount can readily be assessed. The power to award compensation in summary proceedings represents—in cases where the offender's financial circumstances can meet an award—a speedy means by which the victim can be reinstated. An award by magistrates avoids the prospect of a separate civil claim by the victim and, at the lower end, covers situations where the Criminal Injuries Compensation Authority (CICA) cannot make awards (below).

Road traffic accidents

In most cases, compensation arising from road traffic accidents will not be ordered through the magistrates' court 📖✋. However, an order can be made in respect of injury, loss or damage (other than that suffered by dependants as a result of death) due to an accident arising out of the presence of a motor vehicle on a road if it is in respect of:

- damage resulting from an offence under the Theft Act 1968 such as the unlawful taking of a motor vehicle (i.e. compensation may relate to the taken vehicle but not damage caused by it); or
- injury, loss or damage where
  — the offender is uninsured in relation to the vehicle; and
  — compensation is not payable under the Motor Insurers Bureau Agreement. This means that, in respect of property damage, the court is restricted to the first £300 of loss not covered by the MIBA. But this may include any reduction in preferential rates (i.e. loss of no claims bonus).

Fixing the amount

When a court is considering a compensation order, it must satisfy itself that actual loss, damage or injury has resulted from the offence. The court will look at the cost of replacement or repair of goods damaged. Where items are of sentimental value it may be possible to draw common-sense comparisons with other property losses and the likely effect on the victim.

A court can consider loss of earnings following time off work due to a physical attack. It can also look at more intangible matters, such as pain, suffering and any loss of facility. Guidance from Home Office Circulars has, for the greater part, been adopted within the *Magistrates' Court Sentencing Guidelines* (see *Appendix C*) which suggest awards for a range of injuries.

Usually prosecution and defence will try to agree the value of any loss. Where there is a dispute, the court will normally hear evidence presented by the prosecutor who may decide to call the victim to prove the loss, damage or injury, or this may be proved by other evidence such as receipts or a medical report. The offender may then make representations and/or call evidence. The matter need not be proved to the same standard as the offence itself in a criminal trial (i.e. beyond reasonable doubt)—but there must be a proper, information-based and factual basis on which the court can arrive at a figure.

In *Bond v. Chief Constable of Kent* (see page 88), the court stated that where a small sum was involved (£25 in 1982) the usual rule that the amount ordered had to be agreed or proved did not apply when considering anxiety or distress. The impetus behind this seems to be that common sense dictates that small amounts of compensation for real and obvious anxiety or distress occasioned by certain offending (e.g. a brick thrown through a house window, as in Bond's case) are permissible and should be encouraged. However, great care must be taken if courts wish to consider substantial sums of compensation for major psychological problems said to be caused by offending: see *Straightforward cases,* above, and consider judicial advice if necessary. 📖✋

Financial circumstances of the offender

Once the court is satisfied that there has been injury, loss or damage of a given value, its next obligation is to consider the offender's financial circumstances. It must have regard to these in so far as they appear or are known to the court. The Court of Appeal has interpreted this to mean that a compensation order should enable the offender to complete payment within a reasonable time, normally 12 months. This can be extended to up to three years where the circumstances justify it. In many instances, the court will have required the offender to complete a financial circumstances form (see under *Fines* in *Chapter* 4). It cannot be over-emphasised that effective use of compensation often stems from the identification of financial resources which would enable the offender to meet an award—and giving compensation priority as required by law: see *Priority* above.

In reaching its decision, the court may consider any savings or capital which the offender has and can also consider his or her expected ('potential') income. Where the offender can afford to repay only part of the value of the loss, then the court can and should order payment of that part: see, generally, *Priority* above.

Where an offender could sell property (e.g. a car) to pay compensation it is important that the court considers a proper valuation. The offender's own valuation may be 'over-optimistic'—or there may be outstanding credit agreements. Apart from minor differences (e.g. compensation should not be written off without the victim's consent) compensation is enforced in the same way as fines are (*Chapters* 4 and 5).

Compensation ancillary to a custodial sentence

If the offender is sentenced to a custodial sentence there are obvious difficulties. The court will need to consider whether he or she has or will have the means to pay. The Court of Appeal has indicated that it is wrong to make compensation orders which will be a burden on release from custody, as this may lead to further offences to raise the money to pay the order. It is also not generally appropriate to combine a compensation order with a substantial sentence of imprisonment unless immediate funds are available. If the sentence is short then there would seem to be nothing wrong in a court ordering compensation of an amount which would not be considered burdensome on release, e.g. imprisonment for three months and a manageable amount of compensation to be paid thereafter by instalments.

Appeal and review

The victim's entitlement to receive compensation ordered is suspended for 21 days to allow time for an appeal, then until after any appeal is heard. However, enforcement is *not* suspended, since the obligation to pay arises immediately. In circumstances where an appeal is successful, the court will have to return any monies already paid by the offender. A court can also review a compensation order at some future date at the request of the offender, including where: a civil court has decided that the injury, loss or damage was less than the value placed on it by the magistrates' court; the property has been recovered; or the offender's means have deteriorated (seek advice as necessary: 📖✋).

Choices for the victim

In theory victims can sue the offender for damages in the county court or High Court or where there has been a physical injury make a claim to the Criminal Injuries Compensation Authority (CICA) if appropriate. Civil proceedings can be slow and expensive and an unwelcome further burden. An order by magistrates provides the victim with an accessible remedy which avoids expense and delay— and represents a tangible expression of concern.

Some examples of the kind of decisions courts may need to make

Many decisions are straightforward and full compensation is ordered. But magistrates may have to decide: whether to order compensation at all; how much to order; how to balance competing claims of victims; and whether an offender with means should pay more than a joint and equally culpable offender without, e.g.:

(a) Offender A is long-term unemployed, on state benefit. He damages two plate glass windows value £1,000 each. The court has to decide how much compensation he can afford to pay by instalments out of his state benefit.

(b) Offenders B, C and D are charged with damage to property to the amount of £1,500. Offender B does not appear. A warrant is issued for arrest. Offender C enters a plea of guilty, is unemployed, in receipt of state benefit, and married. Offender D who has also pleaded guilty is single, working and earns £400 per week net. The court has to decide whether D should pay the majority, with C paying what he or she can and whether or not between them they should cover the share of the absent B.

(c) Offender E, an adult, is being sentenced on a charge of assault occasioning actual bodily harm: an unprovoked attack on another motorist. The victim received two black eyes. The magistrates decide that in view of the nature of the offence and the offender's record, the sentence should be four months imprisonment. They now need to consider the question of compensation to the victim. Given the probable release date of E, and taking into account his or her present and prospective financial circumstances, should E be required to pay compensation (noting that the amount may be below the CICA minimum (see later) and the victim may, therefore, otherwise have to resort to a civil claim)?

(d) Offender F, who is unemployed and in receipt of state benefits, pleads guilty to two charges of deception. The two separate victims are (i) an elderly pensioner, and (ii) a High Street bank. The pensioner has lost £800. The bank has lost £3,000. The magistrates need to decide whether the whole amount of compensation should be in favour of the pensioner rather than the bank, in view of the offender's limited means.

GENERAL TREATMENT OF VICTIMS

The *Victim's Charter* (1990) outlined the reasonable expectations of victims and how they should be treated. There have since been improvements by way of more sensitive treatment and the extent to which a victim is informed about the progress of his or her case and given the opportunity to provide information to decision-makers.

Victim Support

Victim Support was formed (originally as the National Association of Victims Support Schemes) in 1979. Each year, trained volunteers and staff based in over 400 local areas of England and Wales where schemes are in operation offer help to in excess of a million victims of crimes from burglary to murder. This free and confidential service includes support, practical help (e.g. with home security, insurance claims, CICA claims (below) and information). Victim Support also runs the Court Witness Service, via which trained volunteers offer support and practical information to victims, witnesses and their families before, during and after a trial. The Court Witness Service operates nationwide.

Criminal injuries compensation

The Criminal Injuries Compensation Scheme, originally established in 1964, provides financial compensation to victims of crimes of violence and to those injured in attempting to apprehend offenders or prevent crime. The minimum award is currently £1,000 (March 2003) and injuries meriting lower awards cannot be compensated by the scheme. All applications are made to the Criminal Injuries Compensation Authority (CICA). Compensation for an injury as a result of a crime of violence is intended as an expression of public sympathy and support for an innocent victim. It is not, however, necessary for an offender to have been convicted before an award can be made. Under the scheme, injuries are classified into bands depending on the extent of the injury. There are procedures for review, and in the event of dissatisfaction with the review, the possibility of an appeal to the Criminal Injuries Compensation Appeals Panel which has as its members lawyers, doctors and other people with relevant experience. The original CICA application should normally be lodged no later than two years after the incident.

Compensation and 'restorative justice'

Compensation has become linked with notions of 'restorative justice', i.e. repairing harm and restoring harmony between victims/offenders, an approach now encouraged by government. There is also a Restorative Justice Consortium of interested organizations.

Victims of domestic violence

Special multi-agency and inter-agency arrangements now exist in many parts of the country with a view to preventing domestic violence and coping with the consequences when this is not achieved. In 1999 the Cabinet Office and Home Office jointly published *Living Without Fear* as part of a nationwide initiative to confront the phenomenon.

Justice For All and the Criminal Justice Bill (2002)

An underlying aim of government and a rationale of the White Paper and Criminal Justice Bill is to 'rebalance the criminal justice system' by ensuring justice for victims and that those who commit offences, though entitled to be' treated fairly, do not escape their responsibilities, both to individual victims and the community at large. But, in 2003 a Victims Bill 'to give support, protection and legal rights to information and compensation' to victims (including the creation of a Victims Fund) was 'shelved' due to competing legislative priorities—although a national Victims Advisory Panel was being appointed.

CHAPTER 6

Other Orders of the Court

In addition to the four main levels of sentence outlined in *Chapter 4*, magistrates' courts possess a wide variety of powers to make other orders. This chapter deals with a range of powers not featured elsewhere in *The Sentence of the Court*. Generally: 📖✋.

BINDING OVER

Magistrates have power to bind over an individual to keep the peace. The power—which stems in part from the Justices of the Peace Act 1361—may be exercised in the course of criminal proceedings without formal complaint. Accordingly it may be used at any stage of the proceedings when there are reasonable grounds for believing that there may be a breach of the peace in the future, e.g. disorder in court or a neighbour dispute. A bind over under this ancient law is not dependent on conviction and magistrates should normally seek advice if considering using this power of their own volition 📖✋. A degree of caution may be necessary, e.g. if it is proposed that an acquitted defendant should be bound over.

The most usual way in which the power is considered is following a formal complaint by one person inviting the court to bind over a second person to keep the peace pursuant to section 115 Magistrates' Courts Act 1980. The alleged conduct must be capable of provoking violence and it must be unreasonable. However, it is sufficient to establish a breach of the peace that the natural consequence of the conduct would, if persisted in, be to provoke others to violence, so that some actual danger to the peace is established. Following fair trial principles and other human rights considerations, the defendant should always be told what is in mind and be allowed to address the court before any final decision is made.

Following the case of *Joseph Hashman and Wanda Harrup v. United Kingdom* (2000), CLR 185 to 187, the European Court of Human Rights has indicated that binding over to be of good behaviour is imprecise. Such orders should no longer be made. A further consequence of the Human Rights Act 1998 is that—because they can ultimately involve punishment (even imprisonment, below)—bind over proceedings are likely to be classed as criminal proceedings with all the protections and strict standards that this entails.[1]

People aged 18 but under 21 may be detained and those aged 21 or over may be imprisoned should they refuse to be bound over to keep the peace. Detention or imprisonment will cease if the person concerned subsequently agrees to be bound over. Most defendants *do* promise to behave and to be bound over, whereby they then incur the risk of forfeiting the sum of money to the Crown

---

[1] See, generally, *Human Rights and the Courts*, Waterside Press 1999, at pages 40, 65, 98.

should they misbehave. The order is usually made for a period set by the court, often a year.

COSTS

Magistrates have power to award costs, subject to each case being dealt with on its merits. The basic rule is that costs can—and should normally—be awarded in favour of the successful party, including the Crown Prosecution Service. Costs must always be a reimbursement, i.e. they must not be used as a guise for punishment.

Private prosecutors
Private prosecutors (e.g. the NSPCC, RSPCA, private individuals) may receive an order that their costs be paid out of central funds (public monies held by the justices' chief executive), but not the CPS or other public authorities—since they are funded from the public purse. Such costs in favour of private prosecutors will apply in respect of indictable (including either way) offences only, but can be awarded even if the prosecution is unsuccessful.

Costs against offenders
The court can order a convicted offender to pay just and reasonable costs to the prosecutor. The amount must be stated in the order (and there is no power to refer the matter for taxation, i.e. assessment by the justices' clerk: compare a *Defendant's costs order,* below). An order should only be made where the court is satisfied that the offender has the means (after any compensation and fine) to pay. Costs cannot be imposed if the offender has been ordered to pay a sum not exceeding £5 (whether by way of fine or compensation)—unless the court, in the particular circumstances, considers it right to do so.

The principles governing time for payment of costs are similar to those affecting fines: see *Chapter 4.* It is wrong to order an offender to pay costs if he or she will be unable to pay within a reasonable time (usually, in practice, within 12 months).

The Divisional Court in the case of *R v. Northallerton Magistrates' Court ex parte Dove* (1999) dealt with a challenge to the amount of costs from a defendant who had been fined £1,000 and also ordered to pay £4,624 prosecution costs. In its judgement that court set out a number of propositions which can be summarised as follows:

- the court should ordinarily begin by deciding on the appropriate compensation or fine to reflect the criminality of the defendant's offence, always bearing in mind his or her means and ability to pay, and then consider what, if any, costs he or she should be ordered to pay to the prosecutor. If, when the costs sought by the prosecutor were added to the proposed fine, the total exceeded the sum which in the light of the defendant's means and all other relevant considerations the defendant could reasonably be ordered to pay, it was preferable to achieve an acceptable total by reducing the sum of costs which the defendant was ordered to pay rather than by reducing the fine

- it was for the defendant facing a financial penalty by way of a fine or an order to pay costs to a prosecutor to disclose to magistrates such data relevant to his or her financial position as would enable justices to assess what he or she could reasonably afford to pay. In the absence of such disclosure, justices might draw reasonable inferences as to the defendant's means from evidence they had heard and from all the circumstances of the case; and
- it was incumbent on any court which proposed to make any financial order against a defendant to give him or her a fair opportunity to adduce relevant financial information and make any appropriate submissions. If the court had it in mind to make an unusual or unconventional order potentially adverse to a defendant, it should alert the defendant and his or her advisers to the possibility.

This was a 'non-police' prosecution where the costs that can be claimed are often higher than normal (as they can cover the investigation as well as the process of prosecution) but the principles apply equally to cases brought by the police and presented by the CPS. In the particular case the order for costs was quashed and the matter remitted to the magistrates' court for it to reconsider its decision in the light of the propositions summarised above.

Defendant's costs order (DCO)
Where a case is dismissed, discontinued or withdrawn the court can, and generally will, make a DCO—i.e. an order for payment of the defendant's costs out of central funds (see above). Only exceptionally will a prosecutor be ordered to pay the defendant's costs instead, e.g. where the prosecutor was negligent in failing to deal with some aspect of the case which would have disclosed a sound defence at an early stage.

A defendant who is on a legal representation order may receive a DCO, but only (on taxation) to recover expenses not covered by that order (e.g. travel costs to court).

A DCO is normally made following acquittal or a case being discontinued or withdrawn unless there are positive reasons for not doing so, e.g. where the defendant's own conduct has attracted suspicion and misled the prosecutor into thinking there was a strong case. Where someone is acquitted on some charges but convicted on others, the court has a discretion whether to make a defendant's costs order, or it might order only part of the defendant's costs. In this instance the amount must be specified by the court. The court should always bear in mind that wrongly to refuse a defendant costs could violate the presumption of innocence in Article 6(2) of the European Convention On Human Rights if it reflects any suspicion that the defendant may really be guilty.

Unless the order is for an agreed or a part amount, the figure will be determined by the justices' clerk (as 'taxing officer') after the defence has submitted a detailed account.

Unnecessary or improper acts or omissions
Magistrates may order all or part of the costs to be paid by either party to the other (called an *inter partes* order)—irrespective of the final outcome of the case—if those costs have been incurred as a result of an unnecessary or improper act or

omission, e.g. where one party forgets to warn a witness and the case has to be adjourned. Seek advice: 📖✋

Wasted costs

Magistrates can disallow legal aid costs or order a legal representative to bear costs which are wasted. This means costs incurred as a result of any improper, unreasonable or negligent act or omission on the part of the legal representative. Magistrates should seek advice. 📖✋

RESTITUTION

Where goods have been stolen and someone is convicted of an offence relating to the theft, the court may order restoration of the goods to the person entitled to them (or cash from the sale of goods bought with any such proceeds). Restitution can also be ordered on conviction for dishonest handling, obtaining by deception or blackmail. Goods include all property except land. An order can also be made in respect of TICs: see *Chapter 3*. An order can be made of the court's own volition (there is no need for an application) and may require:

- anyone having possession or control of the goods to restore them to a person entitled to them; or
- any other goods directly or indirectly representing the original stolen goods to be delivered to the person so entitled; or
- any money found on the offender not exceeding the value of the goods to be paid to that person.

The court may order restitution *and* compensation, e.g. for property damage—but summary restitution should only be ordered in clear cases, avoiding difficult questions of law.

DEPRIVATION AND FORFEITURE

When the offence consists of unlawful possession of property, the court may order the defendant to be deprived of that property. A deprivation order can also be made where property has been used to commit an offence or was intended to be so used, whether or not the defendant has been separately convicted of that other offence.

The court must be satisfied that the property has been lawfully seized from the offender, or was in his or her possession or control when apprehended, or when a summons was issued. An order can also be made in respect of TICs: see *Chapter 3*.

'Property' does not include land. The court must have regard to its value and the likely financial and other effects of the order on the offender (together with any other order the court is contemplating). The effect of the order is to deprive the offender of the property—which passes into the possession of the police. This enables the true owner to make an application to the magistrates' court for an order for 'delivery up' of that property. If there is no successful claim, the property will be sold and the proceeds disposed of at the direction of the court.

Where the offence results in personal injury, loss or damage and the court has not been able to make a compensation order (*Chapter 5*) because of the defendant's lack of means, the proceeds of sale resulting from a deprivation order can be used as compensation.

If an offender is convicted of an offence under the Road Traffic Act 1988 which is punishable with imprisonment (such as driving whilst disqualified or an 'excess alcohol' offence), the vehicle used is, by law, to be regarded as having been used for the purpose of facilitating an offence. Thus, the offender may be deprived of the vehicle once the court has considered all relevant factors, including the value of the vehicle and the likely financial and other effects on the offender 📖✋.

A deprivation order is appropriate only in straightforward cases where there would be no difficulty in implementing the order.

Many individual Acts of Parliament provide for forfeiture of specific items on conviction, e.g. the Misuse of Drugs Act 1971; Prevention of Crime Act 1953 (offensive weapons); Obscene Publications Act 1964 and Firearms Act 1968. In some cases the court can also order destruction or disposal of the item concerned.

CRIMINAL CONFISCATION ORDERS

In limited circumstances magistrates can make confiscation orders. They may confiscate the proceeds of certain offences, for example those relating to sex establishments; of supplying or possessing for the purpose of supply videos of unclassified works; and of failure to pay contributions under the Social Security Contributions and Benefits Act 1992. Beyond these special and somewhat restricted powers, Crown Courts (only) can make confiscation orders of a more general nature and in respect of a much wider range of property, funds and assets. Pursuant to the Proceeds of Crime Act 2002 magistrates' courts (who cannot make such orders) can commit to the Crown Court for this purpose alone and even if not committing to that court because their other powers are insufficient. It is important that magistrates make the basis for committal absolutely clear since this affects the powers of the Crown Court. See under *Committal for Sentence* in *Chapter 3* and always seek advice 📖✋.

EXCLUSION ORDERS[2]

Magistrates' courts have power to make 'exclusion orders' where certain offences are committed on licensed premises. The order is designed for offenders who make a serious nuisance of themselves on such premises. Such an order might not be appropriate, e.g. for a one-off minor offence by a first offender. The order is *additional* to the sentence for the offence. The order prohibits the offender from

---

[2] This form of exclusion order is under the Licensed Premises (Exclusion of Certain Persons) Act 1980 and should not be confused with the community sentence exclusion order under the Powers of Criminal Courts (Sentencing) Act 2000: see *Chapter 4*.

entering licensed premises where the offence was committed or other specified licensed premises without the consent of the licensee or someone acting on his or her behalf. The offence has to be on licensed premises and not e.g. outside after the defendant has been ejected.

It is open to the court to make an exclusion order of its own motion, i.e. without an application by the prosecutor or the victim. It is undesirable for an application to be made by someone who is not a victim or party to the proceedings. The proper course for an interested third party is to make representations to the prosecuting authority.

The order may be for not less than three months nor more than two years. A copy is sent to the licensee of each specified premises—and as a matter of good practice to the local police. The licensee or someone acting on his or her behalf may then expel anyone who has entered or whom he or she suspects of entering the premises in breach of the order. A police constable must, at the request of the licensee or staff, assist in expelling anyone the constable suspects of such a breach. Someone who enters premises in breach of an exclusion order is liable, on summary conviction, to a fine not exceeding Level 3 (£1,000) and/or imprisonment for one month. The court must consider whether or not the exclusion order should continue in force—and may terminate or vary it. It is not otherwise affected by conviction for breach of the order.

FOOTBALL BANNING ORDERS

In order to combat a continuing problem of football violence the government strengthened existing legislation in the Football (Disorder) Act 2000. There are now two types of banning order: criminal and civil.

Criminal banning orders
Where someone has been convicted of a football-related offence in connection with a regulated football match (i.e. a match in England and Wales or abroad where one or both of the teams are from the Premier League, Football League or Conference) committed:

- at any regulated football match;
- while entering or leaving the ground;
- while trying to enter or leave the ground; or
- while the accused was on a journey to or from a designated ground

and the court is satisfied that there are reasonable grounds to believe that making a banning order would help prevent violence or disorder at or in connection with regulated football matches the court *must* make an order. If the court is not satisfied that an order is necessary it must give reasons. An order can only be made at the time of sentence and can only be made in addition to a sentence but including a conditional discharge.

Where an immediate custodial sentence is imposed the minimum ban is six years and the maximum ten years. Where any other sentence or discharge is imposed the minimum period is three years and the maximum five years. Under the order the defendant must:

- report to a police station within five days to be photographed;
- surrender his or her passport when regulated games are being played outside England and Wales.

Failure to comply with the requirements of a banning order is a criminal offence carrying six months' imprisonment and/or a fine of £5,000.

Civil banning orders

Here it must appear to the police that the respondent 'has at any time caused or contributed to any violence in the United Kingdom or elsewhere'. Note that violence does *not* have to be football related. The chief of police may then apply by way of a civil complaint. Note that the civil standard of proof applies and hearsay evidence may be used.

An order is justified if the court is satisfied that there are reasonable grounds for believing that a banning order would help prevent football-related violence or disorder. The court can take into account all relevant matters including overseas court or tribunal decisions, deportation or exclusion from a country outside the UK, removal or exclusion from football grounds in the UK or elsewhere and conduct recorded on video or by other means. The 'control period' begins five days before the match and ends with the final whistle. The police may issue a notice which must be in writing and stating the grounds upon which it is made, specifing the magistrates' court at which the person should appear and stating that the person must surrender his or her passport and must not leave England. If the matter is adjourned, bail is on the respondent's own civil recognisance and conditions can be imposed as above.

The court can either make or refuse the application. If an order is not made, the court can award compensation of up to £5,000 out of central funds (i.e. public funds) but only if satisfied that:

- notice should not have been given in the first place;
- the person has suffered consequential loss;
- it is appropriate in respect of the loss.

Where an order is made the minimum period is two years and the maximum three years. The sanctions are the same as for a criminal banning order (i.e. failure to comply with the requirements of a civil banning order is a criminal offence carrying up to six months and/or a fine of £5,000).

DISQUALIFICATION

Disqualification from driving is dealt with in *Chapter 8*. Magistrates may consider other disqualifications in a range of circumstances, e.g.:

- *Companies:* Magistrates can make an order against an offender convicted summarily of an either way offence in connection with the promotion, formation or liquidation of a company (and in certain other situations) prohibiting the offender, without the leave of the court, from being the director etc. of a company for not more than five years.

- *Animals:* Magistrates have various powers of disqualification with regard to keeping animals, such as where cruelty is involved. There are also powers to disqualify people in relation, e.g. to keeping a pet shop or a dangerous wild animal.

Other legislation touches on such diverse areas of human activity as fishing, running a restaurant and operating a gaming club. Under the Food Safety Act 1990, a court may prohibit a proprietor from participating in the management of certain food businesses. There is also power in the Medicines Act 1968 to disqualify offenders from using premises for a pharmacy for up to two years.

As a general rule, the defendant must after conviction and before sentence be given notice of the court's likely intentions and an opportunity to make representations before any disqualification is imposed. Prosecutions for some such offences are quite rare, and it is therefore essential that magistrates seek advice 📖✋.

DEPORTATION

Additional to the sentence for an offence punishable by imprisonment, the court may recommend to the Home Secretary that an offender who is not a British citizen, or a Commonwealth citizen having a right of abode in the UK, should be deported from the UK. This recommendation can only be made after the offender has been served with a notice of liability to deportation. This will usually be the duty of the police. The court has power to grant an adjournment after convicting an offender for the purpose of enabling a notice to be served on him or her. Pursuant to the Human Rights Act 1998 a defendant could argue that his or her rights under Article 3 (no-one shall be subject to torture or inhuman or degrading treatment or punishment) would be breached if a recommendation for deportation is made where it is likely that, if deported, he or she would be subject to treatment prohibited by Article 3—but seek legal advice: 📖✋.

Once a recommendation for deportation is made, the Home Secretary then decides whether or not to deport the offender. In coming to that decision, account will be taken of such factors as the nature of the offence, the length of stay in this country, previous convictions (if any), age, personal history, domestic circumstances and the strength of connections with this country. Any compassionate considerations and representations will also be taken into account. The Home Secretary is unlikely to deport a first-time offender unless the offence (allowing for any TICs) was particularly serious. This is a specialist area and legal advice should be sought (including in relation to European Community nationals to whom extra considerations apply) 📖✋.

POLICE REGISTRATION OF SEX OFFENDERS

Part I of the Sex Offenders Act 1997 imposes a requirement on offenders convicted or cautioned for specific sex offences to notify the police of their name and address and any subsequent changes thereto. The court issues a notice to this effect and gives it to the offender following conviction, certifying that they have been convicted of a qualifying offence. The chairman will need to make an appropriate statement/explanation. Seek advice as to whether an offence is a 'qualifying offence' and concerning the appropriate announcement 📖✋.

The Home Office has advised that registration does not follow either an absolute or conditional discharge and also that it would be unwise to effect registration where a case is committed to the Crown Court for sentence in case that court passes a sentence which does not carry a need for registration. However, both these issues are subject to differing views.

The obligations arise immediately and automatically on conviction and courts can advise the offender of the need to 'register' (the obligation is a local one rather than relating to a single national register) as soon as a guilty plea is entered or a finding of guilt is made. The length of the obligation is based on the sentence imposed. Failure to comply with the provisions is an offence (punishable with a Level 5 fine and/or six months' custody) and will be prosecuted before magistrates.

Sex offender orders

The Crime and Disorder Act 1998 subsequently introduced 'sex offender orders'—whereby if a convicted sex offender acts in such a way as to give cause to believe that serious harm may be caused to the public— the chief officer of police may apply to a magistrates' court for an order imposing prohibitions on the individual concerned. The order is pre-emptive (not unlike a civil injunction). Breach is an either-way offence.

RESTRAINING ORDER: HARASSMENT

The Protection From Harassment Act 1997 creates two offences: a summary offence of causing harassment; and an either-way offence of putting a person in fear of violence. When sentencing for either offence, the court can make an order restraining the defendant from future acts of harassment. This order can be made for a specified period or until a further order. A breach of such an order is itself a separate, either-way offence. The expectation is that the prosecutor will invite the court to make the restraining order, taking account of what is necessary for the victim's or other people's protection. A restraining order can be varied at a future date, but can only be made on the date of the original sentence. It is not the prosecutor's duty to apply for this ancillary order, but merely to remind the magistrates of its existence. As a restraining order is an order ancillary to sentence, a right of appeal against the total sentence (including against the restraining order) is available. Restraining orders can *only* be made following a conviction under the 1997 Act.

REFERRAL ORDER

Normally the issue of a referral order in respect of a juvenile offender arises in the youth court. However, a juvenile may appear alongside an adult in the magistrates' court. Every young offender who pleads guilty and who has not previously been convicted or bound over for an offence must be referred to a youth offending panel. The exceptions are where custody is appropriate, or an absolute discharge, or the court proposes to act under mental health legislation. However, although the adult court could impose an absolute discharge (but not custody) on a youth who is before it (see *Magistrates Bench Handbook, Reference Sheet 12*), practice is usually to remit the youth to a youth court where there will be greater experience in deciding the issues concerned. The court must specify the length of the order (from three to 12 months) on the basis of the seriousness of the offence. The role of youth offending panels is outside the scope of this work but following referral the panel will meet with the offender and devise an 'intervention plan', e.g. programmes and reparation in an attempt to address offending behaviour. Referral orders may also become relevant in the adult court where someone made subject to such an order as a juvenile later appears before it as an adult: 📖✋.

'CRIMINAL' ANTI-SOCIAL BEHAVIOUR ORDER

The Crime and Disorder Act 1998 introduced *civil* anti-social behaviour orders (ASBOs: see *Chapter 1*). They are civil applications, with civil rules of evidence but (by case law) the criminal standard of proof—'beyond reasonable doubt'—applies. Applications for these civil orders can be brought by a range of people, but in practice it will usually be the local authority or the police. ASBOs prohibit specified anti-social acts for a minimum of two years. Breach is an either-way offence carrying six months imprisonment and/or a fine of £5,000 on summary conviction.

A significant development brought about by the Police Reform Act 2002 was to permit courts, on convicting an offender of an offence committed after 2 December 2002 (the commencement date of that part of the Act) to make—ancillary to the main sentence—what is commonly known as a 'criminal ASBO'—or 'CRASBO'. There is no stipulation as to the type of offence of which the defendant must have been convicted but courts will, doubtless, look for some nexus between it and anti-social behaviour. It need not be imprisonable.

The convicting court must be satisfied, in essence, that since 1 April 1999 an offender has acted in an anti-social manner towards persons not of his or her household *and* that an order is necessary to protect people from further such acts. The court can make the order whether or not there has been any application—this may arise if the circumstances of the offence themselves meet the criteria. However, in practice, the prosecutor will probably make applications where appropriate as he or she will have access to other, broader information. It remains to be seen whether prosecutors will try to adduce factors outside the facts of the present or previous offences.

It is possible to suspend the commencement of the CRASBO if the offender is in custody after its imposition. Otherwise the CRASBO operates as a civil ASBO would.

CHAPTER 7

Previous Convictions and Responses

It is the regular practice for prosecutors to submit lists of previous convictions once someone stands convicted of an offence: *Chapter 3*. The relevance of information in such lists turns on the meaning of section 151 Powers of Criminal Courts (Sentencing) Act 2000. This is an area where legal/judicial advice may be desirable in an individual case: 📖✋. The legal provisions govern the place in the sentencing process of:

- previous convictions; and
- responses to previous sentences.

It seems clear, irrespective of any legal rules, that if an offender has previous convictions, particularly if they are for similar offences, then this reduces the extent to which he or she can put forward mitigation. The offender cannot claim to have a 'clean record' or, e.g. where earlier offences are of a similar kind, to have made a genuine mistake or to have failed to comprehend the significance of his or her actions. Similarly, if earlier community sentences have not been complied with it may indicate something about the suitability for the offender of such sentences now: *Chapter 4*.

Origins of the provisions
As indicated in *Chapter 1*, one intention of the Criminal Justice Act 1991 was that courts should pass sentences proportionate to—i.e. 'commensurate' with—the offence or offences of which the offender stood convicted. The original provision, in section 29(1) of the 1991 Act thus provided that:

> An offence shall not be regarded as more serious for the purposes of any provision of [the sentencing provisions of the 1991 Act] by reason of any previous convictions of the offender or any failure of his to respond to previous sentences.

Section 29(2) then stated that:

> Where any aggravating factors of an offence are disclosed by the circumstances of other offences committed by the offender, nothing . . . shall prevent the court from taking those factors into account for the purpose of forming an opinion as to the seriousness of the offence.

Thus, whilst previous convictions or responses could not in themselves affect the seriousness of the present offence, the facts of other offences which actually shed light on the current offence so as to make it more serious could. However, in its application, section 29 proved problematic.

Older common law principles

There were people who thought that section 29 merely set out the principle that an offender should not be sentenced for offences for which he or she had already been punished. The approach adopted by courts until 1991 was that whilst previous convictions might restrict or eliminate the mitigation which could otherwise reduce a sentence (as noted above), a criminal record could not justify a more severe sentence, one *disproportionate* to the seriousness of the present offence. Nonetheless, the government decided to amend the provisions, leading to what became the current law.

The present position

In introducing the current law in 1993, the then Home Secretary stated that the original 1991 version had:

> . . . unnecessarily fettered the hands of the courts and imposed a strait–jacket on their ability to sentence justly in individual cases.

The new version, what later became section 151(1) Powers of Criminal Courts (Sentencing) Act 2000 states:

> . . . in considering the seriousness of any offence, the court may take into account any previous convictions of the offender or any failure of his to respond to previous sentences.

The change of emphasis is clear. But it is not obvious, even today, exactly how the provision alters the approach to be adopted by courts. As long ago as 1993, Lord Taylor, Lord Chief Justice said:

> I believe that the philosophy of the Criminal Justice Act 1991 as it was originally envisaged still holds good. I believe . . . the amendments . . . have improved it and have made it more realistic.

Certainly, a defendant with no previous convictions might claim that the offence was less serious because it stemmed, e.g. from 'a foolish, or spur of the moment decision by someone with an otherwise unblemished record', whereas such convictions would, to the extent that they were relevant to the situation, limit or remove the scope for mitigation. It is less clear to what extent previous convictions can actually increase the seriousness of the present offence (i.e. become an 'aggravating factor')—but, following basic principle, it seems clear that they ought not to be used to justify a sentence wholly disproportionate to that offence. Indeed, an offender would seem to have valid objections under human rights law (*Chapter* 2) if a court did purport, in effect, to sentence him or her again on the basis of matters for which he or she has already been punished. This serves again to emphasise that previous convictions must be examined with great care to ensure that the reasoning process whereby a court concludes that they do in fact make the present offence or offences more serious is valid.

The relevance of past incidents

Section 151 does not mean that *all* previous matters are capable of affecting the seriousness of an offence. The *Magistrates' Court Sentencing Guidelines* (see *Appendix C*) offer the following advice:

> Courts should identify any convictions relevant for this purpose and then consider to what extent they affect the seriousness of the present offence.

Thus even where previous convictions or failures to respond *might* affect seriousness it is still a two stage decision-making process and the question remains: 'To what extent?' should they be taken into account.

Court of Appeal guidance

Commentators have expressed concern that it is now easier for the courts to send minor offenders into custody. It is true to say that, historically, imprisonment has sometimes been a response to persistent minor offending and not justified by the seriousness of the present offence. One general message from the Court of Appeal is that there are some offences which do not pass the custody threshold (the 'so serious' test: *Chapter 4*), notwithstanding that the offender may have a long list of previous convictions for similar offences, e.g. a woman, already on a suspended sentence for burglary, using a false instrument and obtaining property by deception, was sentenced to three months imprisonment for theft of bacon valued at £3.50 from a shop. The Court of Appeal stated that notwithstanding the breach of the suspended prison sentence, and a background of previous offending, the offence did not justify imprisonment: *R v. Wendy Bond* (1994) 5 Cr. App. R. (S.) 430. This suggests that there is a 'seriousness ceiling' for some offences which cannot be exceeded simply on the basis of previous convictions. Arguably, it also suggests that the effect on a sentence will at best be marginal within the usual range for the offence or offences now under consideration (along with all other relevant seriousness factors). Other offences which on the face of it are more serious may now need to be considered in the light of *R v. McInerney* insofar as that case may have implications in relation to the effect of an offender's record. After *R v. McInerney* it becomes arguable that previous convictions can aggravate sentence whatever the other subtleties. During a period of possible adjustment legal advice is essential 📖✋.

Previous responses

Even today there is as yet no comprehensive judicial guidance on the phrase 'response to previous sentences'. At first sight, it is difficult to understand how failures to respond to earlier sentences *can* affect the seriousness of the present offence. One view is that the provision refers to *any* conduct following the imposition of the earlier penalty. Another is that it refers to breach of an existing sentence or a further offence committed during that sentence: see, generally, *Chapter 4*.

Summary of the position

Courts *are* allowed to consider the offender's record and earlier responses to sentence when assessing the seriousness of the present offence or offences—but must adopt a very careful approach when looking at the relevance of previous convictions or responses to the seriousness of the present offence or offences. There remain areas—especially since *R v. McInerney* (see above and *Chapter 4*)—on which clear guidance is needed from the Court of Appeal:

- should a court take previous matters into account if they are similar in type and/or recent, but not if they are different in type and/or were committed a long time ago?
- to what extent *can* previous convictions affect the seriousness of a new offence, i.e. does the current offence set a 'seriousness ceiling' and/or is it the correct rule that sentence should not become wholly disproportionate?
- does a failure to respond to previous sentences include sentences which were completed without a breach or merely sentences which were breached, or still current at the time of a later offence?
- what is the precise connection between previous responses and the seriousness of the present offence?
- at what point might it be claimed that the offender is in fact being sentenced again for matters for which he or she has already been sentenced, in possible contravention of human rights obligations?

Violent and sexual offences: where a different rule applies in many instances
It should be noted that previous convictions may be relevant to the 'protection of the public' test for custody in relation to sexual or violent offences for entirely different reasons. Unlike the 'so serious' test, the 'protection of the public' test involves an assessment of future risk (i.e. of serious harm to the public). Relevant past offences may be an important indicator of the extent of that risk.

CHAPTER 8

Road Traffic Offences

In addition to any penalty imposed, certain motoring offences attract endorsement of the offender's driving licence or disqualification.

ENDORSEMENT

For many traffic offences, the court *must* order that the defendant's driving licence be endorsed with:

- particulars of the offence; and
- the number of points appropriate to that offence.

The only exception is where the court finds 'special reasons' for not endorsing (below). Endorsement means that these particulars and points will be recorded on the licence.[1]

Penalty points

Every endorsable offence carries a number of penalty points, from a minimum of two to a maximum of eleven. Thus, e.g. some common offences and their points are:

Careless or inconsiderate driving	3-9
In charge of a vehicle while unfit due to alcohol or drugs	10
Failing to stop after an accident	5-10
Failing to give particulars/report an accident within 24 hours	5-10
Driving/attempting to drive whilst disqualified	6
Using etc. a motor vehicle whilst uninsured	6-8
Exceeding a speed limit	3-6
Failing to provide a preliminary specimen of breath	4
Failing to comply with traffic lights/directions	3
Construction and use offences	3
Contravention of pedestrian crossing regulations	3
Using a vehicle in a dangerous condition	3

For a full list see *Appendix D*. The chief significance lies in the 'totting up' provisions described under *Obligatory disqualification* on page 109.

'Variable points'

If an offence carries a range of points, the court has a discretion concerning the number to be endorsed—which will depend upon the court's view of the seriousness of the offence.

---

1 If the offender has no licence, this operates as an order to endorse any licence obtained.

Several offences on the same occasion

Where someone is convicted of two or more offences *committed* on the same occasion, the number of points to be endorsed is usually the highest attracted by any one of the offences. Thus e.g. if an offender is convicted of driving while disqualified (six points) and contravening pedestrian crossing regulations (three), then six points would be endorsed. Instead of following this general rule, courts may effectively add the numbers together, i.e. making nine points in the example given. However, the court is obliged to give reasons if it adopts this course which must be announced in open court and recorded in the court register. Seek advice if necessary: 📖✋.

'Special reasons' for not endorsing

As already indicated, when someone is convicted of an endorsable offence, the court *must* order endorsement and the relevant number of points unless it decides—on the basis of evidence—that there are special reasons for not doing so. The court must state in open court any grounds for finding special reasons, and these must be entered in the court register. A special reason means something that is:

- a mitigating or extenuating circumstance
- directly connected with the offence but
- not amounting to a defence in law; and
- which the court ought properly to take into account.

Special reasons must relate to the *offence* (such as a real emergency where there is no alternative: 📖✋), as opposed to the *offender*. So, if the offender puts forward the fact that he or she was hitherto of good character and had driven for many years without being convicted of any offence, this cannot amount to a special reason in law—since it relates to the offender. The onus is on the offender to establish special reasons and he or she must prove them on a balance of probabilities. If the licence is not endorsed, no points are imposed. Seek advice if necessary: 📖✋.

Additionally and quite separately to special reasons, there is a procedure with construction and use offences (e.g. defective brakes, tyres, steering) whereby endorsement can be avoided if the offender establishes that he or she did not know of and had no reasonable cause to suspect the defect. Seek advice if necessary: 📖✋.

The effect of section 143(3) Road Traffic Act 1988 is that in certain circumstances employees driving—in the course of their employment—an uninsured vehicle provided by their employer do not need to resort to special reasons as the provision precludes their conviction in the first place.

Special reasons and appeals

Where the offender is aggrieved by a decision to order penalty points despite his or her assertion that special reasons exist, there is a right of appeal to the Crown Court or to the High Court on a point of law. The prosecutor also has a right of appeal to the High Court if it is contended that the magistrates' decision on this issue is wrong in law.

Penalty points and fixed penalties
Where an offender has accepted a fixed penalty (below), there is no court hearing. If the offence carries a range of points (such as speeding, i.e. 3-6) the number of points imposed is the lowest of the range.

Penalty points when disqualified for a different offence
In *Martin v Director of Public Prosecutions* (1999), *The Times*, November 30, the High Court considered whether, when a court orders disqualification in respect of an offence which carries disqualification (whether mandatory or discretionary (see below)), the court has power to order that—in respect of a separate offence for which the offender appears for sentence at the same time—penalty points which would have been ordered had that separate offence been dealt with on an entirely different occasion should be endorsed on his or her licence. The High Court ruled that no penalty points should be endorsed for the separate offence.

DISQUALIFICATION FROM DRIVING

Disqualification can involve the application of complex legal rules: generally, advice is desirable: 📖✋. There are two kinds:

Discretionary disqualification
The power to disqualify an offender at the court's discretion exists whenever an offence is endorsable (see also *Theft* etc. below). A court considering discretionary disqualification should, over and above any requirements of domestic law and pursuant to the provisions of the European Convention On Human Rights (see *Chapter 2*), warn the parties what is in mind and allow an opportunity for representations. A discretionary disqualification may not be imposed for the same offence if the offender is also liable to be disqualified under the penalty points provisions (see 'Totting up' below), and will not arise where the offence is subject to an *Obligatory disqualification* (see next paragraph).

Obligatory disqualification
Obligatory (or 'mandatory') disqualification arises due to:

- the nature of the offence; or
- the cumulative effect of earlier disqualifications; or
- most frequently in practice under the totting up provisions.

Offences for which the offender must be disqualified
There are several offences for which an offender *must* be disqualified (usually for a minimum of a year):

- driving or attempting to drive whilst unfit through drink or drugs
- driving or attempting to drive with 'excess alcohol' in the blood or urine
- failing or refusing to provide a specimen for analysis after driving
- dangerous driving; and
- aggravated vehicle taking.

In all cases, the court *must* order the defendant to be disqualified for 'such period not less than 12 months' as it thinks fit—unless the court for special reasons (i.e. relating to the offence: see above) thinks fit to order the offender to be disqualified for a shorter period, or not to order a disqualification at all. Where a court convicts someone of one of the offences listed above and orders obligatory disqualification, it cannot endorse a licence with penalty points for other offences of which the offender has been convicted on the same occasion.

The principles affecting special reasons have already been set out in relation to endorsement above—including the requirement to state the grounds for finding any such reasons in open court.

Cumulative effect of earlier disqualifications

A magistrates' court *must* impose a minimum disqualification of two years on an offender on whom more than one disqualification for 56 days or more has been imposed within three years immediately preceding the commission of the offence, if the offence of which he or she has now been convicted involves obligatory disqualification.

This means that an offender who is convicted of any of the offences listed under the heading *Obligatory disqualification* above and who has, within three years immediately preceding the commission of that offence, been the subject of more than one disqualification for a period of 56 days or more, must be disqualified for at least two years.

Along similar lines, where an offender is convicted of a drink/driving offence *committed* within ten years of a previous conviction for such an offence, the minimum period of disqualification is not one year but three years—unless the court decides, for special reasons, to reduce this obligatory disqualification, or not to impose one at all.

See also *Length of totting-up disqualification*, below.

'Totting-up'

In the main, the penalty points system is aimed at the offender who persistently commits relatively minor offences, and who ought to be disqualified because of repeated disregard for the law. Where a driver accumulates 12 or more points within a three year span, he or she must generally be disqualified for a minimum period (usually called a 'totting-up' or 'penalty points' disqualification). In totting-up, the points to be taken into account are:

- those falling to be endorsed for the offence before the court; and
- any that were endorsed on a previous occasion for offences committed within three years of each other, unless already 'wiped clear' by disqualification under the penalty points system (i.e. previous totting-up).

When a court disqualifies the offender under the totting-up provisions, no penalty points are endorsed for the current offence.

Length of totting-up disqualification

The minimum period of a totting-up disqualification is:

- *six months* if no previous disqualification falls to be taken into account; or
- *one year* if one previous disqualification falls to be taken into account; and

- *two years* if more than one previous disqualification falls to be taken into account.

A previous disqualification falls to be taken into account if it was imposed within three years of the *commission* of the latest offence which brought the offender's points total to 12. It need not have been for totting-up (it could have been for an offence involving obligatory disqualification such as drink driving). However, it must have been for 56 days or more and must not have been imposed for stealing a motor vehicle, taking without consent, or going equipped for theft.

'Mitigating circumstances'
Under the totting-up provisions, the offender must be disqualified for one of the minimum statutory periods set out above unless the court is satisfied that there are grounds for mitigating the normal consequences of conviction and sees fit to disqualify for a shorter period, or not to disqualify at all. The onus of establishing mitigating circumstances is on the offender—on a balance of probabilities. No account may be taken of:

- triviality of the offence
- hardship, other than 'exceptional hardship'; or
- circumstances previously taken into account within the three year period.

Mitigating circumstances must not be confused with special reasons (see page 108). Mitigating circumstances are far wider in scope—and, in the ordinary way, they will mainly refer to the *offender*. The exceptional hardship put forward will usually relate e.g. to loss of livelihood if disqualification is imposed. If this plea succeeds and the court reduces the minimum period, or decides not to disqualify, then the offender cannot put forward the same ground again until three years have elapsed. Since mitigating circumstances must be announced in open court and are recorded in the court register, courts can make enquiries as to what grounds were found at an earlier hearing. Although subsequent courts may well ask for a certified extract from an earlier court, most courts place the ultimate onus on the offender to show that any later mitigating circumstances put forward in this three-year period are different from the earlier ones.

Under the penalty points scheme only one disqualification is imposed irrespective of the number of offences. In the event of an appeal against any one or more of the offences, the disqualification will be treated as having been imposed in relation to each endorsable offence. The Crown Court has power to alter sentences imposed by magistrates for several offences, even if the appeal only relates to one of them.

Jones v. Chief Constable of West Mercia Police Authority

A sentencing difficulty can arise where, for instance, a person convicted of speeding at a fairly high level of seriousness invites the court to consider a short disqualification for the offence itself, thus avoiding a possible totting-up disqualification of six months or more had penalty points (3-6) been considered alongside earlier points. The case of *Jones v. Chief Constable of West Mercia Police Authority* (2000) addressed this by saying, in essence, that although the court must start with the offence itself and any discretionary disqualification which might ordinarily be appropriate, the final decision could be seen in the overall context of the driver's record and, if it considered it appropriate, the court could move on to consider variable points and any liability arising under the totting-up scheme.

Theft, taking vehicles without consent and similar offences

The general rule is that there can be no discretionary disqualification unless the offence is endorsable. But courts may impose disqualification in respect of offences of taking a motor vehicle without consent, stealing a motor vehicle or going equipped for the theft of a vehicle—despite the fact that these offences are not in themselves endorsable.

The rule against consecutive disqualifications

Disqualifications cannot be imposed on the same or a subsequent occasion to run consecutively to each other.

Disqualification in absence after notice

An offender cannot be disqualified in his or her absence unless first given the opportunity after conviction of attending court at an adjourned hearing so that he or she can make representations. As an alternative, the court may issue a warrant for the arrest of the defendant but in considering this course of action courts should bear in mind human rights considerations, particularly Article 5 ('liberty and security') and Article 8 ('respect for private and family life') (seek advice: 📖✋).

Commencement of disqualification

Disqualification starts from the moment it is imposed (credit being given by the DVLA for any interim disqualification: see under next heading).

Interim disqualification

Where the court has power to impose an immediate disqualification after conviction it also has power to impose an interim disqualification if:

- committing the defendant to the Crown Court for sentence
- remitting to another magistrates' court for sentence
- deferring sentence: see *Chapter 3*; or
- adjourning after conviction.

Accordingly, when e.g. a magistrates' court adjourns after conviction for a pre-sentence report (see generally *Chapter 9*), or a DVLA print-out (i.e. a computer record of the licence), it may impose an interim disqualification. The DVLA will reduce by the period of the interim disqualification the length of any disqualification imposed by way of sentence at the end of the case. An interim disqualification will automatically last until the case is finalised but, in any event, will not last for more than six months and the court has no power to make a repeat order for the same offence.

'Rehabilitation schemes'—subsequent reduction of a disqualification

Where a defendant is convicted of driving or being in charge when under the influence of drink or drugs, or driving or being in charge with excess alcohol in the blood or urine, or failing to provide a specimen, and is disqualified for a period of not less than 12 months, the court usually offers at the point of sentence to *reduce* the effect of disqualification by three months, or where it is for a longer period than 12 months by a period of not more than one quarter of its length—on the basis that he or she agrees to participate in a rehabilitation course. Such an order can only be made where:

- the court is satisfied that a place on a course is available
- the offender appears to be 17 years of age or older
- the effect of the order is explained to the offender and that he or she is required to pay the fees for the course before it begins; and
- the offender consents to the order being made.

If the offender completes the course successfully and pays the fees involved, a 'certificate of completion' will be forwarded to the supervising court and the reduction in disqualification will take effect. Rehabilitation courses became available to all courts in England and Wales from January 2000.

Disqualification until a test passed

When a court convicts an offender of any road traffic offence—one for which disqualification is obligatory or discretionary—it can order the defendant to be disqualified until he or she passes a driving test. As long as there is no other disqualification in force, the defendant is entitled to drive but must display 'L-plates' and be supervised. If he or she drives without L-plates or supervision, then a charge of driving whilst disqualified can be brought.

The Court of Appeal has repeatedly emphasised that this type of disqualification is not intended as a punishment—but is to protect the public against incompetent drivers or those who fail to use their driving skills properly. Accordingly, the prime reason for considering such an order is the interests of road safety. Orders will generally be in respect of offenders who, through age, infirmity or the circumstances of the offence, display incompetence. Any court disqualifying someone for a long period of time and having misgivings about the offender's ability when the period expires may wish also to consider imposing a disqualification until the offender passes a test.

When the court convicts an offender of dangerous driving, it is not only obliged to disqualify the offender for a minimum of one year but must also order disqualification until an 'extended driving test' is passed. This test is longer and more rigorous than the standard 'L-test', and takes place in a variety of road conditions.

When an offender is convicted of an offence involving obligatory disqualification, or is liable to totting-up, and the court, in its discretion, decides to order disqualification until the offender passes a test, then the test taken by the offender is the extended driving test.

Removal of disqualification

Anyone who has been disqualified (except e.g. for an interim period or until they have passed a test) can apply to the court for the removal of the disqualification and, if successful, disqualification may be lifted from a date specified in the order. The offender may apply:

- if the disqualification was for less than four years, after two years
- if the disqualification was for less than ten years but not less than four years, when half the period has elapsed; or
- in other cases, when a period of five years has elapsed.

If the application is refused, the offender must wait at least three months before reapplying. The court should have regard to the character of the offender and his or her conduct subsequent to the offence, the nature of the offence and any other circumstances. The provisions do not differentiate between *discretionary* and *obligatory* disqualification. Many applications concern three year disqualifications for a second drink/driving offence inside ten years. The offender can apply for the return of his or her licence after two years; but case law indicates that magistrates will need a lot of convincing before removing a disqualification which an earlier court was obliged by law to impose.

Disease or physical disability

There is a mandatory provision of the Road Traffic Offenders Act 1988 whereby—in any proceedings for an offence committed in respect of a motor vehicle—if it appears to the court that the defendant is suffering from any disability or prospective disability, such as is likely to cause his or her driving of a vehicle to be a source of danger to the public, to notify the Secretary of State. There must be sufficient material before the court, e.g. something said by way of mitigation suggesting that the defendant is suffering from a relevant disability or a prospective disability. However, actual conviction is not necessary. Accordingly, a court might use this provision e.g. in respect of a defendant acquitted of careless driving because of a 'dizzy spell', or in respect of someone who is suffering from mental disorder and who is made subject to a hospital order without being convicted (see *Chapter 10*). The Secretary of State has various powers including to revoke the licence.

FIXED PENALTIES: A NOTE[2]

The time, trouble and expense involved in court proceedings can be avoided for some motoring offences by the police offering the alleged offender a fixed penalty fine This offer can be accepted by payment of a fixed sum (below)—which is the end of the matter. If the events are not dealt with in this way, then the usual result is a prosecution in the normal way. The system was extended to a range of offences, from simple parking to some offences that carry endorsement such as speeding, pedestrian crossing offences and construction and use offences involving tyres, steering and brakes. Where there is a range of penalty points (see above) and the fixed penalty procedure is used, the lowest number of points in the range is endorsed. The offer of a fixed penalty is a matter entirely for the police. The procedure in an individual case depends on whether the offence is endorsable or not.

---

[2] Contrast the arrangements for fixed penalties to be issued in respect of a range of 'criminal' offences as noted in *Chapter 1*.

Offence not endorsable

A police constable (or other authorised officer such as a traffic warden) hands a fixed penalty ticket to the driver or, if the driver is absent, attaches it to the vehicle. The defendant has to pay the fixed penalty within 21 days to the relevant justices' chief executive (or within such longer period as is allowed by the ticket). The amount will normally be £30, unless the offence is illegal parking in London, when it is either £40 or £60 depending on the circumstances.

If payment is made within the time limit, that is the end of the matter. If not—and no court hearing is requested—the police may serve a 'notice to owner' upon the registered keeper of the vehicle. This provides a fresh opportunity for the fixed penalty to be paid. If it is not paid, various things can happen:

- the person served may request a hearing (proceedings then commence in the normal way); or
- the person served may satisfy the police by means of a statutory statement of ownership that he or she was not the owner of the vehicle at the material time. He or she will then be taken out of the equation.
- if the person served is the owner but not the driver when the offence occurred, he or she can furnish a statement of ownership together with a statutory statement of facts countersigned by the actual driver. This will enable the police to prosecute the identified driver, if they wish to do so; or
- if there is no response to the notice to the owner the fixed penalty is registered against the owner for enforcement (see *Non-payment*).

Driver present—endorsable offence

The officer requires the driver to produce his or her driving licence. Assuming that the driver is not liable to a totting-up disqualification (above), the constable can offer the alleged offender the option of a fixed penalty and invite him or her to surrender the licence. If the driver does not have the licence with him or her, the constable may issue a provisional fixed penalty notice. The driver then has seven days to produce the notice plus the absent driving licence at any police station. If he or she does this and it is confirmed that no totting-up disqualification is due, the offender will be given a fixed penalty ticket from that police station.

Requesting a hearing

Whenever there is an offer of a fixed penalty, the defendant can, within a time limit, ask for a court hearing. Proceedings are then conducted in the normal way, the defendant being invited to plead guilty or not guilty.

Conditional offer of fixed penalty

A conditional offer scheme is available for all fixed penalty offences (including those which carry endorsement). This allows the police to issue a notice by post to the registered keeper of the vehicle requiring information as to the identity of the driver. The conditional offer is issued to the person identified by the registered keeper as the driver on the occasion when the offence was detected. Should the keeper fail to give information as to the identity of the driver, he or she commits an offence which is itself endorsable. If the driver wishes to take up the offer, he or she will send his or her driving licence and payment to the justices' chief executive named in the notice who will accept payment subject to the driver's licence not disclosing that a totting-up disqualification (above) is due. This relatively new procedure is being phased in—initially only in relation to offences detected by automatic devices.

Non-payment of a fixed penalty—General scheme
If the penalty is unpaid at the end of the period allowed by the ticket, the fixed penalty (£30 non-endorsable offences and £60 endorsable offences: see above) plus 50 per cent of this amount will be registered for enforcement as a fine.

DVLA 'PRINTOUTS'

After conviction and before sentence for any road traffic offence carrying endorsement, the court should obtain either the defendant's driving licence or a printout of the defendant's driving record. Printouts are necessary in all cases where the defendant's licence cannot be obtained—or where one has not been issued. They are obtained from the Driver and Vehicle Licensing Authority (DVLA), Swansea, and contain details of any endorsable offences an individual has been convicted of and a note of disqualifications. The printout also shows sentences and court details.

Sometimes an 'emergency' printout of an offender's driving record can be obtained on the day of the hearing using a computer link to the DVLA. The system automatically requests a printout for every endorsable offence for every hearing.

REVOCATION OF NEW DRIVER'S LICENCE

A main object of the Road Traffic (New Drivers) Act 1995 which came into effect in 1997 is to reduce accidents and injuries involving newly qualified drivers: by mandatory revocation of a driving licence where the new driver accumulates *six or more* penalty points within two years beginning with the day on which he or she first passed a driving test. The driver can then only hold—and drive in accordance with—a provisional licence until he or she has passed a re-test.

Although the court does not order revocation, as a matter of good practice the licence holder should be advised by the court if the points imposed will lead to revocation. Once notified by the court, the DVLA sends a revocation letter to the defendant, which takes effect from five days after the date of issue. Magistrates should be alert to the fact that some defendants may encourage them to impose a short disqualification to circumvent the legislation. A short disqualification (which will not result in *any* penalty points being endorsed on the licence or notified to the DVLA) may be more attractive to the defendant than a re-test.

CHAPTER 9

Pre–sentence Reports

The pre-sentence report—or PSR—is a key decision-making tool in relation to more serious offences. PSRs were introduced by the Criminal Justice Act 1991 which introduced a structured approach whereby the preparation and content of such reports became subject to Home Office National Standards. At the time of writing, the latest standards are those published in 2000. Since the creation of the National Probation Service (NPS) many other strategic matters which were formerly determined locally have become the subject of action and agreement at national or regional level and the nature, content and use of modern PSRs/SSRs is now inescapably linked to the use by the NPS of accredited programmes which are currently being developed with regard to a range of community orders (*Chapter 4*). Also, in recent times, a form of PSR known as a 'specific sentence report'—or SSR—has evolved. This is a more focused form of PSR which, at the request of the court, is directed towards the appropriateness of certain community orders and their suitability for the offender (e.g. lesser community punishment orders (CPOs) or community rehabilitation orders (CROs) with no added requirements (save possibly in relation to accredited programmes)).[1]

BASIC PRINCIPLES

The relevant provisions are now contained in the Powers of Criminal Courts (Sentencing) Act 2000 which defines a PSR as 'a report *in writing*' [italics supplied] which:

(a) with a view to assisting the court in determining the most suitable method of dealing with an offender, is made or submitted by an appropriate officer [further defined as a probation officer or social worker of a local authority social services department in the case of an adult; a member of a youth justice team can also make or submit a PSR if the offender is under 18]; and

(b) contains information as to such matters, presented in such manner, as may be prescribed by rules made by the Secretary of State. (Section 162)

Adjournment periods for PSRs following conviction—usually of 15 working days—have traditionally been included in local *Statements of Preferred Practice* or 'protocols' (see later in this chapter). When it is in the interests of justice, expedited PSRs can be prepared during shorter adjournment periods (and see *Specific Sentence Reports (SSRs)*, below).

---

[1] References to local action etc. should be read in the light of the NPS's nationwide responsibility and influence and its relationship with Probation Boards at local level.

The obligation to consider a PSR

The court *must* consider a PSR when contemplating a custodial sentence or certain community sentences but there is a discretion to dispense with a PSR in an individual case if the court deems one 'unnecessary.' Sentences are not invalidated by failure to obtain a PSR—although on an appeal against sentence the appellate court must obtain a PSR if one was not obtained by the court below (subject to a similar discretion to deem this unnecessary).

For all practical purposes, the former strict legal requirements for reports in all serious cases have been replaced by good sentencing practice—which dictates that a PSR is appropriate whenever a court is considering any of the more severe forms of sentence unless the report could have no real effect on the court's decision. Where magistrates have power to commit for sentence to the Crown Court (see *Chapter 3*), no requirement is placed upon the court to order a PSR even though it will have arrived at a decision to commit because of a feeling that its own powers of punishment are insufficient. However, if a committal for sentence may be a possibility then, if the justices decide to call for a PSR, it is advisable to keep open expressly the option of committing for sentence. Apart from this exception, the situations in which the eventual sentence can be predicted with certainty in the magistrates' court are rare. The following are practical examples of when a PSR *may* be declared unnecessary, i.e. where a defendant:

- is already serving a custodial sentence and a further custodial sentence is envisaged
- is already serving, or has just completed, a community sentence and is reported as suitable for a further such order; or
- stands convicted of an offence which is so obviously very serious that the court would find it impossible to contemplate any option other than a custodial sentence. (This last example may, however, be more likely to occur in the Crown Court).

In cases where a PSR *is* obtained, it forms part of the relevant information which a court should consider before deciding on such important matters as the seriousness of the offence or offences, restriction of liberty and suitability for a particular community order. Among other things, PSRs often signify what demands will be made on the offender by a given sentence (including, again, via accredited programmes). PSRs are also relevant in relation to the risk of the offender re-offending—both generally and, more particularly, in relation to the protection of the public from serious harm from the offender where the court is dealing with a sexual or violent offence.

PREPARATION AND USE OF THE REPORT

Once a PSR is ordered and an adjournment allowed for it to be prepared, the report writer will aim to produce a report that is objective, impartial, free from discriminatory language or 'stereotyping', balanced, verified and factually accurate. Assessment procedures are based on the Offender Assessment System (OASys). This provides a systematic assessment of the nature and the causes of the defendant's offending behaviour, the risk he or she poses to the public and the action which can be taken to reduce the likelihood of reoffending. The PSR will be based on at least one face-to-face interview.

Whatever is said in the PSR (see *Contents of the PSR* below) it remains for *the court* to decide what sentence to impose. Also, where a community sentence *is* appropriate, it is for *the court* to decide whether to impose whatever order may have been proposed by the writer of the report, but, naturally, taking proper account of the contents of the report. There will be times when the court declines to follow even a well-reasoned PSR/SSR. There should be no need for any discord as between the court and the report writer if both have followed correct practice and proper procedures. Human rights obligations compel courts to formulate their own reasons for decisions, whatever views are expressed in a report.

Except in those few cases where it remains a legal requirement (see *Chapter 4*), consent to a community order by the offender is not strictly necessary. However, as suggested in *Chapter 4*, good sentencing practice and a prudent approach point to the desirability of obtaining an expression of the offender's willingness to comply with a proposed order. The National Standard recognises the need for the PSR writer to address both 'motivation' and 'suitability'.

Where the offender does not cooperate at the report stage
The standards indicate that where it has not been possible to complete a PSR (or an SSR as appropriate), for whatever reason, including non-attendance by the offender at interview, the writer should submit written notice to the court giving reasons why the report has not been completed—in effect a form of 'non-report'.

Where a medical report is indicated
This may stem from the facts of an individual case or from something discovered by the writer of a PSR/SSR. In either case, the court can order a separate report into the offender's mental or physical condition. This can pave the way for the court to make a CRO with a requirement of treatment for a mental condition (*Chapter 4*) or to exercise other powers in relation to *Mentally Disordered Offenders* (*Chapter 11*).

CONFIDENTIALITY

Reports are confidential documents (although a ruling early in 2003 held that any admissions of other offences made in a PSR/SSR were admissible on prosecution therefor). Following the Pre-Sentence Report (Prescription of Prosecutors) Order 1998, certain prosecutors are automatically entitled to a copy of the PSR/SSR. Disclosure to other prosecutors is at the discretion of the court. National Standards envisage that a copy will be provided to the court, the defence, the offender and (where required by law) the prosecutor. It is important to note that a PSR/SSR does not represent the interests of any individual or organization.

The contents of the PSR are brought to the attention of the offender by the report writer. This may mean reading it out in private for those who cannot read; including having an interpreter read and translate it to an offender whose first language is not English. A copy of the PSR is given to the offender and to his or her legal representative. It is important post-Human Rights Act 1998 for a court to ensure that the report has been made available to the defendant and that he or she understands and has had a proper opportunity to consider and, where appropriate, comment on it to both the writer and the court, and to make any relevant representations, e.g. if not satisfied that it contains correct data or a valid conclusion.

INITIAL INDICATIONS OF SERIOUSNESS

The case of *R v Gillam* (1981) gave rise to a series of appeal rulings that dealt with what might be called 'legitimate sentencing expectations'. In that case (pursuant to provisions prior to the Criminal Justice Act 1991) the court had adjourned for a report with a view to what was then a community service order (now a CPO) under the 'alternative to custody' approach then in operation. It was held on appeal that, if a court had 'held out' that a certain sentence was specifically under consideration, the defendant could generally expect no higher level of sentence if assessed by the report as being suitable for the order for which the assessment had been ordered. This thinking survived and expanded under the 1991 Act to the following generally applied effect:

- a request for a specific sentence report (SSR: see below) usually signifies that, on the information currently before the court, the court has decided that no higher sentence than a community sentence is appropriate and that sentence will be in the range of community orders covered by the SSR scheme (usually lower level CPOs or CROs)
- a request for a full pre-sentence report (PSR: see below) with a view to a community sentence at large gives rise to a similar *prima facie* expectation that custody will not be imposed if the assessment is positive (and that any community sentence will not be expressed as an 'alternative to custody'
- a request for a PSR which has not ruled out the possibility of custody (i.e. to decide whether or not the 'so serious' etc. test is satisfied) would possibly give the expectation that a committal to the Crown Court for sentence is not under consideration unless new significant new factors emerge.

Courts are encouraged, when ordering a report, to consider carefully, and announce accordingly, the extent of the sentencing range they wish to keep open. Guideline pronouncements are usually employed and the effect recorded on the court file. It is suggested that an 'all options' report (so as not to 'tie the hands' of the next court) is not an appropriate approach for at least the following reasons:

- the ordering of a report is, in itself, arguably a step along the sentencing road and not a precursor to it
- in particular the adjourning court will have had to have decided whether it has already crossed the 'serious enough' threshold for a community sentence (which it can do without a report) and is merely looking for the 'most suitable' community order or whether it wishes to consider crossing the 'so serious' threshold of custody which, by law, *prima facie* requires a PSR

- the defendant has a general right to expect that the court receiving the report (which will, unlike the Crown Court, probably be differently constituted) will apply common sentencing guidelines in a broadly similar way to a similar set of facts
- it is a waste of resources to expect the report writer to have to consider every sentencing option at every level merely because the court has not been specific enough.

If a custodial sentence has, on the face of it, not been ruled out then certain listing and gaolering arrangements might need to be considered for the next hearing. When a court orders a report and grants bail to a defendant previously in custody, case law indicates that no expectation of a non-custodial sentence is created simply by the fact that the court has allowed bail. Nevertheless, good practice calls for a specific warning to this effect.

CONTENTS OF THE PSR

The PSR will start by setting out basic factual information on the offence and the offender (including previous convictions and drawing on other information from the Crown Prosecution Service). There will also be a summary of the sources drawn upon to prepare the report and steps taken to verify information, a note of other potentially useful sources to which it was not possible to have access, and any doubts about the reliability of particular information. Information will then appear under the following main headings:

- **offence analysis**
- **offender assessment**
- **an assessment of the risk of harm to the public and the likelihood of re-offending**
- **a conclusion** (including in appropriate instances a proposal).

Offence analysis
Every PSR will contain an offence analysis as follows:

- an analysis of the offence or offences, highlighting the key features in respect of the nature and circumstances in which it was/they were committed
- an assessment of the offender's culpability and level of premeditation
- an assessment of the consequences of the offence, including what is known of the impact on any victim, either from the CPS papers or from a victim statement where available
- an assessment of the offender's attitude to the offence and awareness of its consequences, including to any victim; and
- an indication of whether or not any positive action has been taken by the offender to make reparation or to address offending behaviour since the offence was committed.

Offender assessment

Similarly each PSR will contain an offender assessment:

- stating the offender's status in relation to:
  - —literacy and numeracy
  - —accommodation
  - —employment
- assessing the implications of any special circumstances, e.g. family crisis, substance abuse or mental illness, which were directly relevant to the offending
- evaluating any patterns of offending including reasons for offending and assessing the outcome of any earlier court interventions, including the offender's response to previous supervision
- where substance abuse is relevant, providing details of the nature of the misuse, and the offender's response to previous or current treatment
- giving consideration to the impact of racism in the offender's behaviour where directly relevant to the offence; and
- including any relevant personal background which may have contributed to the offender's motive for committing the offence.

Assessment of risk of harm to the public and likelihood of reoffending

Every PSR will:

- contain an assessment of the offender's likelihood of reoffending based on the current offence, attitude to it, and other relevant information
- contain an assessment of the offender's risk of causing serious harm to the public; and
- identify any risks of self–harm.

Conclusion

Finally, each PSR will contain a conclusion which:

- evaluates the offender's motivation and ability to change and identifies, where relevant, action required to improve motivation
- explicitly states whether or not an offender is suitable for a community sentence
- makes a clear and realistic proposal for sentence designed to protect the public and reduce reoffending, including for custody where this is necessary
- where the proposal is for a CRO or CPO, includes an outline supervision plan containing:
  - —a description of the purposes and desired outcomes of the proposed sentence
  - —the methods envisaged and interventions likely to be undertaken, including attendance at accredited programmes[2] where appropriate

---

[2] Increasingly it seems, courts may be expected to understand what is meant by a particular form of accredited programme—concerning which the NPS has, e.g. issued *Probation Circulars* and *NPS Briefings*. See the example in relation to CPOs/Enhanced Community Punishment (ECP) in *Chapter 4*.

—the level of supervision envisaged (which for offenders at high risk of causing serious harm to the public is likely to be higher than the minimum required by the standards)

- where a specific condition is imposed, sets out the requirement precisely as it is proposed to appear in any order, and gives a likely start date
- where the proposal is for a curfew order, includes details of the suitability of the proposed curfew address and its likely effects on others living at the offender's address
- for all serious sexual or violent offences, provides advice on the appropriateness of extended supervision; and
- where custody is a likely option, identifies any anticipated effects on the offender's family circumstances, current employment or education.

When a custodial sentence is passed, a copy of the order is normally sent to the NPS/Social Services Department representative in the custodial institution and OASys (above) follows through to custody and post-release supervision (see *Chapter 10*).

SPECIFIC SENTENCE REPORTS (SSRs)

Magistrates have a wide discretion to sentence adults without a PSR where they consider one to be unnecessary, but, as indicated earlier in this chapter, it is normally good practice to seek the benefit of information in such a report. There are circumstances where a court may well not require a full PSR but might wish to seek the advice of the National Probation Service on a particular community sentencing option (or options) that it has in mind. Consideration of a CPO is a typical example of where this advice may be sought and there is, in fact, in this instance an obligation to obtain information by way of a 'CPO assessment' (as it is generally known) dealing with the offender's suitability for the order and the availability of work under it if made. Strictly speaking, in contrast to the position in relation to a PSR proper, such an assessment need not be in writing.

The concept of the specific sentence report (SSR) has thus evolved. Where a community penalty is in mind (but not custody: SSRs are primarily directed towards lesser CPOs and CROs without added requirements (other than accredited programmes)) an SSR can be requested. SSRs reduce delay and make better use of resources, and cases can be disposed of sooner—sometimes on the same day as a plea or a verdict of guilty.

An SSR writer who has, or who discovers, concerns that a risk assessment in an SSR report may not be adequate, or that there are other issues needing to be further explored, will advise the court to request a full PSR. The National Standards contain the following advice:

The purpose of a specific sentence report (SSR) is to provide information about the offender and offence(s) so as to assist the sentencing court to determine the offender's suitability for a specific sentence envisaged by the court. It is a PSR for the formal purposes of the Powers of Criminal Courts (Sentencing) Act 2000 and is used to speed up the provision of information to the court to allow sentencing without delay and is most likely to be used where the court envisages a CPO of up to 100 hours or CRO without additional requirements [subject to local extensions]. An SSR shall:

- be based on an initial assessment of risk of serious harm and likelihood of reoffending
- be a written report, even where presented orally to the court . . .
- clearly set out the offender's suitability for a particular penalty as requested by the court
- other than in exceptional circumstance, be available to the court on the day requested; and
- recommend an adjournment for a full PSR if the writer believes further investigation is required.

Some NPS areas are considering whether it is possible to complete a shortened form of PSR (as opposed to an SSR) on the day of the hearing, thus addressing those cases which fall between SSR's (where limited enquiry and assessment are required) and full PSRs (where substantial enquiry and assessment are still needed).

LOCAL PROTOCOLS

An effect of National Standards is to require the NPS to agree protocols or 'working understandings' with courts and other agencies, something which, historically speaking, largely occurred locally and which now happens against the backdrop of national direction. The position is covered by Probation Circular 12/2003 which talks of a 'Communications Strategy for Sentencers'. In particular it is important for there to be understandings about court pronouncements when calling for a PSR/SSR, adjournments and the management and enforcement of community orders (where the modern approach is to take a firm stance in order to ensure effectiveness).

Summary of Early Release Provisions

Prisoners aged 18 years and over [1]

LENGTH OF SENTENCE	TYPE OF EARLY RELEASE SCHEME	REGIME (↓ Start of Sentence — 1/2)	REGIME (1/2 — 2/3)	(3/4 → Sentence Expiry Date)
Under 12 months	Automatic Unconditional Release ('AUR')	• Custody • If serving 3 months or more eligible for Home Detention Curfew ('HDC')	• Released automatically and unconditionally • 'At Risk'[2]	
12 months or more but less than 4 years	Automatic Conditional Release ('ACR')	• Custody • Eligible for Home Detention Curfew ('HDC') given that serving more than 3 months	• Released automatically • Post-Release Licence Supervision Conditions • 'At Risk'	'At Risk'
4 years or more	Discretionary Conditional Release ('DCR') on Parole *or* Non-Parole Licence	• Custody • No eligibility for Home Detention Curfew ('HDC')	• Custody • Eligible for Discretionary Release on Parole—supervision continues to three quarters stage • 'At Risk'　　　• Released Automatically in any event (i.e. Non-Parole Licence) • Post-Release Licence Supervision Conditions • 'At Risk'	'At Risk'

1 All prisoners aged under 22 years will always have a minimum of 3 months' post-release supervision by virtue of section 65 Criminal Justice Act 1991.

2 'At Risk' = At risk of return for all or part of balance of sentence if convicted of further imprisonable offence before Sentence Expiry Date.

CHAPTER 10

Early Release of Prisoners

A system for the early release of sentenced prisoners on parole or other form of supervision has been in place in England and Wales since 1968. The rationale behind early release schemes is to ensure good behaviour by the prisoner during the custodial sentence and afterwards by, e.g.:

- encouraging compliance with the prison regime
- providing a target and focus for a rehabilitation programme; and
- removing pressure on crowded prison resources (see, in particular, now, release on *Home Detention Curfew*, below).

It should be stressed at the outset that the sentencer must not artificially increase the length of any custodial sentence in an attempt to secure the actual time to be 'spent behind bars'. The sentencing requirements of the Powers of Criminal Courts (Sentencing) Act 2000, as outlined in *Chapter 4* of this handbook and amplified by case law, are to impose any custodial sentence, and to fix its particular duration, based solely on the seriousness of the offence or the need to protect the public (as applicable). Any reduction which an offender may subsequently acquire, either by right or under a discretionary scheme (such as home detention curfew: see later in this chapter), is generally a matter for the post-sentence process not the sentencer.

However, this is not to say that magistrates and other sentencers can totally disregard the practical effect of imposing custodial sentences. On occasions, imposing further custodial sentences consecutively to earlier ones can have the cumulative effect of altering, to the offender's disadvantage, the early discharge provisions which would otherwise apply. Sentencers must, therefore, be alive to the issue and consider the appropriateness of the overall sentencing position 📖✋.

The former Lord Chief Justice, Lord Bingham, indicated that courts sentencing people to custody should, at that time, give the offender an indication of how long the sentence will actually be in practice and how the release date will be calculated. This requires careful phrasing (and sometimes careful calculation). Advice should always be sought 📖✋.

There is statutory provision, not yet brought into general effect but piloted by a number of magistrates' courts, whereby magistrates would be required formally to determine the early release date at the time of imposing sentence. The pilot courts reported the considerable problems which inevitably arose, especially when there were so many other issues and pressures to be addressed at the point of sentence. Whereas it is clearly appropriate for a newly-sentenced prisoner to have an early indication of when his or her release might occur, it is equally important that this is calculated carefully and when in possession of all information as to when the offender was held in any form of custody in the proceedings prior to sentence. The expected expansion of more powerful and interactive computerisation in the criminal justice system might make it easier for early release calculations to be made at the point of sentence.

Previous law saw early release based on time an offender might be able to earn by way of remission for good behaviour. The Criminal Justice Act 1991 provided a more definite scheme whereby the early release date and the basic terms thereof are now generally determined at the outset. Thereafter the early release date can be put back if the offender fails to behave appropriately in the lead-up to release.

The offender's early release date is ultimately calculated by reference to a number of factors such as:

- his or her age[1]
- length of sentence
- credit for any time spent on remand in custody
- any 'added days' for prison disciplinary offences
- whether the release comes within the 'automatic' or 'discretionary' criteria (below); and
- whether the further discretionary home detention curfew provisions are applicable and actually operating (below).

The calculation will, therefore, often be complex. However, one aspect of facilitating the quick and timely calculation of early release dates is already within the control of magistrates' courts. When remanding in custody for a number of offences it is to the offender's definite and appropriate benefit if magistrates consider all offences before them and remand in custody on all offences which justify such a remand. All such offences will therefore appear on the remand warrant and form part of the record by which the prison authorities, who presently have the task, will calculate the early release date. There have been occasions where the remand warrant has shown only one of many offences and that one allegation has later, e.g. been withdrawn. An offender then sentenced to a custodial sentence for other offences in the same proceedings could well lose credit for time spent on remand as those other offences will not have appeared on the face of the remand record as held by HM Prison Service.

AUTOMATIC UNCONDITIONAL RELEASE

Automatic unconditional release (AUR) generally applies where the offender:

- is classed as a *short-term prisoner* (i.e. serving a term of custody for less than four years); and
- is actually serving a term of *less than 12 months*; and
- has reached the half-way stage of the sentence.

---

[1] This chapter deals with offenders aged 18 years or over at the time when they were sentenced. Slightly different provisions apply to offenders who were under 18 years of age at that point in time. Nonetheless, such people may appear before the adult magistrates' court aged 18 or over for breach of licence conditions, but it would make this basic outline unduly complex to add and explain the differences here: seek advice 📖✌.

The basis of the release will be:

- *unconditional* i.e. there will be no licence with conditions controlling the prisoner's movements or activities; but
- subject to the possibility of return under section 116 Powers of Criminal Courts (Sentencing) Act 2000 (see below) to serve some or all of the outstanding term if the offender is convicted of an offence committed during what would have been the full term of the sentence—known as being 'at risk'.

AUTOMATIC CONDITIONAL RELEASE

Automatic conditional release (ACR) generally applies where the offender:

- is classed as a *short-term prisoner* (i.e. serving a term of custody for less than four years); and
- is actually serving a term of *12 months or more* (and clearly less than four years); and
- has reached the half-way stage.

The basis of the release will:

- be *conditional*, i.e. subject to a licence with conditions which may vary from case to case but which will cover matters such as residence, movement, activities, rehabilitation and supervision by the National Probation Service
- provide for such licence to run to the three-quarters stage of the original full term (or to the end of the original full term in the case of sexual or violent offenders who may, by reason of the nature of their offence, be subject to an 'extended sentence' under section 85 Powers of Criminal Courts (Sentencing) Act 2000 whereby the sentencing court felt and ordered that an extended period of post-release licence appeared necessary on the facts of the case)
- be subject to action for breach of such licence conditions (see below); and will
- be subject to the possibility of return, under section 116 of the 2000 Act (below), to serve some or all of the outstanding term if the offender is convicted of an offence committed during what would have been the full term of the sentence.

NON-PAROLE DATE RELEASE (NPD)

NPD release is automatic and generally applies where the offender:

- is classed as a *long-term prisoner* (i.e. serving a term of custody of four years or more; and
- has reached the two-thirds stage (i.e. the date when the period for discretionary release on parole has met up with the point where release would otherwise be automatic, albeit conditional—see below); and

- release on parole under DCR (below) has not already started and run through the two-thirds stage.

The basis of release will:

- be *conditional*, i.e. subject to a licence with conditions which may vary from case to case but which will cover matters such as residence, movement, activities and supervision by the National Probation Service
- provide for such licence to run to the three-quarters stage of the original full term (or to the end of the original full term in the case of sexual or violent offenders who may, by reason of the nature of their offence, be subject to an 'extended sentence' under section 85 of the 2000 Act whereby the sentencing court felt and ordered that an extended period of post-release licence appeared necessary on the facts of the case)
- be subject to action for breach of such licence conditions (see below); and
- be subject to the possibility of return, under section 116 of the 2000 Act (see below) to serve some or all of the outstanding term if the offender is convicted of an offence committed during what would have been the full term of the sentence.

DISCRETIONARY CONDITIONAL RELEASE

There is a further and discretionary power to release *long-term* prisoners on parole licence with conditions before the two-thirds point, i.e. on discretionary conditional release (DCR), sometimes known as 'parole licence'. This power arises at or after the half-way stage and then, if granted, runs through the two-thirds point when NPD as above would otherwise have come into play. The parole licence will run through to the three-quarters stage in the usual way as if NPD had otherwise operated.

LIFE SENTENCE ETC. PRISONERS

The provisions for the early release of people serving life sentences are somewhat different from those for other prisoners and are not covered in this book. Special provisions apply to lifers and offenders under 18 years (the latter ordered to be detained at Her Majesty's pleasure for certain grave crimes: see further in *Appendix F*).[2]

---

[2] For a general treatment of the regime and arrangements for this high risk group see *Murderers and Life Imprisonment: Detention, Treatment, Safety and Risk*, Eric Cullen and Tim Newell, Waterside Press, 1998. Clearly, magistrates are not involved in imposing such sentences and also do not deal with any failures by released lifers to comply with the terms of their release. However, magistrates' courts may, on occasions, have to sentence lifers who have re-offended following early release and may feel the need to take this aspect of the offence into account in assessing its overall seriousness.

BREACH OF LICENCE CONDITIONS

The combined effect of sections 38 and 39 Criminal Justice Act 1991 taken together with provisions in the 2000 Act deal with the powers on breach of licence.

Short-term prisoners (original offence committed *prior to 1 January 1999*)

- breach is a summary offence carrying a level 3 fine (£1,000). Absolute or conditional discharges are also available as are those community orders which do not require the offence (in this case the breach offence) to carry imprisonment
- in addition, the balance of the licence can be suspended for up to six months and the offender returned to custody for the period of suspension
- the National Probation Service will usually prosecute the offence (note that this is a full-blown prosecution as for any other form of criminal offence and all the usual resulting considerations apply)
- because the breach offence itself does not carry imprisonment, the power to issue a warrant for the offender's arrest will not ordinarily be available and cases may often have to be heard in the absence of offenders if they do not otherwise attend
- however, if recall is ordered in an offender's absence, the offender is deemed to be 'unlawfully at large' and liable to arrest without warrant; and
- as time goes by, this form of breach action will disappear as the new form, as outlined below, becomes more common.

Short-term prisoners (original offence committed *on or after 1 January 1999*)

- new provisions now make such prisoners, in common with long-term prisoners who breach their licence conditions, liable to direct recall by the Secretary of State on the recommendation of the Parole Board; and
- such cases should, therefore, no longer come before magistrates' courts although it will always be advisable to check the dates of the original offences where any breaches of licence conditions by short-term prisoners are alleged before magistrates.

Long-term prisoners (irrespective of when original offence committed)

- all breaches of licence are already covered by direct recall by the Secretary of State on the recommendation of the Parole Board.

COMMISSION OF NEW OFFENCE ON RELEASE

Where an offender commits a further offence while on early release, the 'at-risk' provisions of section 116 Powers of Criminal Courts (Sentencing) Act 2000 have the following effects:

- a prisoner convicted of any offence punishable with imprisonment committed between the point of early release and the point at which the custodial sentence would otherwise have run its full course is liable to recall under section 116 by the sentencing court
- the period of recall will start from the date it is ordered
- the length of the recall will be for such period as may be felt appropriate but the maximum must be based on the period from the commission of the new offence up to the time when the sentence would otherwise have reached its full term; and
- magistrates are, in any event, restricted to six months but do have a power to send the matter (and with it the new offence) to the Crown Court which will have the full powers. **NB** In such cases the magistrates should take legal advice concerning their various powers to commit to the Crown Court for sentence/to be dealt with so as to make sure that they have used the most appropriate and relevant ones and thereby given the Crown Court all necessary powers 📖✋.

BREACH BY OFFENDERS UNDER 22

Under section 65 Criminal Justice Act 1991, all offenders aged *under 22 years of age at the time of release* (be it early or otherwise) from a young offender institution (now replaced for those under 18 years with detention and training orders) will always be subject to some form of supervision for at least three months.

This will often be by way of a licence which happens to run for at least that period. However, if there is no licence or it expires before the three months point, section 65 will provide for supervision by a probation officer (or a member of a youth offending team (YOT)). This supervision will arise immediately if there is no early release on licence or will come into play, if the licence is for less than three months, at the end of the licence period. In this case the supervision will last until a date three months from the date of release.

In respect of a section 65 order for supervision:

- breach is made a criminal offence and will usually be prosecuted by the National Probation Service (or YOT) and all the usual factors relating to criminal prosecutions apply
- the offence carries a level 3 fine (£1,000) *or* 'an appropriate custodial sentence' not exceeding 30 days
- 'appropriate custodial sentence' means imprisonment for those aged 21 years or over and detention in a young offender institution for those aged 18 years but under 21 years; and
- because of the above, there will be a need to take into account the usual ancillary factors relating to the imposition of custodial sentences such as finding the offence to be 'so serious', to give reasons for that decision and the opportunity for legal representation.

HOME DETENTION CURFEW (HDC)

Since the Crime and Disorder Act 1998, it has been possible for certain prisoners to be considered for release before their usual automatic release date if they observe a curfew for the time from the new early release date up to the time when automatic release would otherwise arise. This is geared towards releasing from prison, as a lead up to automatic release, those offenders who are not thought to be a danger. The need to reduce congestion in prisons is implicit in the measures. The main aspects of these provisions are:

- they apply only to *short-term* prisoners (see above) serving at least three months (and, of course, under four years)
- they apply only to offenders aged *18 years or over*
- release is at the discretion of the Home Secretary
- many types of offender are automatically precluded by statute
- Category A prisoners and sex offenders are *prima facie* presumed unsuitable
- the period of HDC varies from 14 days to two months, depending on the length of the original sentence
- the release is on licence and includes specific curfew terms and address(es)
- the curfew is monitored by electronic tagging similar to that for curfew orders made directly as a community sentence on sentencing for an offence (see *Chapter 4*); and
- breaches of the tagging aspect of the HDC (unlike other breaches of the licence) never come before the courts but are dealt with directly through the Parole Board.

Magistrates may, however, find it desirable to take legal advice if they are presented with an offender who is already subject to HDC facing a new charge (or who is also subject to ACR, above). There may well be issues of proposed bail conditions conflicting with the HDC requirements and offending during the HDC period may possibly be considered an aggravating factor in sentencing 📖✍.

They should also note that the discretion to offer HDC is generally not considered favourably when the offender still has time to serve for fine default. Magistrates may again wish to take advice when ordering custody for fine default, especially where to be consecutive to other custodial sentences for offences 📖✍.

ROLE OF THE NATIONAL PROBATION SERVICE

The work of the National Probation Service (NPS) here is covered by National Standards which provide the following aims for supervising probation officers:

- address and reduce offending behaviour
- challenge the offender to accept responsibility for the crimes committed and their consequences

- contribute to the protection of the public
- motivate and assist the offender towards a greater sense of personal responsibility and discipline; and
- aid reintegration as a law-abiding member of the community.

The NPS has, as part of this process, the responsibility of reporting breaches to the Parole Board or of instigating breach prosecutions where that course of action remains (see above).

EARLY RELEASE: HUMAN RIGHTS ISSUES

Broadly speaking, the same human rights considerations arise when dealing with people who are at risk of being returned to custody or sentenced for breach of their licence as apply to other criminal proceedings—and because liberty may be directly affected they should be applied to the highest standard and with no cutting of corners 'because the defendant is a serving (albeit currently released) prisoner'. Similar issues arise for HM Prison Service and those of its staff who are charged with making relevant decisions affecting release including in relation to 'prison adjudications' for disciplinary offences and 'added days' (above).

CHAPTER 11

Mentally Disordered Offenders

Dealing with mentally disordered offenders (MDOs)—a term widely used to encompass any alleged offender presenting any kind of perceived mental problem—gives rise to complex issues which warrant greater consideration than is possible here. These complexities manifest themselves in both the medical conditions encountered (and their diagnosis) and also in the legal provisions which may fall to be considered in relation to criminal justice processes. It should also be noted that the Mental Health Act 1983 (the main statutory provision dealing with mental health issues in general) has detailed civil provisions which, on occasions, may be applied to MDOs without reference to criminal proceedings. Equally, the issue will sometimes arise whether or not offending behaviour is directly attributable to the offender's mental condition, when courts will usually require expert medical assistance.

There is a clear tension, on the one hand, between recognising and working with an illness which happens to manifest itself mentally rather than physically and, on the other, protecting the public from any criminal manifestations of mental disorder. This tension is often exacerbated by an apparent lack of access to appropriate medical facilities. Much effort has been directed in recent times by governments towards managing such tensions and providing more appropriate and co-ordinated overall strategies and services. In 1999, the Labour government published a Green Paper, *Reform of the Mental Health Act 1983*, which was heralded as outlining major changes in the way mental health issues, including those resulting in offending behaviour, are dealt with. Immediate change now seems unlikely.

Courts will wish to ensure that defendants who are believed to be mentally disordered are legally represented if at all possible.

Scale of the problem
Although individual magistrates are unlikely to deal with, let alone sentence, a high number of MDOs, and particularly those with major medical problems, it is worth noting some earlier statistics that put the matter into perspective nationwide:

- 64 per cent of male prisoners have some form of mental health problem
- 50 per cent of female prisoners have some form of mental health problem
- on average, three killings are committed each month in the UK by mentally ill people; and
- annually, criminal courts as a whole order the compulsory admission of some 1,000 convicted people to mental health service facilities.

Those statistics also suggest that:

- at least three million people in the UK are affected by anxiety states
- dementia affects 700,000 elderly people in the UK (but is not exclusively a condition experienced by the elderly)

- there are at least 250,000 manic depressives in the UK (of which some 60 per cent are female)
- schizophrenia affects at least 250,000 people in the UK (fairly evenly divided between males and females); and
- on average some 80 mentally ill people commit suicide in the UK every month.

MULTI-AGENCY/INTER-AGENCY STRATEGIES

Nowadays, multi-agency MDO groups adopt an inter-agency (or 'partnership') approach to issues affecting mentally disordered offenders. Such groups have a broad range of functions which include the co-ordination of all main local agencies which may interact with MDOs and also the provision of advice and other related services to criminal courts. Membership typically includes representatives from agencies such as the following:

- Mental Health Services
- Police
- National Probation Service
- Social Services
- Crown Prosecution Service
- Education Service
- Magistrates' Court
- Crown Court
- Housing Department
- Local Law Society; and
- Youth Offending Team (YOT: which deals mainly with people under 18 years of age).

DIVERSION FROM THE CRIMINAL PROCESS

Especially following the arrival of the local multi-agency MDO groups (above), much emphasis has been placed on, and energy invested in, the diversion of MDOs from the criminal justice process where treatment is considered more appropriate than punishment. This process starts at the point of the initial criminal investigation and extends right up to the start of any criminal prosecution, and possibly goes even beyond this, into the formal proceedings at any point before conviction.

SERVICES LINKED TO MAGISTRATES' COURTS

MDO groups provide in particular (and where appropriate and feasible) some form of duty or on-call psychiatric officer for police custody centres (i.e. suitably structured cells where prisoners are questioned, charged and held) and magistrates' courts to which these centres produce newly-charged defendants. In busy city courts this could, for instance, be a duty psychiatrist and in others an on-call community forensic psychiatric nurse (CFPN). Such people can help with matters such as:

- identifying mental health problems in people arrested
- suggesting diversion where this may possibly be appropriate
- arranging referral to mental health services on diversion; and
- linking courts with local mental health services to obtain reports or to seek provision for treatment under court orders.

FITNESS TO PLEAD

The question of a defendant's fitness to plead may occasionally arise and detailed legal advice should be sought in all such cases 📖✋.

INSANITY AS A DEFENCE

Where insanity is specifically pleaded as a defence (a rare occurrence, especially in magistrates' courts, because the consequences, i.e. long-term detention in a secure hospital, far outweigh any likely penalty) detailed legal advice should always be sought 📖✋.

TERMINOLOGY: MAGISTRATES' COURTS

As intimated above, specific medical conditions and their diagnosis will often be complex. However, the Mental Health Act 1983 recognises four specific forms of 'mental disorder':

- mental illness
- psychopathic disorder
- severe mental impairment; and
- mental impairment.

The definition and identification of each of these will require expert and detailed medical input and advice which, on occasions, may conflict in terms of diagnosis, extent of disorder, possible treatment and the likelihood of success. Nevertheless, it is these four conditions which generally give rise to both the civil and criminal based powers to deal with people with a mental condition. In terms of the criminal courts, such conditions usually give rise, under the Mental Health Act 1983, to the possibility on conviction of:

- a hospital order; or
- a guardianship order.

Both of these are discussed below.

Personality disorder

The term 'personality disorder' is often encountered. It is used to reflect a wide range of behavioural scenarios that do not involve mental illness as such. Personality disorders are not usually susceptible to treatment by medication, but more often require some form and degree of cognitive behavioural therapy. It is in this area that magistrates may most often experience MDOs in the widest sense of the term—and when the possibility of a community rehabilitation order (CRO) may arise with a requirement for treatment (by a psychiatrist, other medical practitioner or chartered psychologist) or for individual and/or group work with a probation officer (see, generally, *Chapter 4*).

POWERS RE MENTALLY DISORDERED PEOPLE

Although, clinically speaking, it may be inappropriate to look at sentencing powers as a range of 'pigeon holes' into which the mentally disordered offender and his or her offence need to be fitted, magistrates may often have to face up to this form of approach, and there will then be a need to try to harmonise medical and sentencing approaches.

If MDOs are not diverted before or during the arrest and prosecution process (above) then, on conviction, magistrates' courts have the following basic options:

- to sentence in the ordinary way relying on the standard range of sentences, including a CRO with a requirement for treatment (by a psychiatrist, other registered medical practitioner or chartered psychologist) or individual or group work with a probation officer (see, generally, *Chapter 4*)
- to make a hospital order
- to make a guardianship order; or
- to commit the offender to the Crown Court with a view to a hospital order being made with a restriction on discharge (magistrates having no power to add such a restriction).

Each of these options is considered below.

Information before exercising powers in respect of mentally disordered offenders

It can be appreciated that, when considering sentence in respect of a person believed to be mentally disordered, there is a special need (and in certain situations a legal obligation 📖🖐) to instigate and consider detailed investigations and reports.

Although the National Probation Service, the community forensic psychiatric nurse and the offender's general medical practitioner amongst others may be able to offer much direct or indirect information on the offender's apparent mental condition, magistrates will usually need a formal medical report, especially if some court order for treatment is envisaged.

In such cases, any report will have to be provided by a 'registered medical practitioner' (who must be 'approved for the purposes of section 12 Mental Health Act 1983 as having special experience in the diagnosis or treatment of mental disorder'). Lists of people so approved are usually drawn up and circulated on a regional basis by the relevant mental health authorities. It should be noted that a psychologist (as opposed to a psychiatrist) may not necessarily be a registered medical practitioner for the above purposes 📖✋.

Magistrates, on convicting a defendant believed to have mental problems, can (and *must* if they feel that such enquiry ought to be made or if a *custodial sentence* is under consideration: *Chapter 4*) order reports from at least one section 12 approved registered medical practitioner.

If such an offender is released on bail, then specific bail conditions to secure the offender's co-operation must be applied pursuant to section 11 Powers of Criminal Courts (Sentencing) Act 2000 and these will be above and beyond any other conditions appropriate to the individual case 📖✋.

Courts may approach the medical services direct or—in practice quite often—through a probation officer (who is likely to be asked to provide a linked pre-sentence report (PSR)) in consultation with the local community forensic psychiatric nurse (CFPN).

If the defendant is remanded in custody HM Prison Service will usually make the necessary arrangements. In this event, the prison authorities, rather than the court, will meet any costs of the doctor or doctors involved.

Such medical reports place a substantial burden on what is a fairly limited and costly medical resource and courts may well wish to give the matter extra careful consideration when a defence solicitor (who may have been refused authority to incur the cost of such reports under a legal representation order) invites a court to order medical reports.

SENTENCING IN THE ORDINARY WAY

As already indicated, the full range of standard sentencing options will generally be available in respect of mentally disordered people, subject to any inherent criteria in such orders or disposals and their appropriateness in the circumstances of the case and for the offender. It should be remembered that the normal seriousness or protection of the public tests apply and courts cannot 'short circuit' these just because someone appears to need medical support. Even, e.g. where the offence is 'serious enough' for a community sentence, the court will still need to conclude that a particular disposal (such as a CRO with a requirement for treatment for a mental condition: see *Chapter 4*) is the most suitable community sentence for the offender. Neither should custody be imposed purely because of the presence of a mental disorder or any perceived difficulty about its treatment in the community, or in securing the provision of such treatment.

It is easy to see that—but for the legal framework for sentencing—the court might be compelled towards such outcomes, but courts must follow the full reasoning process before using mental health or other powers. This is additionally important following the Human Rights Act 1998, if only because the offender may be vulnerable in the sense that he or she may have difficulty in fully understanding what is happening, or in responding effectively.

HOSPITAL ORDER

The effect of a hospital order is that the convicted offender will be compulsorily admitted within 28 days to an appropriate hospital for treatment. If admission cannot be immediate (e.g. lack of a bed) the offender will be held for the relevant part of the 28 day period in a specified 'place of safety' (often, but not necessarily, a prison or remand centre). The period of admission will initially be a maximum of 12 months, but there is provision (not involving a return to court) for the subsequent early discharge of, or extension to, this period.

The relevant medical and legal criteria and procedures require detailed legal advice (📖✋) but the following key points should be noted:

- the offence must be imprisonable on summary conviction
- reports (written or oral) are required from two registered medical practitioners
- at least one such practitioner must be approved for the purposes of section 12 Mental Health Act 1983 (see above)
- the magistrates must be satisfied, on the strength of the two reports, that the offender is suffering from mental illness, psychopathic disorder, severe mental impairment or mental impairment (Note: Difficulties clearly arise where the two practitioners both identify a mental disorder but do not agree on its location within one of the above four categories. In that event a hospital order would not, without more, be possible)
- the nature or degree of the specific mental disorder within the above four categories must make detention in hospital for treatment appropriate and, in the case of psychopathic disorder or mental impairment (but not severe mental impairment) such treatment must be likely to alleviate the offender's condition
- the court must be of the opinion, having regard to all the circumstances including the nature of the offence and the character and antecedents of the offender, and to the other available methods of dealing with him or her, that a hospital order is the most suitable method of disposing of the case
- the court has to be satisfied on the written or oral evidence of the person who will be in charge of the treatment (or of some other person representing the hospital managers) that admission to a specified hospital within 28 days has been arranged; and
- fines, imprisonment and CROs are specifically precluded on the making of a hospital order although other sentences and ancillary orders are possible (but are rarely appropriate).

GUARDIANSHIP ORDER

A guardianship order places the offender under the guardianship of a local authority social services department or of an individual who is approved by the local authority for this purpose. The purpose of such an order is to enable the mentally disordered offender to receive community care where such care could not otherwise be provided without the use of compulsory powers.

It should be noted, however, that treatment cannot be given under the order (in contrast to the position under civil powers or a hospital order) without the offender's consent and the order itself does not empower the offender's detention. He or she can, however, be required:

- to live at a specified place
- to attend specified places at specified times for medical treatment to be considered
- to attend at specified places at specified times for occupation, education or training; and
- to allow access by a doctor, approved social worker or other specified persons.

The pre-conditions for guardianship orders closely mirror those for hospital orders.

Guardianship orders initially last for six months but can be renewed and are particularly useful where the mentally disordered offender would benefit from occupation, training and education in the community.

RESTRICTION ORDERS

As already noted, a hospital order does not in itself prevent the offender discharging himself or herself, and magistrates' courts cannot add a condition restricting this. However, the Crown Court does have such a power and magistrates can commit the offender to the Crown Court for this purpose. In simple terms, the Crown Court's powers to make an order restricting discharge arises where a hospital order in itself appears appropriate *and* there is a risk of further offending coupled with a need to protect the public from serious harm from the mentally disordered offender.

The restriction on discharge will be for an indefinite or specified period.

Any committal to the Crown Court must be in custody and any powers to remand to a hospital or to make an interim hospital order (see below) do not apply.

REMANDS TO HOSPITAL/INTERIM ORDERS

As well as being able to remand on bail (with specific set conditions) and to remand in custody for the preparation of any necessary medical reports, magistrates can, in certain circumstances, also remand to a specified hospital for the preparation of full medical reports. In brief, they must be satisfied, on the written or oral report of one registered medical practitioner, that there is reason to suspect that the defendant, charged with or convicted of an offence punishable with imprisonment on summary conviction, is suffering from mental illness, psychopathic disorder, severe mental impairment or mental impairment.

The power to remand an unconvicted defendant arises only where such a defendant consents to such a remand.

In all circumstances the magistrates must be satisfied that it would be impracticable for a report on the offender's mental condition to be prepared on bail and that the specified hospital will receive the offender.

Other important procedural provisions apply and detailed legal advice should always be sought if such a remand is to be considered 📖✋.

Furthermore, where magistrates have convicted an offender and, having received all the necessary reports and considered all the necessary statutory provisions, feel that a hospital order is an immediate possibility they may, subject to certain further conditions, make an interim hospital order to check whether a full hospital order or some other disposal is most appropriate. Again, in such circumstances, detailed legal advice is essential 📖✋.

HOSPITAL ORDERS WITHOUT A CONVICTION

In certain circumstances, magistrates' courts can make a hospital order without convicting the defendant. This power arises where the defendant admits or is proved to have committed the act or omission charged (known as the *actus reus* element of the offence) but any mental element such as intent (the *mens rea*) is not necessarily made out. This power can also, in certain circumstances, be exercised where an either-way offence might otherwise have to be heard before the Crown Court. The criteria and procedures for making a hospital order without convicting the defendant are otherwise essentially as for making such an order following conviction, but this special power is not something which arises frequently and will always require a court to take detailed legal advice 📖✋.

HUMAN RIGHTS ISSUES

All the human rights issues which affect criminal proceedings and sentencing (*Chapter 2*) apply to mentally disordered offenders with special force and significance due to their vulnerability and possible lack of communicative powers. Under the European Convention the following aspects become relevant with regard to mentally disordered offenders, particularly in view of Article 5 ('right to liberty and security'):

- ordering compulsory admission to hospital under a hospital order
- ordering treatment without or against the individual's consent
- whether the procedures for the monitoring and review of hospital orders by the authorities to check the continuing need for detention based on the existence and severity of the disorder meet those requirements which provide for a right to challenge detention before a court (Article 5(4)); and
- the lack of a right to bail where a defendant is committed to the Crown Court with a view to a hospital order with an order restricting discharge, especially given that the basis of the committal will be founded on a need for treatment rather than punishment.

It will be especially important to ensure that there is a clear and significant link between any suggested mental disorder and the particular offending.

CHAPTER 12

Judicial Advice

Sentencing has become increasingly complex due in no small measure to an increasing amount of relevant legislation. This has created a range of new offences and introduced fresh rules, procedures and sentencing considerations. Whilst sentencing now takes place within the broad framework outlined in *Chapter 4*, there are often further legal considerations. Courts are also required to give valid reasons or explanations for a range of sentence-related decisions. This aspect has been given an added impetus by virtue of the Human Rights Act 1998 (*Chapter 2*).

LAW PRACTICE AND PROCEDURE

The law in relation to sentencing is found not only in Acts of Parliament and Statutory Instruments (SIs), but also in rulings of the Court of Appeal (Criminal Division) and the High Court. These courts interpret sentencing legislation and occasionally give general guidance.

The Court of Appeal has emphasised that its decisions in relation to appeals against sentence serve as examples of how a particular offender ought to have been dealt with in relation to a given offence. What are known as 'guideline judgments'—i.e. rulings which deal with sentencing issues in a more general way—are clearly of greater import than an isolated appeal ruling. Many rulings of the higher courts are contained in law reports,[1] whilst any significant developments are noted in the regular legal journals.

In addition, non-binding guidance on a range of matters is issued by ministers of the Crown acting within their particular fields of responsibility. Thus, the Home Secretary is responsible for criminal policy, including the development of legislation affecting the sentences available to courts. Home Office circulars an information bulletrins—issued to courts and others—often outline the official stance.

Established practice in an area or locality is also something which affects the way in which sentence decisions are arrived at.

It is the responsibility of legal advisers to magistrates to be conversant with all such matters—and particularly with current developments. They are all professionals who receive special training in this regard. Their specialities include criminal law, evidence, procedure, sentencing and the principles of judicial decision-making.

---

[1] These are validated/recognised accounts which can be cited in court for or against a given proposition. Magistrates may occasionally encounter a 'transcript', especially where the proceedings of the higher court have gone 'unreported'. Lawyers/advisers are trained to identify the higher court's 'reasons for deciding' (or *ratio decidendi:* often shortened to *ratio*) past appeals and to apply that reasoning to the facts of other, later, cases; also to recognise what is *binding* and what is merely *persuasive*.

THE JUSTICES' CLERK

The justices' clerk—as legal and judicial adviser to the bench—is under a duty to ensure that magistrates receive all appropriate advice including advice on sentencing.[2] In 2000, the duties of justices' clerks and court legal advisers were the subject of a *Practice Direction (Justices: Clerk to Court)* issued by Lord Woolf, Lord Chief Justice. Under this direction the justices' clerk is responsible for:

a. the legal advice tendered to the justices within the area;
b. the performance of any of the [relevant] functions . . . of his or her staff acting as legal advisers;
c. ensuring that competent advice is available to justices when . . . not personally present in court;
d. the effective delivery of case management and the reduction of unnecessary delay.

Paragraph (3) of the direction states that it is the responsibility of an adviser to provide magistrates with any advice they require properly to perform their functions whether or not they have requested it, on:

(i)   questions of law (including European Court of Human Rights jurisprudence) ;
(ii)   questions of mixed law and fact;
(iii)   matters of practice and procedure;
(iv)   the range of penalties available;
(v)   any relevant decisions of the superior courts or other guidelines;
(vi)   other issues relevant to the matter before the court;
(vii) the appropriate decision-making structure to be applied in any given case.

Paragraph (4) emphasises that he or she must not play any part in making findings of fact but may assist the bench by reminding them of the evidence etc. and paragraph (5) that he or she may ask questions of a witness and the parties in order to clarify 'any issue in the case'. Above all, perhaps, paragraph (6) provides that '. . . a legal adviser has a duty to ensure that every case is conducted fairly'.

The principle of open court and advice in the retiring room
Paragraph 8 of the direction states that:

At any time, justices are entitled to receive advice to assist them in discharging their responsibilities . . . This should ordinarily be done in open court. Where the justices request their adviser to join them in the retiring room, this request should be made in the presence of the parties in court. Any legal advice given to the justices other than in open court should be clearly stated to be provisional and the adviser should subsequently repeat the substance of the advice in open court and give the parties an opportunity to make any representations they wish on that provisional advice. The legal adviser should then state in open court whether the provisional advice is confirmed or if it is varied the nature of the variation.

---

2 For a more rounded description of the role of the justices' clerk and his or her relationship to the bench, justices' chief executive, magistrates' courts committee and his or her own staff, see *Introduction to the Magistrates' Court*, Bryan Gibson, Waterside Press, 2001.

The justices' clerk or legal adviser must thus advise *on request*, but he or she can also act of his or her *own initiative*—and, in effect, must do so if the magistrates are about to go wrong in law. He or she may be invited into the magistrates' private retiring room but should never go there automatically and normally not unless specifically asked to do so. This invitation should only occur where there is a genuine need for legal advice or support and for this to be given in private. This said, there is a duty to interrupt magistrates' deliberations—whether taking place in public or in private—if not to do so would be likely to result in some legal or judicial error being made.

The modern approach as sanctioned by the *Practice Direction* mentioned above—and in keeping with human rights considerations—is for advice to be given or repeated in open court where it can be heard by all concerned. The parties can then comment on the advice if they so wish. This is an aspect of ensuring a fair trial and safeguarding the principle of open court. There are, of course, limitations: magistrates may wish to express personal doubts or reservations, or work their way towards a decision by discussion and an exchange of thoughts (ideally following decision-making structures of the kind referred to earlier in this handbook)—when common sense indicates that such exchanges should occur in the retiring room. The central point is that nothing should happen which leaves a party ignorant of some relevant consideration or which inappropriately denies him or her an opportunity to influence the court's decision by way of representations.[3]

Enforcement proceedings

The *Practice Direction* also covers the situation where the legal adviser is dealing with enforcement proceedings (see, generally, *Chapter 4*) which following the Access to Justice Act 1999 are ultimately for the justices' chief executive to bring before the court. The legal adviser must not seek to 'prosecute' (as often tended to happen in the past when such matters were the responsibility of the justices' clerk) whilst the direction acknowledges, but does not seek to comment on the practice in some areas whereby another member of staff is allocated to the task of prosecuting enforcement cases, other than to say this does not breach human rights law.[4]

PERSONAL LIABILITY

Justices were warned by Lord Taylor, the late Lord Chief Justice, that if they failed to take appropriate advice on a settled legal point they could be held personally liable for the costs of any appeal. The case in question concerned an everyday matter, i.e. whether 'special reasons' for not endorsing a driving licence existed (*Chapter 8*) and salient advice—which was wrongly rejected—had been given both orally and in writing. This emphasises the constant need to be alert to the possibility that judicial advice may be essential even in 'run-of-the-mill' cases.

---

[3] Justices are entitled to receive advice and assistance in the retiring room when drafting their reasons. This does not need to be repeated in open court. However, it is important to note that this advice is being given at a time when the decision (e.g. the verdict) has already been made.

[4] A justices' clerk (or some other staff member) can be authorised to act in that capacity by the justices' chief executive delegating the function. Quite obviously, no-one can properly act in the dual capacity of prosecutor and impartial adviser.

Appendix A: National Mode of Trial Guidelines

FOREWORD

The National Mode of Trial Guidelines were first produced in 1990. They have proved extremely useful and helpful to magistrates having to decide whether or not to commit 'either way' offences to the Crown Court for trial. Now, they have been revised and brought up to date by the Secretariat of the Criminal Justice Consultative Council. The Secretariat and all those who have assisted them, from the Home Office, the Lord Chancellor's Department, the Law Officers' Department, the Crown Prosecution Service, the Magistrates' Association and the Justices' Clerks' Society are to be congratulated and thanked for their work.

It must be recognised that in this field as in others, guidelines are offered by way of assistance not as directions. That said, those who have the difficult decisions to make on Mode of Trial will find these revised guidelines most helpful. I commend them wholeheartedly.

Taylor CJ Lord Chief Justice of England

NATIONAL MODE OF TRIAL GUIDELINES 1995[1]

The purpose of these guidelines is to help magistrates decide whether or not to commit 'either way' offences for trial in the Crown Court. Their object is to provide guidance not direction. They are not intended to impinge upon a magistrate's duty to consider each case individually and on its own particular facts.

These guidelines apply to all defendants aged 18 and above.

General Mode of Trial Considerations
Section 19 of the Magistrates' Court Act 1980 requires magistrates to have regard to the following matters in deciding whether an offence is more suitable for summary trial or trial on indictment:

1. the nature of the case
2. whether the circumstances make the offence one of a serious character
3. whether the punishment which a magistrates' court would have power to inflict for it would be adequate
4. any other circumstances which appear to the court to make it more suitable for the offence to be tried in one way rather than the other
5. any representations made by the prosecution or the defence.

Certain general observations can be made:

a. the court should never make its decision on the grounds of convenience or expedition
b. the court should assume for the purpose of deciding mode of trial that the prosecution version of the facts is correct

c. the fact that the offences are alleged to be specimens is a relevant consideration; the fact that the defendant will be asking for other offences to be taken into consideration, if convicted, is not
d. where cases involve complex questions of fact or difficult questions of law, including difficult issues of disclosure of sensitive material, the court should consider committal for trial
e. where two or more defendants are jointly charged with an offence each has an individual right to elect his mode of trial. [This follows the decision in *R v Brentwood Justices ex parte Nicholls*.]
f. *In general, except where otherwise stated, either way offences should be tried summarily unless the court considers that the particular case has one or more of the features set out in the following pages and that its sentencing powers are insufficient.*
g. The court should also consider its power to commit an offender for sentence, under Section 38 of the Magistrates' Courts Act 1980, as amended by Section 25 of the Criminal Justice Act 1991, if information emerges during the course of the hearing which leads them to conclude that the offence is so serious, or the offender such a risk to the public, that their powers to sentence him are inadequate. This amendment means that committal for sentence is no longer determined by reference to the character or antecedents of the defendant.

FEATURES RELEVANT TO INDIVIDUAL OFFENCES

Note: Where reference is made in these guidelines to property or damage of 'high value' it means a figure equal to at least twice the amount of the limit (currently £5,000) imposed by statute on a magistrates' court when making a compensation order.

Burglary

> Cases should be tried summarily unless the court considers that one or more of the following features is present in the case and that its sentencing powers are insufficient.
>
> Magistrates should take account of their powers under S25 of the Criminal Justice Act 1991 to commit for sentence.
>
> *Note: See paragraph (g) above.*

1. Dwelling House

1. Entry in the daytime when the occupier (or another) is present
2. Entry at night of a house which is normally occupied, whether or not the occupier (or another) is present
3. The offence is alleged to be one of a series of similar offences
4. When soiling, ransacking, damage or vandalism occurs
5. The offence has professional hallmarks
6. The unrecovered property is of high value (see above for definition of high value)

Note: Attention is drawn to para 28(c) of Schedule 1 of the Magistrates' Courts Act 1980, by which offences of burglary in a dwelling cannot be tried summarily if any person in the dwelling was subjected to violence or the threat of violence.

---

[1] The National Mode of Trial Guidelines have not been updated since. It is important that they are applied in the light of the developments described in this handbook, especially in relation to custodial sentences, mode of trial and plea before venue: see principally Chapters 3 and 4.

Burglary

Cases should be tried summarily unless the court considers that one or more of the following features is present in the case and that its sentencing powers are insufficient.

Magistrates should take account of their powers under S25 of the Criminal Justice Act 1991 to commit for sentence.

Note: See paragraph (g) on page 2 of these guidelines.

2. Non-Dwellings
1. Entry of a pharmacy or doctor's surgery
2. Fear is caused or violence is done to anyone lawfully on the premises (e.g. night-watchman; security guard)
3. The offence has professional hallmarks
4. Vandalism on a substantial scale
5. The unrecovered property is of high value (see page 2 above for definition of high value)

Theft and Fraud

Cases should be tried summarily unless the court considers that one or more of the following features is present in the case and that its sentencing powers are insufficient.

Magistrates should take account of their powers under S25 of the Criminal Justice Act 1991 to commit for sentence.

Note: See paragraph (g) on page 2 of these guidelines.

1. Breach of trust by a person in a position of substantial authority, or in whom a high degree of trust is placed
2. Theft or fraud which has been committed or disguised in a sophisticated manner
3. Theft or fraud committed by an organized gang
4. The victim is particularly vulnerable to theft or fraud e.g. the elderly or infirm
5. The unrecovered property is of high value (see page 2 of these guidelines for definition of high value)

Handling

Cases should be tried summarily unless the court considers that one or more of the following features is present in the case and that its sentencing powers are insufficient.

Magistrates should take account of their powers under S25 of the Criminal Justice Act 1991 to commit for sentence.

Note: See paragraph (g) on page 2 of these guidelines.

1. Dishonest handling of stolen property by a receiver who has commissioned the theft
2. The offence has professional hallmarks
3. The property is of high value (see page 2 of these guidelines for definition of high value)

Social Security Frauds

Cases should be tried summarily unless the court considers that one or more of the following features is present in the case and that its sentencing powers are insufficient.

Magistrates should take account of their powers under S25 of the Criminal Justice Act 1991 to commit for sentence.

Note: See paragraph (g) on page 2 of these guidelines.

1. Organized fraud on a large scale
2. The frauds are substantial and carried out over a long period of time

Violence (Sections 20 and 47 of the Offences Against the Person Act 1861)

Cases should be tried summarily unless the court considers that one or more of the following features is present in the case and that its sentencing powers are insufficient.

Magistrates should take account of their powers under S25 of the Criminal Justice Act 1991 to commit for sentence.

Note: See paragraph (g) on page 2 of these guidelines.

1. The use of a weapon of a kind likely to cause serious injury
2. A weapon is used and serious injury is caused
3. More than minor injury is caused by kicking, head butting or similar forms of assault
4. Serious violence is caused to those whose work has to be done in contact with the public or who are likely to face violence in the course of their work
5. Violence to vulnerable people eg the elderly and infirm
6. The offence has clear racial motivation

Note: The same considerations apply to cases of **domestic violence**.

Public Order Act Offences

Cases should be tried summarily unless the court considers that one or more of the following features is present in the case and that its sentencing powers are insufficient.

Magistrates should take account of their powers under S25 of the Criminal Justice Act 1991 to commit for sentence.

Note: See paragraph (g) on page 2 of these guidelines.

1. Cases of **Violent Disorder** should generally be committed for trial

2. Affray
1. Organized violence or use of weapons
2. Significant injury or substantial damage
3. The offence has clear racial motivation
4. An attack upon police officers, prison officers, ambulance men, firemen and the like

Violence to and Neglect of Children

Cases should be tried summarily unless the court considers that one or more of the following features is present in the case and that its sentencing powers are insufficient.

Magistrates should take account of their powers under S25 of the Criminal Justice Act 1991 to commit for **sentence**.

Note: See paragraph (g) on page 2 of these guidelines.

1. Substantial injury
2. Repeated violence or serious neglect, even if the physical harm is slight
3. Sadistic violence e.g. deliberate burning or scalding

Indecent Assault

Cases should be tried summarily unless the court considers that one or more of the following features is present in the case and that its sentencing powers are insufficient.

Magistrates should take account of their powers under S25 of the Criminal Justice Act 1991 to commit for **sentence**.

Note: See paragraph (g) on page 2 of these guidelines.

1. Substantial disparity in age between victim and defendant, and the assault is more than trivial
2. Violence or threats of violence
3. Relationship of trust or responsibility between defendant and victim
4. Several similar offences, and the assaults are more than trivial
5. The victim is particularly vulnerable
6. Serious nature of the assault

Unlawful Sexual Intercourse

Cases should be tried summarily unless the court considers that one or more of the following features is present in the case and that its sentencing powers are insufficient.

Magistrates should take account of their powers under S25 of the Criminal Justice Act 1991 to commit for **sentence**.

Note: See paragraph (g) on page 2 of these guidelines.

1. Wide disparity of age
2. Breach of position of trust
3. The victim is particularly vulnerable

Drugs

1. **Class A**

   a. Supply; possession with intent to supply
   These cases should be committed for trial

   b. Possession
   Should be committed for trial unless the amount is consistent only with personal use

2. **Class B**

   a. Supply; possession with intent to supply
   Should be committed for trial unless there is only small scale supply for no payment

   b. Possession
   Should be committed for trial when the quantity is substantial and not consistent only with personal use

Dangerous Driving

Cases should be tried summarily unless the court considers that one or more of the following features is present in the case and that its sentencing powers are insufficient.

Magistrates should take account of their powers under S25 of the Criminal Justice Act 1991 to commit for **sentence**.

Note: See paragraph (g) on page 2 of these guidelines.

1. Alcohol or drugs contributing to dangerousness
2. Grossly excessive speed
3. Racing
4. Prolonged course of dangerous driving
5. Degree of injury or damage sustained
6. Other related offences

Criminal Damage

Cases should be tried summarily unless the court considers that one or more of the following features is present in the case and that its sentencing powers are insufficient.

Magistrates should take account of their powers under S25 of the Criminal Justice Act 1991 to commit for **sentence**.

Note: See paragraph (g) page 2 of these guidelines.

1. Deliberate fire-raising
2. Committed by group
3. Damage of a high value
4. The offence has clear racial motivation

Note: Offences set out in Schedule 2 of the Magistrates' Courts Act 1980 (which includes offences of criminal damage which do not amount to arson) must be tried summarily if the value of the property damaged or destroyed is £5,000 or less.

Appendix B: Considerations Affecting Decisions Whether or Not to Commit to the Crown Court for Sentence (Revised 2003)

INTRODUCTION

The plea before venue procedure introduced by section 49 Criminal Procedure and Investigations Act 1996 (see Chapter 3) requires a magistrates' court, when a defendant aged 18 or over *intimates* a guilty plea in relation to an *either way offence*, either:

• to proceed to sentence using its own powers; or
• to commit to the Crown Court for sentence.

The Basic Consideration

The basic question is whether:

• on the basis of the information available to the magistrates' court
• the maximum sentencing powers available to magistrates of six months per offence (or possibly 12 months in aggregate where there are two or more either way offences) are sufficient in relation to the offence (or offences) in respect of which a guilty plea (or pleas) has (or have) been intimated.

This in turn requires the court to consider the seriousness of the offence or, if the offence is a violent or sexual offence and custody a prospect, the need to protect the public from serious harm from the offender: see *The Sentence of the Court, Chapter 4.* Following an intimation of a guilty plea to an either way offence, magistrates thus need to consider:

• those indications of gravity contained in the *National Mode of Trial Guidelines* as reproduced in *Appendix A* of this handbook
• the *Magistrates' Court Sentencing Guidelines* as reproduced in *Appendix C*
• whatever specific advice may be given by court legal advisers about guidance from the higher courts
• the extent of any credit which ought to be allowed for an early guilty plea: *The Sentence of the Court, Chapter 1.* Note in this context that, in recent times, some discounts allowed in the Crown Court have, exceptionally, been up to one half ▢❦.

General Guidance

The guidance set out in the following pages is based upon Court of Appeal rulings and should be borne in mind in relation to the particular offences as listed. Everything said is now subject, in particular, to developments in the cases of *R v. Kefford* (2002) and *R v. McInerney* (2002) and any broader implications which flow from those rulings: see, *The Sentence of the Court, Chapter 4* ▢❦.

• See the case of *R v. McInerney* mentioned in *Chapter 4* and the chart concerning burglary reproduced in that chapter.

• It appears from *R v. McInerney* that among other things:
—the guideline starting point for certain domestic burglaries is now a community penalty
—this may be displaced in certain circumstances by factors such as:
  • the possible lack of efficacy of a community sentence in the particular circumstances
  • the existence of previous convictions, especially for domestic burglary.

Seek legal advice ▢❦.

Burglary: Dwelling

• Domestic burglary has always been regarded as a very serious offence. Sneak thefts (sometimes called 'walk-in' thefts) are the only burglaries of dwellings which, historically speaking, may not merit consideration whether to commit to the Crown Court for sentence.

Burglary: Non-Dwelling

• The *National Mode of Trial Guidelines* are highly relevant in deciding whether to send a defendant to the Crown Court for sentence.

• Any burglary of commercial premises where £1,000[1] or more is taken would normally indicate the need for the offender to be sentenced in the Crown Court.

• 'Ram-raiding' also indicates Crown Court.

• Where there is more than one charge (i.e. two or more non-dwelling burglaries) and it is clear that the offences have been committed whilst on bail, this would be another indication that the matter should be sent to the Crown Court for sentence.

• The court should always look at elements of planning and preparation, even if only a small amount has been taken.

• In respect of all types of burglary, the defendant's record is very relevant. Any suggestion that the defendant is a 'professional' indicates that the appropriate venue for sentence is the Crown Court.

Theft

• Systematic picking of pockets will normally indicate the Crown Court for sentence. This includes a defendant with one or two present offences who has a long record of such offences, including, e.g. thefts of purses or handbags.

• Thieves who steal from shops should go to the Crown Court where there is evidence of careful planning and the incident involves removal of goods of significant value.

• Thieves of livestock should be sent to the Crown Court for sentence. However, unlicensed fishers can be dealt with by magistrates when sentencing levels are well within magistrates' powers.

• Thieves who steal from phone boxes can normally be sentenced by magistrates unless there are indications of considerable difficulties caused by the prevalence of the offences.

• Thieves who steal lorries and cars for commercial gain should normally be sentenced at the Crown Court.

---

[1] All figures quoted in the text were first promulgated in 1998. Allowance should presumably be made for inflation over the five years since that time: ▢❦.

Drugs

a) Cannabis

(i) Supply/possession with intent to supply

- The Court of Appeal has cast doubts on the usefulness of street value as a guide. If the defendant is a wholesaler and is dealing with 400 grammes or more then the matter should normally go to the Crown Court for sentence. At a lower level, where retailing is on a smaller scale, the matter should be sent to the Crown Court for sentence where the defendant is offering to supply in a general way rather than to a small group of friends. Where the evidence shows commercial supply (e.g. bags, wraps, scales, cash) this is generally an indication that the matter should go to the Crown Court for sentence. Sales to schoolchildren are another indication that the matter is serious and should go to the Crown Court.

(ii) Possession

- Normally magistrates' powers of sentencing are sufficient.

(iii) Cultivation

- If it is clear that cultivation is solely for personal use then magistrates' powers of sentencing are sufficient. However, if there is a substantial amount of drugs involved, committal to the Crown Court for sentence is justified.

- If cultivation is for commercial use then this should normally point towards the Crown Court for sentence.

b) Heroin

(i) Supply/possession with intent to supply

- Cases of this nature should normally go to the Crown Court for sentence. There have been many fatal overdoses and the Court of Appeal has said that the prevalence of an offence is capable of aggravating its seriousness.

(ii) Simple possession

- Where the drug is for the defendant's own use and there is a plea of guilty, magistrates' sentencing powers may be sufficient.

c) LSD

(i) Supply/possession with intent to supply

- This should normally be sent to the Crown Court for sentence unless it is clear that a minimal amount was involved in the supply/intended supply, i.e. fewer than ten doses.

(ii) Possession

- The same comments as under *Heroin* above.

d) Ecstasy (MDMA)

(i) Supply/possession with intent to supply

- Unless the circumstances are exceptional, defendants should normally be sent to the Crown Court for sentence.

(ii) Possession

- If the drug is for the defendant's own use and there is a plea of guilty, the magistrates' sentencing powers may be sufficient.

e) Amphetamine

The same comments as under *Ecstasy* above.

Theft in breach of trust: *R v Barrick* (1985) (7 Cr. App. R. (S)) (as expanded on in *R v Clark, The Times,* 4 December 1997) is the guideline case concerning general considerations and parameters. The court should consider: (i) the amount involved; (ii) the period covered by the offence or offences; (iii) whether money taken was spent on necessities or luxuries; (iv) the effect on the victim; (v) the impact on public confidence; (vi) the effect on work colleagues; (vii) the effect on the offender; (viii) the offender's own history; (ix) any help given to police.

Monetary threshold: Case law (and the *National Mode of Trial Guidelines*) indicate that magistrates' sentencing powers are not necessarily bound by a comparison with the upper compensation limit of £5,000 per offence and they may, if appropriate, sentence for offences where the value involved is up to £10,000. Where the victim is very vulnerable, e.g. an old person, some lesser amount may justify a committal to the Crown Court for sentence.

Handling Stolen Goods

- If the goods involved are the proceeds of major crime, this will indicate that the matter should be sent to the Crown Court for sentence.

- Isolated handling by someone of good character can still be an indication that the matter should go to the Crown Court for sentence where the goods are over £10,000 in value.

- If the defendant is a 'regular' handler of proceeds of burglary, this indicates the Crown Court should sentence, especially if the court concludes it is dealing with a 'professional' handler.

Abstracting Electricity

- Sentence will normally be within magistrates' powers. Accordingly these offences are unlikely to be sent to the Crown Court for sentence unless committed over a very long period and there is high value, e.g. £10,000 plus, or evidence suggests commercial methods/organization.

Making Off Without Paying

- Magistrates' sentencing powers would normally be sufficient.

'Going Equipped' for Theft, Burglary or Cheat

- Usually this offence can be sentenced summarily. However, if the items involved are obviously for a dwelling-house burglary (or some other serious offence such as large scale theft, or mortgage fraud) which would justify committal to the Crown Court for sentence in its own right, then committal for sentence may be appropriate.

Criminal Damage

a) Arson

Magistrates should be reluctant to sentence in any case involving arson of a building. Damage must be minimal. Arson of other items may be sentenced by magistrates but they need to be satisfied that the fire could not have spread more widely.

b) Other forms of damage

- Where the damage exceeds £10,000 and is clearly intentional (rather than reckless), then magistrates ought to consider sending the case to the Crown Court for sentence.

- Where the decision to commit for sentence may be finely balanced, any allegation of racist behaviour will be a pointer towards the matter being sent to the Crown Court for sentence. Similarly where there is a religious aspect: see *Chapter 3*.

Indecent Assault

- If the victim is a young girl the case ought to go to the Crown Court.
- Similarly, if the indecency is serious, e.g. touching the child with defendant's penis.
- Any suggestion of attempted penetration or use of force also indicates that the matter should be sent to the Crown Court for sentence; and digital interference with the vagina also indicates Crown Court for sentence.
- If there is any suggestion that the defendant is not of full adult capacity, the offence may be appropriate for sentence by magistrates.
- Where the victim is an adolescent girl who 'consents', consideration should still be given to sending the matter to the Crown Court for sentence where there are features such as digital interference or oral sex.
- Impulsive touching unaccompanied by threats may justify sentencing in the magistrates' court.

Unlawful Sexual Intercourse

The following factors may point to a committal for sentence:

- Wide disparity of age as between offender and victim.
- Breach of a position of trust.
- The victim being particularly vulnerable (e.g. young, old, infirm, mentally disadvantaged).

'Malicious Wounding': Grievous Bodily Harm (section 20)

- Offences under section 18 Offences Against the Person Act 1861 (wounding with *intent*) are *not* triable by magistrates. As a general rule, the closer a section 20 ('malicious wounding') offence is to a section 18 offence, then the stronger the case for committing the defendant to the Crown Court for sentence.
- Kicking to the head, especially if repeated, should lead to the conclusion that the matter be sent to the Crown Court for sentence. The same can be said of the use of a glass ('glassing'), where two year sentences of imprisonment are a regular feature of Court of Appeal decisions. It makes little difference whether the glass is held or thrown if it leads in either case to injury to the face.
- The use of a weapon likely to cause serious injury should again lead to the conclusion that the matter be sent to the Crown Court for sentence. Case law also suggests that head-butting, and the use of feet or teeth is considered as akin to the use of a weapon.

Violent Disorder

- The *National Mode of Trial Guidelines* recommend that magistrates should decline jurisdiction. Only in rare cases should intimation of a guilty plea lead magistrates to *sentence* for this offence. It would need to be low level disorder, bordering on affray, and a mild affray at that.
- The larger the group of people involved in the disorder, the more likely it is that committal for sentence should follow.

Possessing an Offensive Weapon

- Where the weapon is offensive *per se* (e.g. a flick knife) then a sentence in the region of three to six months imprisonment is within Court of Appeal guidelines and accordingly magistrates may wish to proceed to sentence.

Committal to the Crown Court for a Confiscation Order

Section 70 Proceeds of Crime Act 2002 (in force from 24 March 2003) provides—as part of an extensive package of measures aimed at confiscating proceeds of criminal activity in the widest sense—a process in relation to the proceeds of crime and offences before magistrates. On conviction, the prosecutor may ask the magistrates' court to commit the defendant to the Crown Court (on bail or in custody) so that the Crown Court may make a criminal confiscation order (a power which magistrates do not themselves possess). Once such a request is made, the magistrates *must* commit for sentence under these provisions.

It is most important that the magistrates indicate the basis of the committal, i.e. whether or not they would otherwise commit for sentence—i.e. for a greater sentence—or whether they are only committing the case to the Crown Court because they themselves lack the power to make a confiscation order. Without a clear statement that the committal is for the former purpose, the Crown Court will be restricted (other than with respect to making a confiscation order) to magistrates' maximum powers.

The overall provisions are novel, lengthy and complex: 𝟙𝟙⁰.

MAGISTRATES' COURT SENTENCING GUIDELINES

Implementation date: 1 September 2000

These Magistrates Courts Sentencing Guidelines have been produced by a Working Party which met throughout 1999 and the early part of 2000. The members of the Working Party are:

Andrew Ashworth, Vinerian Professor of English Law: University of Oxford

Maureen Bateman, Chairman of the Sentencing Committee: Magistrates' Association (from January 2000)

Michael Calvert, Chairman of the Sentencing Committee: Magistrates' Association (to December 1999)

Anne Fuller OBE JP, Chairman: Magistrates' Association (to November 1999)

Penelope Hewitt, Chairman: Society of Stipendiary Magistrates for England and Wales

Gaynor Houghton-Jones, Junior Vice President: Justices' Clerks' Society; Justices' Clerk: Bow Street and Horseferry Road

John James JP, Deputy Chairman: Magistrates Association (from November 1999)

Rachel Lipscomb JP, Deputy Chairman: Magistrates' Association (from November 1999)

Harry Mawdsley JP, Chairman: Magistrates' Association (from November 1999)

Graham Parkinson, Chief Metropolitan Stipendiary Magistrate

Roy Taylor JP, Deputy Chairman: Magistrates Association (to November 1999)

George Tranter, Council Member: Justices' Clerks' Society; Justices Clerk for Wrexham

Arthur Winnington, Chairman of the Road Traffic Committee: Magistrates' Association

Brian Worcester-Davis OBE JP, Deputy Chairman: Magistrates' Association (to November 1999).

These Guidelines have the support of the Lord Chancellor and the former Lord Chief Justice.

They are of course only guidelines – they do not curtail your independent discretion to impose the sentences you think are right, case by case. But they exist to help you in that process. To give you a starting point. To give you more information in reaching your decisions. And, importantly, they help to assist the magistracy to maintain an overall consistency of approach.

I think it most important that, within discretionary limits, magistrates' courts up and down the country should endeavour to approach sentencing with a measure of consistency, and I have no doubt that these Guidelines will contribute powerfully to that end.

The Rt Hon Lord Bingham of Cornhill

Alphabetical list of contents

IMPORTANT: THIS USER GUIDE IS AN INTEGRAL PART OF THE GUIDELINES — PLEASE READ IT

Introduction

These Sentencing Guidelines cover offences with which magistrates deal regularly and frequently in the adult criminal courts. They provide a sentencing structure which sets out how to:

• establish the seriousness of each case
• determine the most appropriate way of dealing with it

The Sentencing Guidelines provide a method for considering individual cases and a Guideline from which discussion should properly flow; but they are **not a tariff and should never be used as such.**

Using the sentencing structure

The sentencing structure used for these Guidelines was established by the Criminal Justice Act 1991. This reaffirms the principle of 'just deserts' so that any penalty must reflect the seriousness of the offence for which it is imposed and the personal circumstances of the offender. Magistrates must always start the sentencing process by taking full account of all the circumstances of the offence and making a judicial assessment of the seriousness category into which it falls.

In every case, the Criminal Justice Act 1991 requires sentencers to consider:

• Is discharge or a fine appropriate?
• Is the offence serious enough for a community penalty?
• Is it so serious that only custody is appropriate?

If the last, in either way cases, justices will also need to consider if magistrates' courts' powers are appropriate.

The format of the Sentencing Guidelines

1. CONSIDER THE SERIOUSNESS OF THE OFFENCE

Magistrates must always make an assessment of seriousness following the structure of the Criminal Justice Act 1991. However, the Sentencing Guidelines do give a starting point guideline for each offence.

Where this guideline is discharge or fine, a suggested starting point guideline fine is also given. Refer to the guidance on pages 69, 70 and 85.

Where the starting point guideline is a community penalty, refer to the guidance on pages 72 and 73.

Where the starting point guideline is custody, think in terms of weeks or months and discount as appropriate for a timely guilty plea. Refer to page 66 for further guidance.

For some either way offences the guideline is 'are **magistrates' sentencing powers appropriate?**'. This indicates that magistrates should be considering whether the seriousness of the offence is such that six months (or twelve months in the case of two or more offences) is insufficient, so that the case must be committed to the Crown Court (consult the clerk with regard to Crown Court sentencing and guideline cases). If the case is retained in the magistrates' court a substantial custodial sentence is likely to be necessary.

It should be noted that if magistrates consider (say) nine months to be the appropriate sentence, to be reduced for a timely guilty plea to six months, then the case falls within their powers and must be retained. Subject to offender mitigation, six months would appear to be the appropriate sentence.

2. CONSIDER AGGRAVATING AND MITIGATING FACTORS

Make sure that all aggravating and mitigating factors are considered. The lists in the Sentencing Guidelines are neither exhaustive nor a substitute for the personal judgment of magistrates. Factors which do not appear in the Guidelines may be important in individual cases.

If the offence was racially aggravated, the court must treat that fact as an aggravating factor under statute (s.82 Crime and Disorder Act 1998).

If the offence was committed while the offender was on bail, the court must treat that as an aggravating factor under statute (s. 29 Criminal Justice Act 1991, as amended).

Consider previous convictions, or any failure to respond to previous sentences, in assessing seriousness. Courts should identify any convictions relevant for this purpose and then consider to what extent they affect the seriousness of the present offence.

3. TAKE A PRELIMINARY VIEW OF SERIOUSNESS, THEN CONSIDER OFFENDER MITIGATION

When an initial assessment of the seriousness of the offence has been formed, consider the offender.

The Guidelines set out some examples of offender mitigation but there are frequently others to be considered in individual cases. Any offender mitigation that the court accepts must lead to some downward revision of the provisional assessment of seriousness, although this revision may be minor.

A previous criminal record may deprive the defendant of being able to say that he is a person of good character.

4. CONSIDER YOUR SENTENCE

The law requires that the court reduces the sentence for a timely guilty plea but this provision should be used with judicial flexibility. A timely guilty plea may attract a sentencing discount of up to one third but the precise amount of discount will depend on the facts of each case and a last minute plea of guilty may attract only a minimal reduction.

Discount may be given in respect of the amount of a fine or periods of community service or custody. Periods of mandatory disqualification or mandatory penalty points cannot be reduced for a guilty plea.

5. DECIDE YOUR SENTENCE

Remember that magistrates have a duty to consider the award of compensation in all appropriate cases, and to give reasons if compensation is not awarded. See page 75 to 77, Section Three.

Agree the form of words that the Chairman will use when announcing sentence. See the Magistrates' Association *Pronouncements in Court* for examples.

Affray

Public Order Act 1986 s.3
Triable either way – see Mode of Trial Guidelines
Penalty: Level 5 and/or 6 months

CONSIDER THE SERIOUSNESS OF THE OFFENCE
(INCLUDING THE IMPACT ON THE VICTIM)

IS IT SERIOUS ENOUGH FOR A COMMUNITY PENALTY?

IS IT SO SERIOUS THAT ONLY CUSTODY IS APPROPRIATE?

GUIDELINE: → *IS IT SO SERIOUS THAT ONLY CUSTODY IS APPROPRIATE?*
ARE MAGISTRATES' SENTENCING POWERS APPROPRIATE?

⊕ CONSIDER AGGRAVATING AND MITIGATING FACTORS ⊖

for example
Busy public place
Group action
Injuries caused
People actually put in fear
Vulnerable victim(s)
This list is not exhaustive

for example
Offender acting alone
Provocation
Did not start the trouble
Stopped as soon as the police arrived
This list is not exhaustive

If racially aggravated, or offender is on bail, this offence is more serious.
If offender has previous convictions, their relevance and any failure to respond to previous
sentences must be considered – they may increase the seriousness

TAKE A PRELIMINARY VIEW OF SERIOUSNESS, THEN CONSIDER
WHETHER THE CASE SHOULD BE COMMITTED FOR SENTENCE,
THEN CONSIDER OFFENDER MITIGATION

CONSIDER COMMITTAL OR YOUR SENTENCE

for example
Age, health (physical or mental)
Co-operation with police
Voluntary compensation
Evidence of genuine remorse

Compare it with the suggested guideline level of sentence and reconsider
your reasons carefully if you have chosen a sentence at a different level.
Consider a discount for a timely guilty plea.

DECIDE YOUR SENTENCE
NB. COMPENSATION – Give reasons if not awarding compensation

Remember: These are GUIDELINES only

Aggravated Vehicle-Taking

Theft Act 1968 s. 12A as inserted by
Aggravated Vehicle-taking Act 1992
Triable either way – but in certain cases
summarily only – consult clerk.
Penalty: Level 5 and/or 6 months
Must endorse and disqualify at least 12 months

CONSIDER THE SERIOUSNESS OF THE OFFENCE
(INCLUDING THE IMPACT ON THE VICTIM)

IS DISCHARGE OR FINE APPROPRIATE?

IS IT SERIOUS ENOUGH FOR A COMMUNITY PENALTY?

GUIDELINE: → *IS IT SO SERIOUS THAT ONLY CUSTODY IS APPROPRIATE?*
ARE MAGISTRATES' SENTENCING POWERS APPROPRIATE?

⊕ CONSIDER AGGRAVATING AND MITIGATING FACTORS ⊖

for example
Competitive driving: racing, showing off
Disregard of warnings eg from passengers
or others in vicinity
Group action
Police chase
Pre-meditated
Serious injury/damage
Serious risk
Trying to avoid detection or arrest
Vehicle destroyed
This list is not exhaustive

for example
No competitiveness/racing
Passenger only
Single incident of bad driving
Speed not excessive
Very minor injury/damage
This list is not exhaustive

If racially aggravated, or offender is on bail, this offence is more serious.
If offender has previous convictions, their relevance and any failure to respond to previous
sentences must be considered – they may increase the seriousness

TAKE A PRELIMINARY VIEW OF SERIOUSNESS, THEN
CONSIDER OFFENDER MITIGATION

CONSIDER YOUR SENTENCE

for example
Health (physical or mental)
Co-operation with police
Voluntary compensation
Evidence of genuine remorse

Compare it with the suggested guideline level of sentence and reconsider
your reasons carefully if you have chosen a sentence at a different level.
Consider a discount for a timely guilty plea.

DECIDE YOUR SENTENCE
NB. COMPENSATION – Give reasons if not awarding compensation

Remember: These are GUIDELINES only

Animal Cruelty

Protection of Animals Act 1911, s.1
Triable only summarily
Penalty: Level 5 and/or 6 months with powers to deprive ownership of the relevant animal and disqualify from keeping all or any animals

CONSIDER THE SERIOUSNESS OF THE OFFENCE

IS DISCHARGE OR FINE APPROPRIATE?

GUIDELINE: → *IS IT SERIOUS ENOUGH FOR A COMMUNITY PENALTY?*

IS IT SO SERIOUS THAT ONLY CUSTODY IS APPROPRIATE?

✚ CONSIDER AGGRAVATING AND MITIGATING FACTORS ❶

for example
Adult involving children
Animal(s) kept for livelihood
Committed over a period or involving several animals
Deriving pleasure from torturing or frightening
Disregarded warnings of others
Group action
Offender in position of special responsibility towards the animal
Premeditated/Deliberate
Prolonged neglect
Serious injury or death
Use of weapon
This list is not exhaustive

for example
Ignorance of appropriate care
Impulsive
Minor injury
Offender induced by others
Single incident
This list is not exhaustive

If offender is on bail, this offence is more serious
If offender has previous convictions, their relevance and any failure to respond to previous sentences must be considered – they may increase the seriousness

TAKE A PRELIMINARY VIEW OF SERIOUSNESS, THEN CONSIDER OFFENDER MITIGATION

for example
Age, health (physical or mental)
Co-operation with police
Evidence of genuine remorse

CONSIDER YOUR SENTENCE

Compare it with the suggested guideline level of sentence and reconsider your reasons carefully if you have chosen a sentence at a different level.
Consider a discount for a timely guilty plea.
Always consider disqualifying the offender from having custody of animals, or depriving him or her of owning the animal concerned.

DECIDE YOUR SENTENCE

Remember: These are GUIDELINES only

Assault – Actual Bodily Harm

Offences Against the Person Act 1861 s.47
Triable either way – see Mode of Trial Guidelines
Penalty: Level 5 and/or 6 months

CONSIDER THE SERIOUSNESS OF THE OFFENCE
(INCLUDING THE IMPACT ON THE VICTIM)

IS DISCHARGE OR FINE APPROPRIATE?

IS IT SERIOUS ENOUGH FOR A COMMUNITY PENALTY?

IS IT SO SERIOUS THAT ONLY CUSTODY IS APPROPRIATE?

GUIDELINE: → *ARE MAGISTRATES' SENTENCING POWERS APPROPRIATE?*

✚ CONSIDER AGGRAVATING AND MITIGATING FACTORS ❶

for example
Deliberate kicking or biting
Extensive injuries (may be psychiatric)
Headbutting
Group action
Offender in position of authority
On hospital/medical premises
Premeditated
Victim particularly vulnerable
Victim serving the public
Weapon
This list is not exhaustive

for example
Minor injury
Provocation
Single blow
This list is not exhaustive

If offender is on bail, this offence is more serious
If offender has previous convictions, their relevance and any failure to respond to previous sentences must be considered – they may increase the seriousness

TAKE A PRELIMINARY VIEW OF SERIOUSNESS, THEN CONSIDER WHETHER THE CASE SHOULD BE COMMITTED FOR SENTENCE, THEN CONSIDER OFFENDER MITIGATION

for example
Age, health (physical or mental)
Co-operation with police
Voluntary compensation
Evidence of genuine remorse

CONSIDER COMMITTAL OR YOUR SENTENCE

Compare it with the suggested guideline level of sentence and reconsider your reasons carefully if you have chosen a sentence at a different level.
Consider a discount for a timely guilty plea.

DECIDE YOUR SENTENCE

NB. COMPENSATION – Give reasons if not awarding compensation

Remember: These are GUIDELINES only

Assault on a Police Officer

Police Act 1996 s.89
Triable only summarily
Penalty: Level 5 and/or 6 months

CONSIDER THE SERIOUSNESS OF THE OFFENCE
(INCLUDING THE IMPACT ON THE VICTIM)

IS IT SERIOUS ENOUGH FOR A COMMUNITY PENALTY?

GUIDELINE: → *IS IT SO SERIOUS THAT ONLY CUSTODY IS APPROPRIATE?*

IS DISCHARGE OR FINE APPROPRIATE?

➕ CONSIDER AGGRAVATING AND MITIGATING FACTORS ➊

for example	for example
Any injuries caused	Impulsive action
Gross disregard for police authority	Unaware that person was a police officer
Group action	*This list is not exhaustive*
Premeditated	
This list is not exhaustive	

If racially aggravated, or offender is on bail, this offence is more serious
If offender has previous convictions, their relevance and any failure to respond to previous sentences must be considered – they may increase the seriousness

TAKE A PRELIMINARY VIEW OF SERIOUSNESS, THEN CONSIDER OFFENDER MITIGATION

for example
Age, health (physical or mental)
Co-operation with police
Voluntary compensation
Evidence of genuine remorse

CONSIDER YOUR SENTENCE

Compare it with the suggested guideline level of sentence and reconsider your reasons carefully if you have chosen a sentence at a different level.
Consider a discount for a timely guilty plea.

DECIDE YOUR SENTENCE

NB. COMPENSATION – Give reasons if not awarding compensation

Remember: These are GUIDELINES only

Breach of a community order

Criminal Justice Act 1991 sch. 2
A fine – maximum £1,000
A Community Service Order (up to 60 hours)
A Curfew Order
In certain circumstances, an Attendance Centre Order
Revocation of Order and re-sentence for original offence
Commit a Crown Court Order to be dealt with at Crown Court

CONSIDER THE SERIOUSNESS OF THE OFFENCE

➕ CONSIDER AGGRAVATING AND MITIGATING FACTORS ➊

for example	for example
No attempt to start the sentence	Completed a significant part of the order
Unco-operative	*This list is not exhaustive*
This list is not exhaustive	

CONSIDER OFFENDER MITIGATION
(including timely admission)

DECIDE IF THE ORDER SHOULD CONTINUE

IF THE ORDER SHOULD CONTINUE

Is a fine appropriate? (Starting Point B)

Is a community service order appropriate?

Where the order is a probation order, is an attendance centre order appropriate?

Is a curfew order appropriate?

IF THE ORDER SHOULD NOT CONTINUE AND IT IS A MAGISTRATES' COURT ORDER:

Revoke and re-sentence for original sentence (see relevant guideline)

NB. IF THE ORDER WAS MADE BY THE CROWN COURT, MAY FINE AND ALLOW ORDER TO CONTINUE, OR COMMIT TO CROWN COURT TO BE DEALT WITH (CONSULT CLERK)

For further guidance, refer to the summary National Standards guide, and to the booklet, *Community Penalties and the Court – Towards Good Practice.*

Remember: These are GUIDELINES only

Burglary (Dwelling)

Theft Act 1968 s.9
Triable either way – see Mode of Trial Guidelines
Penalty: Level 5 and/or 6 months

CONSIDER THE SERIOUSNESS OF THE OFFENCE
(INCLUDING THE IMPACT ON THE VICTIM)

IS IT DISCHARGE OR FINE APPROPRIATE?
IS IT SERIOUS ENOUGH FOR A COMMUNITY PENALTY?
IS IT SO SERIOUS THAT ONLY CUSTODY IS APPROPRIATE?
GUIDELINE: → ARE MAGISTRATES' SENTENCING POWERS APPROPRIATE?

➕ CONSIDER AGGRAVATING AND MITIGATING FACTORS ➊

for example

At night
Forcible entry
Group offence
People in house
Occupants frightened
Professional operation
Repeat victimisation
Soiling, ransacking, damage
This list is not exhaustive

for example
Low value
Nobody frightened
No damage or disturbance
No forcible entry
Opportunist
This list is not exhaustive

If racially aggravated, or offender is on bail, this offence is more serious
If offender has previous convictions, their relevance and any failure to respond to previous sentences must be considered – they may increase the seriousness

TAKE A PRELIMINARY VIEW OF SERIOUSNESS, THEN CONSIDER WHETHER THE CASE SHOULD BE COMMITTED FOR SENTENCE, THEN CONSIDER OFFENDER MITIGATION

for example
Age, health (physical or mental)
Co-operation with police
Voluntary compensation
Evidence of genuine remorse

CONSIDER COMMITTAL OR YOUR SENTENCE

Compare it with the suggested guideline level of sentence and reconsider your reasons carefully if you have chosen a sentence at a different level.
Consider a discount for a timely guilty plea.

DECIDE YOUR SENTENCE
NB. COMPENSATION – Give reasons if not awarding compensation

Remember: These are GUIDELINES only

Burglary (Non-dwelling)

Theft Act 1968 s.9
Triable either way – see Mode of Trial Guidelines
Penalty: Level 5 and/or 6 months

CONSIDER THE SERIOUSNESS OF THE OFFENCE
(INCLUDING THE IMPACT ON THE VICTIM)

IS IT DISCHARGE OR FINE APPROPRIATE?
GUIDELINE: → IS IT SERIOUS ENOUGH FOR A COMMUNITY PENALTY?
IS IT SO SERIOUS THAT ONLY CUSTODY IS APPROPRIATE?
ARE MAGISTRATES' SENTENCING POWERS APPROPRIATE?

➕ CONSIDER AGGRAVATING AND MITIGATING FACTORS ➊

for example
Forcible entry
Group offence
Harm to business
Night time
Occupants frightened
Professional operation
Repeat victimisation
School premises
Soiling, ransacking, damage
This list is not exhaustive

for example
Low value
Nobody frightened
No damage or disturbance
No forcible entry
This list is not exhaustive

If racially aggravated, or offender is on bail, this offence is more serious
If offender has previous convictions, their relevance and any failure to respond to previous sentences must be considered – they may increase the seriousness

TAKE A PRELIMINARY VIEW OF SERIOUSNESS, THEN CONSIDER OFFENDER MITIGATION

for example
Age, health (physical or mental)
Co-operation with police
Voluntary compensation
Evidence of genuine remorse

CONSIDER YOUR SENTENCE

Compare it with the suggested guideline level of sentence and reconsider your reasons carefully if you have chosen a sentence at a different level.
Consider a discount for a timely guilty plea.

DECIDE YOUR SENTENCE
NB. COMPENSATION – Give reasons if not awarding compensation

Remember: These are GUIDELINES only

Class A Drugs – Possession

Misuse of Drugs Act 1971
Triable either way – see Mode of Trial Guidelines
Penalty: Level 5 and/or 6 months

CONSIDER THE SERIOUSNESS OF THE OFFENCE

IS IT SERIOUS ENOUGH FOR A COMMUNITY PENALTY?
IS IT SO SERIOUS THAT ONLY CUSTODY IS APPROPRIATE?
ARE MAGISTRATES' SENTENCING POWERS APPROPRIATE?

GUIDELINE: → *IS DISCHARGE OR FINE APPROPRIATE?*

⊕ CONSIDER AGGRAVATING AND MITIGATING FACTORS ⓘ

for example	**for example**
An amount other than a very small quantity	Very small quantity
This list is not exhaustive	*This list is not exhaustive*

If offender has previous convictions, their relevance and any failure to respond to previous sentences must be considered – they may increase the seriousness

If offender is on bail, this offence is more serious

TAKE A PRELIMINARY VIEW OF SERIOUSNESS, THEN CONSIDER OFFENDER MITIGATION

for example
Age, health (physical or mental)
Co-operation with police
Evidence of genuine remorse

CONSIDER YOUR SENTENCE

Compare it with the suggested guideline level of sentence and reconsider your reasons carefully if you have chosen a sentence at a different level. Consider a discount for a timely guilty plea. Consider forfeiture and destruction.

DECIDE YOUR SENTENCE

Remember: These are GUIDELINES only

Class A Drugs – Production, Supply

Misuse of Drugs Act 1971
Triable either way – see Mode of Trial Guidelines
Penalty: Level 5 and/or 6 months

CONSIDER THE SERIOUSNESS OF THE OFFENCE
(INCLUDING THE IMPACT ON THE VICTIM)

IS IT SERIOUS ENOUGH FOR A COMMUNITY PENALTY?
IS IT SO SERIOUS THAT ONLY CUSTODY IS APPROPRIATE?
ARE MAGISTRATES' SENTENCING POWERS APPROPRIATE?

GUIDELINE: → *IS DISCHARGE OR FINE APPROPRIATE?*

⊕ CONSIDER AGGRAVATING AND MITIGATING FACTORS ⓘ

for example	**for example**
Commercial production	Small amount
Large amount	*This list is not exhaustive*
Deliberate adulteration	
Venue, eg, prisons, educational establishments	
Sophisticated operation	
Supply to children	
This list is not exhaustive	

If offender has previous convictions, their relevance and any failure to respond to previous sentences must be considered – they may increase the seriousness

If offender is on bail, this offence is more serious

TAKE A PRELIMINARY VIEW OF SERIOUSNESS, THEN CONSIDER WHETHER THE CASE SHOULD BE COMMITTED FOR SENTENCE, THEN CONSIDER OFFENDER MITIGATION

for example
Age, health (physical or mental)
Co-operation with police
Evidence of genuine remorse

CONSIDER COMMITTAL OR YOUR SENTENCE

Compare it with the suggested guideline level of sentence and reconsider your reasons carefully if you have chosen a sentence at a different level. Consider a discount for a timely guilty plea. Consider forfeiture and destruction.

DECIDE YOUR SENTENCE

Remember: These are GUIDELINES only

Class B Drugs – Supply:
Possession with intent to supply

Misuse of Drugs Act 1971
Triable either way – see Mode of Trial Guidelines
Penalty: Level 5 and/or 3 months

CONSIDER THE SERIOUSNESS OF THE OFFENCE
(INCLUDING THE IMPACT ON THE VICTIM)

GUIDELINE: →
IS DISCHARGE OR FINE APPROPRIATE?
IS IT SERIOUS ENOUGH FOR A COMMUNITY PENALTY?
IS IT SO SERIOUS THAT ONLY CUSTODY IS APPROPRIATE?
ARE MAGISTRATES' SENTENCING POWERS APPROPRIATE?

➕ CONSIDER AGGRAVATING AND MITIGATING FACTORS ➊

for example
Commercial production
Large amount
Venue, eg. prisons, educational
establishments
Deliberate adulteration
This list is not exhaustive

for example
No commercial motive
Small amount
This list is not exhaustive

If offender is on bail, this offence is more serious
If offender has previous convictions, their relevance and any failure to respond to previous sentences must be considered – they may increase the seriousness

TAKE A PRELIMINARY VIEW OF SERIOUSNESS, THEN CONSIDER WHETHER THE CASE SHOULD BE COMMITTED FOR SENTENCE, THEN CONSIDER OFFENDER MITIGATION

for example
Age, health (physical or mental)
Co-operation with police
Evidence of genuine remorse

CONSIDER COMMITTAL OR YOUR SENTENCE

Compare it with the suggested guideline level of sentence and reconsider your reasons carefully if you have chosen a sentence at a different level. Consider a discount for a timely guilty plea. Consider forfeiture and destruction.

DECIDE YOUR SENTENCE

Remember: These are GUIDELINES only

© The Magistrates' Association   12   *Issue September 2000*

Class B Drugs – Possession

Misuse of Drugs Acts 1971
Triable either way – see Mode of Trial Guidelines
Penalty: Level 4 and/or 3 months

CONSIDER THE SERIOUSNESS OF THE OFFENCE

GUIDELINE: →
IS DISCHARGE OR FINE APPROPRIATE?
IS IT SERIOUS ENOUGH FOR A COMMUNITY PENALTY?
IS IT SO SERIOUS THAT ONLY CUSTODY IS APPROPRIATE?
ARE MAGISTRATES' SENTENCING POWERS APPROPRIATE?

GUIDELINE FINE — STARTING POINT B

➕ CONSIDER AGGRAVATING AND MITIGATING FACTORS ➊

for example
Large amount
This list is not exhaustive

for example
Small amount
This list is not exhaustive

If offender is on bail, this offence is more serious
If offender has previous convictions, their relevance and any failure to respond to previous sentences must be considered – they may increase the seriousness

TAKE A PRELIMINARY VIEW OF SERIOUSNESS, THEN CONSIDER OFFENDER MITIGATION

for example
Age, health (physical or mental)
Co-operation with police
Evidence of genuine remorse

CONSIDER YOUR SENTENCE

Compare it with the suggested guideline level of sentence and reconsider your reasons carefully if you have chosen a sentence at a different level. Consider a discount for a timely guilty plea. Consider forfeiture and destruction.

DECIDE YOUR SENTENCE

Remember: These are GUIDELINES only

© The Magistrates' Association   11   *Issue September 2000*

Common Assault

Criminal Justice Act 1988 s.39
Triable only summarily
Penalty: Level 5 and/or 6 months

CONSIDER THE SERIOUSNESS OF THE OFFENCE
(INCLUDING THE IMPACT ON THE VICTIM)

IS IT DISCHARGE OR FINE APPROPRIATE?

GUIDELINE: → *IS IT SO SERIOUS ENOUGH FOR A COMMUNITY PENALTY?*
IS IT SO SERIOUS THAT ONLY CUSTODY IS APPROPRIATE?

 CONSIDER AGGRAVATING AND MITIGATING FACTORS

for example
Group action
Injury
Offender in position of authority
On hospital/medical premises
Premeditated
Victim particularly vulnerable
Victim serving the public
Weapon
This list is not exhaustive

for example
Impulsive
Minor injury
Provocation
Single blow
This list is not exhaustive

If offender is on bail, this offence is more serious
If offender has previous convictions, their relevance and any failure to respond to previous sentences must be considered – they may increase the seriousness

TAKE A PRELIMINARY VIEW OF SERIOUSNESS, THEN CONSIDER OFFENDER MITIGATION

for example
Age, health (physical or mental)
Co-operation with police
Voluntary compensation
Evidence of genuine remorse

CONSIDER YOUR SENTENCE

Compare it with the suggested guideline level of sentence and reconsider
your reasons carefully if you have chosen a sentence at a different level.
Consider a discount for a timely guilty plea.

DECIDE YOUR SENTENCE
NB. COMPENSATION – Give reasons if not awarding compensation

Remember: These are GUIDELINES only

Criminal Damage

Criminal Damage Act 1971 s.1
Triable either way or summarily only. Consult Clerk
Penalty: Either way – Level 5 and/or 6 months
Summarily – Level 4 and/or 3 months

CONSIDER THE SERIOUSNESS OF THE OFFENCE
(INCLUDING THE IMPACT ON THE VICTIM)

IS IT DISCHARGE OR FINE APPROPRIATE?

GUIDELINE: → *IS IT SERIOUS ENOUGH FOR A COMMUNITY PENALTY?*
IS IT SO SERIOUS THAT ONLY CUSTODY IS APPROPRIATE?
ARE MAGISTRATES' SENTENCING POWERS APPROPRIATE?

GUIDELINE FINE — STARTING POINT C

 CONSIDER AGGRAVATING AND MITIGATING FACTORS

for example
Deliberate
Group offence
Serious damage
This list is not exhaustive

for example
Impulsive action
Minor damage
Provocation
This list is not exhaustive

If offender is on bail, this offence is more serious
If offender has previous convictions, their relevance and any failure to respond to previous sentences must be considered – they may increase the seriousness

TAKE A PRELIMINARY VIEW OF SERIOUSNESS, THEN CONSIDER OFFENDER MITIGATION

for example
Age, health (physical or mental)
Co-operation with police
Voluntary compensation
Evidence of genuine remorse

CONSIDER YOUR SENTENCE

Compare it with the suggested guideline level of sentence and reconsider
your reasons carefully if you have chosen a sentence at a different level.
Consider a discount for a timely guilty plea.

DECIDE YOUR SENTENCE
NB. COMPENSATION – Give reasons if not awarding compensation

Remember: These are GUIDELINES only

Drunk and Disorderly

Criminal Justice Act 1967 s.91
Triable only summarily
Penalty: Level 3

CONSIDER THE SERIOUSNESS OF THE OFFENCE

GUIDELINE: → IS DISCHARGE OR FINE APPROPRIATE?

IS IT SERIOUS ENOUGH FOR A COMMUNITY PENALTY?

(PROBATION AND CURFEW ORDERS ARE THE ONLY AVAILABLE COMMUNITY PENALTIES FOR THIS OFFENCE)

GUIDELINE FINE — STARTING POINT A

➕ CONSIDER AGGRAVATING AND MITIGATING FACTORS ➖

for example
Offensive language or behaviour
On hospital/medical premises
With group
This list is not exhaustive

for example
Induced by others
No significant disturbance
Not threatening
This list is not exhaustive

If racially aggravated, or offender is on bail, this offence is more serious
If offender has previous convictions, their relevance and any failure to respond to previous sentences must be considered – they may increase the seriousness

TAKE A PRELIMINARY VIEW OF SERIOUSNESS, THEN
CONSIDER OFFENDER MITIGATION

for example
Health (physical or mental)
Co-operation with police
Evidence of genuine remorse

CONSIDER YOUR SENTENCE

Compare it with the suggested guideline level of sentence and reconsider your reasons carefully if you have chosen a sentence at a different level.
Consider a discount for a timely guilty plea.

DECIDE YOUR SENTENCE

Remember: These are GUIDELINES only

Cultivation of Cannabis

Misuse of Drugs Act 1971
Triable either way – see Mode of Trial Guidelines
Penalty: Level 5 and/or 6 months

CONSIDER THE SERIOUSNESS OF THE OFFENCE
(INCLUDING THE IMPACT ON THE VICTIM)

GUIDELINE: → IS DISCHARGE OR FINE APPROPRIATE?

IS IT SERIOUS ENOUGH FOR A COMMUNITY PENALTY?
IS IT SO SERIOUS THAT ONLY CUSTODY IS APPROPRIATE?
ARE MAGISTRATES' SENTENCING POWERS APPROPRIATE?

GUIDELINE FINE — STARTING POINT B

➕ CONSIDER AGGRAVATING AND MITIGATING FACTORS ➖

for example
Commercial cultivation
Large quantity
This list is not exhaustive

for example
For personal use
Not commercial
Not responsible for planting
Small scale cultivation
This list is not exhaustive

If offender is on bail, this offence is more serious
If offender has previous convictions, their relevance and any failure to respond to previous sentences must be considered – they may increase the seriousness

TAKE A PRELIMINARY VIEW OF SERIOUSNESS, THEN
CONSIDER OFFENDER MITIGATION

for example
Age, health (physical or mental)
Co-operation with police
Evidence of genuine remorse

CONSIDER YOUR SENTENCE

Compare it with the suggested guideline level of sentence and reconsider your reasons carefully if you have chosen a sentence at a different level. Consider forfeiture and destruction.
Consider a discount for a timely guilty plea.

DECIDE YOUR SENTENCE

Remember: These are GUIDELINES only

Evasion of Duty

Customs and Excise Management Act 1979 s.170
Triable either way – see Mode of Trial Guidelines
Penalty: 6 months and/or £5000/ or 3 times the
value of the goods (whichever is the greater)

CONSIDER THE SERIOUSNESS OF THE OFFENCE

IS IT SERIOUS ENOUGH FOR A COMMUNITY PENALTY?

IS IT SO SERIOUS THAT ONLY CUSTODY IS APPROPRIATE?

GUIDELINE: → *ARE MAGISTRATES' SENTENCING POWERS APPROPRIATE?*

CONSIDER AGGRAVATING AND MITIGATING FACTORS

for example
Organiser
More than one journey
Commercial operation
Sophisticated operation
Imports two or more dutiable goods
This list is not exhaustive

for example
Supply to restricted group
Small quantity of goods
This list is not exhaustive

If offender is on bail, this offence is more serious

*If offender has previous convictions, their relevance and any failure to respond to previous
sentences must be considered – they may increase the seriousness*

TAKE A PRELIMINARY VIEW OF SERIOUSNESS, THEN CONSIDER WHETHER THE CASE SHOULD BE COMMITTED FOR SENTENCE, THEN CONSIDER OFFENDER MITIGATION

for example
Age, health (physical or mental)
Co-operation with police
Voluntary payment of duty
Evidence of genuine remorse

CONSIDER COMMITTAL OR YOUR SENTENCE

*Compare it with the suggested guideline level of sentence and reconsider
your reasons carefully if you have chosen a sentence at a different level.
Consider a discount for a timely guilty plea.*

DECIDE YOUR SENTENCE

Remember: These are GUIDELINES only

Failure to surrender to bail

Bail Act 1976 s.6
Triable only summarily
Penalty: Level 5 and/or 3 months

CONSIDER THE SERIOUSNESS OF THE OFFENCE

GUIDELINE: → *IS DISCHARGE OR FINE APPROPRIATE?*

IS IT SERIOUS ENOUGH FOR A COMMUNITY PENALTY?

IS IT SO SERIOUS THAT ONLY CUSTODY IS APPROPRIATE?

GUIDELINE FINE — STARTING POINT B

CONSIDER AGGRAVATING AND MITIGATING FACTORS

for example
Leaves jurisdiction
Wilful evasion
Appears after arrest
This list is not exhaustive

for example
Appears late on day of hearing
Genuine misunderstanding
Voluntary surrender
This list is not exhaustive

Previous convictions for this offence increase the seriousness

TAKE A PRELIMINARY VIEW OF SERIOUSNESS, THEN CONSIDER OFFENDER MITIGATION

for example
Age, health (physical or mental)
Co-operation with police
Evidence of genuine remorse

CONSIDER YOUR SENTENCE

*Compare it with the suggested guideline level of sentence and reconsider
your reasons carefully if you have chosen a sentence at a different level.
Consider a discount for a timely guilty plea.*

DECIDE YOUR SENTENCE

Remember: These are GUIDELINES only

Going Equipped for Theft etc.

Theft Act s.25
Triable either way – see Mode of Trial Guidelines
Penalty: Level 5 and/or 6 months
May disqualify where committed with reference
to the theft or taking of the vehicle

CONSIDER THE SERIOUSNESS OF THE OFFENCE

IS DISCHARGE OR FINE APPROPRIATE?

GUIDELINE: → **IS IT SERIOUS ENOUGH FOR A COMMUNITY PENALTY?**
IS IT SO SERIOUS THAT ONLY CUSTODY IS APPROPRIATE?
ARE MAGISTRATES' SENTENCING POWERS APPROPRIATE?

CONSIDER AGGRAVATING AND MITIGATING FACTORS

for example
Premeditated
Group action
Sophisticated
Specialised equipment
Number of items
People put in fear
This list is not exhaustive

for example

If offender is on bail, this offence is more serious
If offender has previous convictions, their relevance and any failure to respond to previous
sentences must be considered – they may increase the seriousness

TAKE A PRELIMINARY VIEW OF SERIOUSNESS, THEN
CONSIDER OFFENDER MITIGATION

for example
Age, health (physical or mental)
Co-operation with police
Evidence of genuine remorse

CONSIDER YOUR SENTENCE

Compare it with the suggested guideline level of sentence and reconsider
your reasons carefully if you have chosen a sentence at a different level.
Consider a discount for a timely guilty plea.

DECIDE YOUR SENTENCE

Remember: These are GUIDELINES only

Handling Stolen Goods

Theft Act 1968 s.22
Triable either way – see Mode of Trial Guidelines
Penalty: Level 5 and/or 6 months

CONSIDER THE SERIOUSNESS OF THE OFFENCE
(INCLUDING THE IMPACT ON THE VICTIM)

IS DISCHARGE OR FINE APPROPRIATE?

GUIDELINE: → **IS IT SERIOUS ENOUGH FOR A COMMUNITY PENALTY?**
IS IT SO SERIOUS THAT ONLY CUSTODY IS APPROPRIATE?
ARE MAGISTRATES' SENTENCING POWERS APPROPRIATE?

CONSIDER AGGRAVATING AND MITIGATING FACTORS

for example
Adult involving children
High value
Organiser or distributor
This list is not exhaustive

for example
For personal use
Impulsive action
Low value
No financial gain
Not part of a sophisticated operation
Single item
This list is not exhaustive

If offender is on bail, this offence is more serious
If offender has previous convictions, their relevance and any failure to respond to previous
sentences must be considered – they may increase the seriousness

TAKE A PRELIMINARY VIEW OF SERIOUSNESS, THEN
CONSIDER OFFENDER MITIGATION

for example
Age, health (physical or mental)
Co-operation with police
Voluntary compensation
Evidence of genuine remorse

CONSIDER YOUR SENTENCE

Compare it with the suggested guideline level of sentence and reconsider
your reasons carefully if you have chosen a sentence at a different level.
Consider a discount for a timely guilty plea.

DECIDE YOUR SENTENCE

NB. COMPENSATION – Give reasons if not awarding compensation

Remember: These are GUIDELINES only

Harassment, Alarm or Distress

Public Order Act 1986 s.5
Triable only summarily
Penalty: Level 3

CONSIDER THE SERIOUSNESS OF THE OFFENCE
(INCLUDING THE IMPACT ON THE VICTIM)

GUIDELINE: →

IS DISCHARGE OR FINE APPROPRIATE?

IS IT SERIOUS ENOUGH FOR A COMMUNITY PENALTY?

(PROBATION AND CURFEW ORDERS ARE THE ONLY AVAILABLE COMMUNITY PENALTIES FOR THIS OFFENCE)

GUIDELINE FINE — STARTING POINT B

 CONSIDER AGGRAVATING AND MITIGATING FACTORS

for example	**for example**
Group action	Stopped as soon as police arrived
Vulnerable victim	Trivial incident
This list is not exhaustive	*This list is not exhaustive*

If offender is on bail, this offence is more serious

If offender has previous convictions, their relevance and any failure to respond to previous sentences must be considered – they may increase the seriousness

TAKE A PRELIMINARY VIEW OF SERIOUSNESS, THEN CONSIDER OFFENDER MITIGATION

for example
Age, health (physical or mental)
Co-operation with police
Voluntary compensation
Evidence of genuine remorse

CONSIDER YOUR SENTENCE

Compare it with the suggested guideline level of sentence and reconsider your reasons carefully if you have chosen a sentence at a different level.
Consider a discount for a timely guilty plea.

DECIDE YOUR SENTENCE
NB. COMPENSATION – *Give reasons if not awarding compensation*

Remember: These are GUIDELINES only

© The Magistrates' Association

21

Issue September 2000

Harassment, Alarm or Distress with Intent

Public Order Act 1986 s.4A
Triable only summarily
Penalty: Level 5 and/or 6 months

CONSIDER THE SERIOUSNESS OF THE OFFENCE
(INCLUDING THE IMPACT ON THE VICTIM)

IS DISCHARGE OR FINE APPROPRIATE?

IS IT SERIOUS ENOUGH FOR A COMMUNITY PENALTY?

GUIDELINE: → *IS IT SO SERIOUS THAT ONLY CUSTODY IS APPROPRIATE?*

 CONSIDER AGGRAVATING AND MITIGATING FACTORS

for example	**for example**
Football hooliganism	Short duration
Group action	*This list is not exhaustive*
High degree of planning	
Night time offence	
Victims specifically targeted	
Weapon	
This list is not exhaustive	

If offender is on bail, this offence is more serious

If offender has previous convictions, their relevance and any failure to respond to previous sentences must be considered – they may increase the seriousness

TAKE A PRELIMINARY VIEW OF SERIOUSNESS, THEN CONSIDER OFFENDER MITIGATION

for example
Age, health (physical or mental)
Co-operation with police
Voluntary compensation
Evidence of genuine remorse

CONSIDER YOUR SENTENCE

Compare it with the suggested guideline level of sentence and reconsider your reasons carefully if you have chosen a sentence at a different level.
Consider a discount for a timely guilty plea.

DECIDE YOUR SENTENCE
NB. COMPENSATION – *Give reasons if not awarding compensation*

Remember: These are GUIDELINES only

© The Magistrates' Association

22

Issue September 2000

Harassment
Conduct causing harassment

Protection from Harassment Act 1997. s.2
Triable only summarily
Penalty: Level 5 and/or 6 months

CONSIDER THE SERIOUSNESS OF THE OFFENCE
(INCLUDING THE IMPACT ON THE VICTIM)

IS DISCHARGE OR FINE APPROPRIATE?

IS IT SERIOUS ENOUGH FOR A COMMUNITY PENALTY?

GUIDELINE: → *IS IT SO SERIOUS THAT ONLY CUSTODY IS APPROPRIATE?*

❶

➕ CONSIDER AGGRAVATING AND MITIGATING FACTORS

for example
Disregard of warning
Excessive persistence
Interference with employment/business
Invasion of victim's home
Involvement of others
Use of violence or grossly offensive material
Where photographs or images of a personal nature are involved
This list is not exhaustive

for example
Initial provocation
Short duration
This list is not exhaustive

If offender is on bail, this offence is more serious
If offender has previous convictions, their relevance and any failure to respond to previous sentences must be considered – they may increase the seriousness

TAKE A PRELIMINARY VIEW OF SERIOUSNESS, THEN
CONSIDER OFFENDER MITIGATION

for example
Age, health (physical or mental)
Co-operation with police
Evidence of genuine remorse

CONSIDER YOUR SENTENCE

Compare it with the suggested guideline level of sentence and reconsider your reasons carefully if you have chosen a sentence at a different level.
Consider a discount for a timely guilty plea.
Restraining order – consider making an order in addition to the sentence to protect the victim or any named person from further conduct which would amount to harassment.

DECIDE YOUR SENTENCE
NB. COMPENSATION – Give reasons if not awarding compensation

Remember: These are GUIDELINES only

© *The Magistrates' Association* 24 *Issue September 2000*

Harassment
Conduct causing fear of violence

Protection from Harassment Act 1997. s.4
Triable either way
Penalty: Level 5 and/or 6 months

CONSIDER THE SERIOUSNESS OF THE OFFENCE
(INCLUDING THE IMPACT ON THE VICTIM)

IS DISCHARGE OR FINE APPROPRIATE?

IS IT SERIOUS ENOUGH FOR A COMMUNITY PENALTY?

GUIDELINE: → *IS IT SO SERIOUS THAT ONLY CUSTODY IS APPROPRIATE?*
ARE MAGISTRATES' SENTENCING POWERS APPROPRIATE?

❶

➕ CONSIDER AGGRAVATING AND MITIGATING FACTORS

for example
Disregard of warning
Excessive persistence
Interference with employment/business
Invasion of victim's home
Involvement of others
Threat to use weapon or substance (including realistic imitations)
Use of violence or grossly offensive material
Where photographs or images of a personal nature are involved
This list is not exhaustive

for example
Initial provocation
Short duration
This list is not exhaustive

If offender is on bail, this offence is more serious
If offender has previous convictions, their relevance and any failure to respond to previous sentences must be considered – they may increase the seriousness

TAKE A PRELIMINARY VIEW OF SERIOUSNESS, THEN
CONSIDER OFFENDER MITIGATION

for example
Age, health (physical or mental)
Co-operation with police
Evidence of genuine remorse

CONSIDER YOUR SENTENCE

Compare it with the suggested guideline level of sentence and reconsider your reasons carefully if you have chosen a sentence at a different level.
Consider a discount for a timely guilty plea.
Restraining order – consider making an order in addition to the sentence to protect the victim or any named person from further conduct which would amount to harassment, or which would cause the fear of violence.

DECIDE YOUR SENTENCE
NB. COMPENSATION – Give reasons if not awarding compensation

Remember: These are GUIDELINES only

© *The Magistrates' Association* 23 *Issue September 2000*

Indecent Assault

Sexual Offences Act 1956 ss.14&15
Triable either way – see Mode of Trial Guidelines
Penalty: Level 5 and/or 6 months

CONSIDER THE SERIOUSNESS OF THE OFFENCE
(INCLUDING THE IMPACT ON THE VICTIM)

GUIDELINE: → *IS IS SO SERIOUS THAT ONLY CUSTODY IS APPROPRIATE?*

IS IT SERIOUS ENOUGH FOR A COMMUNITY PENALTY?
IS IT DISCHARGE OR FINE APPROPRIATE?
ARE MAGISTRATES' SENTENCING POWERS APPROPRIATE?

CONSIDER AGGRAVATING AND MITIGATING FACTORS

for example
Age differential
Breach of trust
Injury (may be psychiatric)
Prolonged assault
Very young victim
Victim deliberately targeted
Victim serving public
Vulnerable victim
This list is not exhaustive

for example
Slight contact
This list is not exhaustive

If racially aggravated, or offender is on bail, this offence is more serious

TAKE A PRELIMINARY VIEW OF SERIOUSNESS, THEN CONSIDER WHETHER THE CASE SHOULD BE COMMITTED FOR SENTENCE, THEN CONSIDER OFFENDER MITIGATION

If offender has previous convictions, their relevance and any failure to respond to previous sentences must be considered – they may increase the seriousness

CONSIDER COMMITTAL OR CONSIDER YOUR SENTENCE

for example
Age, health (physical or mental)
Co-operation with police
Voluntary compensation
Evidence of genuine remorse

Compare it with the suggested guideline level of sentence and reconsider your reasons carefully if you have chosen a sentence at a different level.
Consider a discount for a timely guilty plea.

DECIDE YOUR SENTENCE

Remember: These are GUIDELINES only

Making off without Payment

Theft Act 1978 s.3
Triable either way – see Mode of Trial Guidelines
Penalty: Level 5 and/or 6 months

CONSIDER THE SERIOUSNESS OF THE OFFENCE
(INCLUDING THE IMPACT ON THE VICTIM)

GUIDELINE: →

IS IT SERIOUS ENOUGH FOR A COMMUNITY PENALTY?
IS IT DISCHARGE OR FINE APPROPRIATE?
IS IS SO SERIOUS THAT ONLY CUSTODY IS APPROPRIATE?
ARE MAGISTRATES' SENTENCING POWERS APPROPRIATE?

GUIDELINE FINE – STARTING POINT B

CONSIDER AGGRAVATING AND MITIGATING FACTORS

for example
Deliberate plan
High value
Two or more involved
Victim particularly vulnerable
This list is not exhaustive

for example
Impulsive action
Low value
This list is not exhaustive

If racially aggravated, or offender is on bail, this offence is more serious

TAKE A PRELIMINARY VIEW OF SERIOUSNESS, THEN CONSIDER OFFENDER MITIGATION

If offender has previous convictions, their relevance and any failure to respond to previous sentences must be considered – they may increase the seriousness

CONSIDER YOUR SENTENCE

for example
Age, health (physical or mental)
Co-operation with police
Voluntary compensation
Evidence of genuine remorse

Compare it with the suggested guideline level of sentence and reconsider your reasons carefully if you have chosen a sentence at a different level.
Consider a discount for a timely guilty plea.

DECIDE YOUR SENTENCE

NB. COMPENSATION – Give reasons if not awarding compensation

Remember: These are GUIDELINES only

Obstructing a Police Officer

Police Act 1996 s.89(2)
Triable only summarily
Penalty: Level 3 and/or 1 month

CONSIDER THE SERIOUSNESS OF THE OFFENCE
(INCLUDING THE IMPACT ON THE VICTIM)

GUIDELINE: →
IS DISCHARGE OR FINE APPROPRIATE?
IS IT SERIOUS ENOUGH FOR A COMMUNITY PENALTY?
IS IT SO SERIOUS THAT ONLY CUSTODY IS APPROPRIATE?

GUIDELINE FINE — STARTING POINT B

➊ **CONSIDER AGGRAVATING AND MITIGATING FACTORS**

for example
Group action
Premeditated
This list is not exhaustive

for example
Genuine misjudgement
Impulsive action
Minor obstruction
This list is not exhaustive

If racially aggravated, or offender is on bail, this offence is more serious
If offender has previous convictions, their relevance and any failure to respond to previous
sentences must be considered – they may increase the seriousness

TAKE A PRELIMINARY VIEW OF SERIOUSNESS, THEN
CONSIDER OFFENDER MITIGATION

for example
Age, health (physical or mental)
Subsequent co-operation with police
Evidence of genuine remorse

CONSIDER YOUR SENTENCE

Compare it with the suggested guideline level of sentence and reconsider
your reasons carefully if you have chosen a sentence at a different level.
Consider a discount for a timely guilty plea.

DECIDE YOUR SENTENCE

Remember: These are GUIDELINES only

Obtaining by Deception

Theft Act 1968 s.15
Triable either way – see Mode of Trial Guidelines
Penalty: Level 5 and/or 6 months

CONSIDER THE SERIOUSNESS OF THE OFFENCE
(INCLUDING THE IMPACT ON THE VICTIM)

GUIDELINE: →
IS DISCHARGE OR FINE APPROPRIATE?
IS IT SERIOUS ENOUGH FOR A COMMUNITY PENALTY?
IS IT SO SERIOUS THAT ONLY CUSTODY IS APPROPRIATE?
ARE MAGISTRATES' SENTENCING POWERS APPROPRIATE?

➊ **CONSIDER AGGRAVATING AND MITIGATING FACTORS**

for example
Committed over lengthy period
Large sums or valuable goods
Two or more involved
Victim particularly vulnerable
This list is not exhaustive

for example
Impulsive action
Short period
Small sum
This list is not exhaustive

If offender is on bail, this offence is more serious
If offender has previous convictions, their relevance and any failure to respond to previous
sentences must be considered – they may increase the seriousness

TAKE A PRELIMINARY VIEW OF SERIOUSNESS, THEN
CONSIDER OFFENDER MITIGATION

for example
Age, health (physical or mental)
Co-operation with police
Voluntary compensation
Evidence of genuine remorse

CONSIDER YOUR SENTENCE

Compare it with the suggested guideline level of sentence and reconsider
your reasons carefully if you have chosen a sentence at a different level.
Consider a discount for a timely guilty plea.

DECIDE YOUR SENTENCE

NB. COMPENSATION – Give reasons if not awarding compensation

Remember: These are GUIDELINES only

Possession of a Bladed Instrument

Criminal Justice Act 1988 s.139
Triable either way – see Mode of Trial Guidelines
Penalty: Level 5 and/or 6 months

CONSIDER THE SERIOUSNESS OF THE OFFENCE
(INCLUDING THE IMPACT ON THE VICTIM)

IS IT SERIOUS ENOUGH FOR A COMMUNITY PENALTY?
IS DISCHARGE OR FINE APPROPRIATE?

GUIDELINE: → IS IT SO SERIOUS THAT ONLY CUSTODY IS APPROPRIATE?
ARE MAGISTRATES' SENTENCING POWERS APPROPRIATE?

 CONSIDER AGGRAVATING AND MITIGATING FACTORS

for example	for example
Location of offence	Acting out of genuine fear
Group action or joint possession	No attempt to use
People put in fear/weapon brandished	Not premeditated
Planned use	*This list is not exhaustive*
This list is not exhaustive	

If racially aggravated, or offender is on bail, this offence is more serious
If offender has previous convictions, their relevance and any failure to respond to previous sentences must be considered – they may increase the seriousness

TAKE A PRELIMINARY VIEW OF SERIOUSNESS, THEN CONSIDER OFFENDER MITIGATION

for example
Age, health (physical or mental)
Co-operation with police
Voluntary compensation
Evidence of genuine remorse

CONSIDER YOUR SENTENCE

Compare it with the suggested guideline level of sentence and reconsider your reasons carefully if you have chosen a sentence at a different level.
Consider a discount for a timely guilty plea.

DECIDE YOUR SENTENCE

Remember: These are GUIDELINES only

Possessing an Offensive Weapon

Prevention of Crime Act 1953 s.1
Triable either way – see Mode of Trial Guidelines
Penalty: Level 5 and/or 6 months

CONSIDER THE SERIOUSNESS OF THE OFFENCE
(INCLUDING THE IMPACT ON THE VICTIM)

IS IT SERIOUS ENOUGH FOR A COMMUNITY PENALTY?
IS DISCHARGE OR FINE APPROPRIATE?

GUIDELINE: → IS IT SO SERIOUS THAT ONLY CUSTODY IS APPROPRIATE?
ARE MAGISTRATES' SENTENCING POWERS APPROPRIATE?

 CONSIDER AGGRAVATING AND MITIGATING FACTORS

for example	for example
Group action or joint possession	Acting out of genuine fear
Location of offence	No attempt to use
People put in fear/weapon brandished	Not premeditated
Planned use	*This list is not exhaustive*
Very dangerous weapon	
This list is not exhaustive	

If racially aggravated, or offender is on bail, this offence is more serious
If offender has previous convictions, their relevance and any failure to respond to previous sentences must be considered – they may increase the seriousness

TAKE A PRELIMINARY VIEW OF SERIOUSNESS, THEN CONSIDER OFFENDER MITIGATION

for example
Age, health (physical or mental)
Co-operation with police
Voluntary compensation
Evidence of genuine remorse

CONSIDER YOUR SENTENCE

Compare it with the suggested guideline level of sentence and reconsider your reasons carefully if you have chosen a sentence at a different level.
Consider a discount for a timely guilty plea.

DECIDE YOUR SENTENCE

Remember: These are GUIDELINES only

Racially Aggravated Assault – Actual Bodily Harm

Offences Against the Person Act 1861 s.47
Crime and Disorder Act 1998 s.29
Triable either way – see Mode of Trial Guidelines
Penalty: Level 5 and/or 6 months

CONSIDER THE SERIOUSNESS OF THE OFFENCE
(INCLUDING THE LEVEL OF RACIAL AGGRAVATION AND THE IMPACT ON THE VICTIM)

IS IT SERIOUS ENOUGH FOR A DISCHARGE OR FINE APPROPRIATE?

IS IT SERIOUS ENOUGH FOR A COMMUNITY PENALTY?

IS IT SO SERIOUS THAT ONLY CUSTODY IS APPROPRIATE?

GUIDELINE: → *ARE MAGISTRATES' SENTENCING POWERS APPROPRIATE?*

➕ CONSIDER AGGRAVATING AND MITIGATING FACTORS ➖

for example
Deliberate kicking or biting
Extensive injuries (may be psychiatric)
Headbutting
Group action
Offender in position of authority
On hospital/medical premises
Premeditated
Victim particularly vulnerable
Victim serving the public
Weapon
This list is not exhaustive

for example
Minor injury
Provocation
Single blow
This list is not exhaustive

If offender is on bail, this offence is more serious
If offender has previous convictions, their relevance and any failure to respond to previous sentences must be considered – they may increase the seriousness

TAKE A PRELIMINARY VIEW OF SERIOUSNESS, THEN CONSIDER WHETHER THE CASE SHOULD BE COMMITTED FOR SENTENCE, THEN CONSIDER OFFENDER MITIGATION

for example
Age, health (physical or mental)
Co-operation with police
Voluntary compensation
Evidence of genuine remorse

CONSIDER COMMITTAL OR YOUR SENTENCE

Compare it with the suggested guideline level of sentence and reconsider your reasons carefully if you have chosen a sentence at a different level.
Consider a discount for a timely guilty plea.

DECIDE YOUR SENTENCE
NB. COMPENSATION – Give reasons if not awarding compensation

Remember: These are GUIDELINES only

© The Magistrates' Association   31   *Issue September 2000*

Racially Aggravated Common Assault

Criminal Justice Act 1988 s.39
Crime and Disorder Act 1998 s.29
Triable either way – see Mode of Trial Guidelines
Penalty: Level 5 and/or 6 months

CONSIDER THE SERIOUSNESS OF THE OFFENCE
(INCLUDING THE LEVEL OF RACIAL AGGRAVATION AND THE IMPACT ON THE VICTIM)

IS DISCHARGE OR FINE APPROPRIATE?

IS IT SERIOUS ENOUGH FOR A COMMUNITY PENALTY?

IS IT SO SERIOUS THAT ONLY CUSTODY IS APPROPRIATE?

GUIDELINE: → *IS IT SO SERIOUS THAT ONLY CUSTODY IS APPROPRIATE?*
ARE MAGISTRATES' SENTENCING POWERS APPROPRIATE?

➕ CONSIDER AGGRAVATING AND MITIGATING FACTORS ➖

for example
Group action
Injury
Offender in position of authority
On hospital/medical premises
Premeditated
Victim particularly vulnerable
Victim serving the public
Weapon
This list is not exhaustive

for example
Impulsive
Minor injury
Provocation
Single blow
This list is not exhaustive

If offender is on bail, this offence is more serious
If offender has previous convictions, their relevance and any failure to respond to previous sentences must be considered – they may increase the seriousness

TAKE A PRELIMINARY VIEW OF SERIOUSNESS, THEN CONSIDER OFFENDER MITIGATION

for example
Age, health (physical or mental)
Co-operation with police
Voluntary compensation
Evidence of genuine remorse

CONSIDER YOUR SENTENCE

Compare it with the suggested guideline level of sentence and reconsider your reasons carefully if you have chosen a sentence at a different level.
Consider a discount for a timely guilty plea.

DECIDE YOUR SENTENCE
NB. COMPENSATION – Give reasons if not awarding compensation

Remember: These are GUIDELINES only

© The Magistrates' Association   32   *Issue September 2000*

Racially Aggravated Criminal Damage

Criminal Damage Act 1971 s.1
Crime and Disorder Act 1998 s.30
Triable either way – see Mode of Trial Guidelines
Penalty: Level 5 and/or 6 months

CONSIDER THE SERIOUSNESS OF THE OFFENCE
(INCLUDING THE LEVEL OF RACIAL AGGRAVATION AND THE IMPACT ON THE VICTIM)

IS IT SERIOUS ENOUGH FOR A COMMUNITY PENALTY?

GUIDELINE: → *IS IT SO SERIOUS THAT ONLY CUSTODY IS APPROPRIATE?*

IS DISCHARGE OR FINE APPROPRIATE?

ARE MAGISTRATES' SENTENCING POWERS APPROPRIATE?

CONSIDER AGGRAVATING AND MITIGATING FACTORS

for example
Deliberate
Group offence
Serious damage
This list is not exhaustive

for example
Impulsive action
Minor damage
Provocation
This list is not exhaustive

If offender is on bail, this offence is more serious
If offender has previous convictions, their relevance and any failure to respond to previous sentences must be considered – they may increase the seriousness

TAKE A PRELIMINARY VIEW OF SERIOUSNESS, THEN CONSIDER OFFENDER MITIGATION

for example
Age, health (physical or mental)
Co-operation with police
Voluntary compensation
Evidence of genuine remorse

CONSIDER YOUR SENTENCE

Compare it with the suggested guideline level of sentence and reconsider your reasons carefully if you have chosen a sentence at a different level.
Consider a discount for a timely guilty plea.

DECIDE YOUR SENTENCE
NB. COMPENSATION – Give reasons if not awarding compensation

Remember: These are GUIDELINES only

Issue September 2000

Racially Aggravated Harassment, Alarm or Distress

Public Order Act 1986 s.5
Crime and Disorder Act 1998 s.31
Triable only summarily
Penalty: Level 4

CONSIDER THE SERIOUSNESS OF THE OFFENCE
(INCLUDING THE LEVEL OF RACIAL AGGRAVATION AND THE IMPACT ON THE VICTIM)

IS DISCHARGE OR FINE APPROPRIATE?

GUIDELINE: → *IS IT SERIOUS ENOUGH FOR A COMMUNITY PENALTY?*

(PROBATION AND CURFEW ORDERS ARE THE ONLY AVAILABLE COMMUNITY PENALTIES FOR THIS OFFENCE)

CONSIDER AGGRAVATING AND MITIGATING FACTORS

for example
Group action
Vulnerable victim
This list is not exhaustive

for example
Stopped as soon as police arrived
Trivial incident
This list is not exhaustive

If offender is on bail, this offence is more serious
If offender has previous convictions, their relevance and any failure to respond to previous sentences must be considered – they may increase the seriousness

TAKE A PRELIMINARY VIEW OF SERIOUSNESS, THEN CONSIDER OFFENDER MITIGATION

for example
Age, health (physical or mental)
Co-operation with police
Voluntary compensation
Evidence of genuine remorse

CONSIDER YOUR SENTENCE

Compare it with the suggested guideline level of sentence and reconsider your reasons carefully if you have chosen a sentence at a different level.
Consider a discount for a timely guilty plea.

DECIDE YOUR SENTENCE
NB. COMPENSATION – Give reasons if not awarding compensation

Remember: These are GUIDELINES only

Issue September 2000

Racially Aggravated Harassment
Conduct causing fear of violence

Protection from Harassment Act 1997, s.4
Crime and Disorder Act 1998 2.32
Triable either way – see Mode of Trial Guidelines
Penalty: Level 5 and/or 6 months

CONSIDER THE SERIOUSNESS OF THE OFFENCE
(INCLUDING THE LEVEL OF RACIAL AGGRAVATION AND THE IMPACT ON THE VICTIM)

IS IT DISCHARGE OR FINE APPROPRIATE?
IS IT SERIOUS ENOUGH FOR A COMMUNITY PENALTY?
IS IT SO SERIOUS THAT ONLY CUSTODY IS APPROPRIATE?
GUIDELINE: → ARE MAGISTRATES' SENTENCING POWERS APPROPRIATE?

➕ CONSIDER AGGRAVATING AND MITIGATING FACTORS ➖

for example	for example
Disregard of warning	Initial provocation
Excessive persistence	Short duration
Interference with employment/business	*This list is not exhaustive*
Invasion of victim's home	
Involvement of others	
Threat to use weapon or substance (including realistic imitations)	
Use of violence or grossly offensive material	
Where photographs or images of a personal nature are involved	
This list is not exhaustive	

If offender is on bail, this offence is more serious
If offender has previous convictions, their relevance and any failure to respond to previous sentences must be considered – they may increase the seriousness

TAKE A PRELIMINARY VIEW OF SERIOUSNESS, THEN CONSIDER WHETHER THE CASE SHOULD BE COMMITTED FOR SENTENCE, THEN CONSIDER OFFENDER MITIGATION

for example
Age, health (physical or mental)
Co-operation with police
Evidence of genuine remorse

CONSIDER COMMITTAL OR YOUR SENTENCE

Compare it with the suggested guideline level of sentence and reconsider your reasons carefully if you have chosen a sentence at a different level.
Consider a discount for a timely guilty plea.
Restraining order – consider making an order in addition to the sentence to protect the victim or any named person from further conduct which would amount to harassment, or which would cause the fear of violence.

DECIDE YOUR SENTENCE
NB. COMPENSATION – Give reasons if not awarding compensation

Remember: These are GUIDELINES only

Racially Aggravated Harassment, Alarm or Distress with Intent

Public Order Act 1986 s.4A
Crime and Disorder Act 1998 s.31
Triable either way – see Mode of Trial Guidelines
Penalty: Level 5 and/or 6 months

CONSIDER THE SERIOUSNESS OF THE OFFENCE
(INCLUDING THE LEVEL OF RACIAL AGGRAVATION AND THE IMPACT ON THE VICTIM)

IS IT DISCHARGE OR FINE APPROPRIATE?
IS IT SERIOUS ENOUGH FOR A COMMUNITY PENALTY?
IS IT SO SERIOUS THAT ONLY CUSTODY IS APPROPRIATE?
GUIDELINE: → ARE MAGISTRATES' SENTENCING POWERS APPROPRIATE?

➕ CONSIDER AGGRAVATING AND MITIGATING FACTORS ➖

for example	for example
Football hooliganism	Short duration
Group action	*This list is not exhaustive*
High degree of planning	
Night time offence	
Victims specifically targeted	
Weapon	
This list is not exhaustive	

If offender is on bail, this offence is more serious
If offender has previous convictions, their relevance and any failure to respond to previous sentences must be considered – they may increase the seriousness

TAKE A PRELIMINARY VIEW OF SERIOUSNESS, THEN CONSIDER WHETHER THE CASE SHOULD BE COMMITTED FOR SENTENCE, THEN CONSIDER OFFENDER MITIGATION

for example
Age, health (physical or mental)
Co-operation with police
Voluntary compensation
Evidence of genuine remorse

CONSIDER COMMITTAL OR YOUR SENTENCE

Compare it with the suggested guideline level of sentence and reconsider your reasons carefully if you have chosen a sentence at a different level.
Consider a discount for a timely guilty plea.

DECIDE YOUR SENTENCE
NB. COMPENSATION – Give reasons if not awarding compensation

Remember: These are GUIDELINES only

Racially Aggravated Harassment
Conduct causing harassment

Protection from Harassment Act 1997, s.2
Crime and Disorder Act 1998 s.32
Triable either way – see Mode of Trial Guidelines
Penalty: Level 5 and/or 6 months

CONSIDER THE SERIOUSNESS OF THE OFFENCE
(INCLUDING THE LEVEL OF RACIAL AGGRAVATION AND THE IMPACT ON THE VICTIM)

IS IT SERIOUS ENOUGH FOR A COMMUNITY PENALTY?

GUIDELINE: → *IS IT SO SERIOUS THAT ONLY CUSTODY IS APPROPRIATE?*
IS IT DISCHARGE OR FINE APPROPRIATE?
ARE MAGISTRATES' SENTENCING POWERS APPROPRIATE?

 CONSIDER AGGRAVATING AND MITIGATING FACTORS

for example
Disregard of warning
Excessive persistence
Interference with employment/business
Invasion of victim's home
Involvement of others
Use of violence or grossly offensive
material
Where photographs or images of a
personal nature are involved
This list is not exhaustive

for example
Initial provocation
Short duration
This list is not exhaustive

If offender is on bail, this offence is more serious
If offender has previous convictions, their relevance and any failure to respond to previous
sentences must be considered – they may increase the seriousness

TAKE A PRELIMINARY VIEW OF SERIOUSNESS, THEN
CONSIDER OFFENDER MITIGATION

for example
Age, health (physical or mental)
Co-operation with police
Evidence of genuine remorse

CONSIDER YOUR SENTENCE

Compare it with the suggested guideline level of sentence and reconsider
your reasons carefully if you have chosen a sentence at a different level.
Consider a discount for a timely guilty plea.
Restraining order – consider making an order in addition to the sentence to protect the victim
or any named person from further conduct which would amount to harassment.

DECIDE YOUR SENTENCE
NB. COMPENSATION – Give reasons if not awarding compensation

Remember: These are GUIDELINES only

Racially Aggravated Threatening Behaviour

Public Order Act 1986 s.4
Crime and Disorder Act 1998 s.32
Triable either way – see Mode of Trial Guidelines
Penalty: Level 5 and/or 6 months

CONSIDER THE SERIOUSNESS OF THE OFFENCE
(INCLUDING THE LEVEL OF RACIAL AGGRAVATION AND THE IMPACT ON THE VICTIM)

IS IT SERIOUS ENOUGH FOR A COMMUNITY PENALTY?

GUIDELINE: → *IS IT SO SERIOUS THAT ONLY CUSTODY IS APPROPRIATE?*
IS IT DISCHARGE OR FINE APPROPRIATE?
ARE MAGISTRATES' SENTENCING POWERS APPROPRIATE?

 CONSIDER AGGRAVATING AND MITIGATING FACTORS

for example
Group action
On hospital/medical premises
People put in fear
Victim serving the public
Vulnerable victim
This list is not exhaustive

for example
Minor matter
Short duration
This list is not exhaustive

If offender is on bail, this offence is more serious
If offender has previous convictions, their relevance and any failure to respond to previous
sentences must be considered – they may increase the seriousness

TAKE A PRELIMINARY VIEW OF SERIOUSNESS, THEN
CONSIDER OFFENDER MITIGATION

for example
Age, health (physical or mental)
Co-operation with police
Voluntary compensation
Evidence of genuine remorse

CONSIDER YOUR SENTENCE

Compare it with the suggested guideline level of sentence and reconsider
your reasons carefully if you have chosen a sentence at a different level.
Consider a discount for a timely guilty plea.

DECIDE YOUR SENTENCE
NB. COMPENSATION – Give reasons if not awarding compensation

Remember: These are GUIDELINES only

School Non-Attendance

Education Act 1996 s.444
Penalty: Level 3

CONSIDER THE SERIOUSNESS OF THE OFFENCE

GUIDELINE: → **IS DISCHARGE OR FINE APPROPRIATE?**

IS IT SERIOUS ENOUGH FOR A COMMUNITY PENALTY?

(NB. PROBATION/CURFEW AND PARENTING ORDERS ARE THE ONLY AVAILABLE COMMUNITY PENALTIES FOR THIS OFFENCE)

GUIDELINE FINE — STARTING POINT B

+ **CONSIDER AGGRAVATING AND MITIGATING FACTORS** **!**

for example
Harmful effect on other children in the family
Lack of parental effort to ensure attendance
Parental collusion
This list is not exhaustive

for example
Parent has complained of bullying, drugs etc.
Parental unawareness
Physical or mental health of child
This list is not exhaustive

If offender is on bail, this offence is more serious

If offender has previous convictions, their relevance and any failure to respond to previous sentences must be considered – they may increase the seriousness

TAKE A PRELIMINARY VIEW OF SERIOUSNESS, THEN CONSIDER OFFENDER MITIGATION

for example
Age, health (physical or mental)
Co-operation with the Education Authority
Evidence of genuine remorse

CONSIDER YOUR SENTENCE

Compare it with the suggested guideline level of sentence and reconsider your reasons carefully if you have chosen a sentence at a different level.
Consider a discount for a timely guilty plea.
Consider a parenting order where appropriate.

DECIDE YOUR SENTENCE

Remember: These are GUIDELINES only

Racially Aggravated Wounding – Grievous Bodily Harm

Offences Against the Person Act 1861 s.20
Crime and Disorder Act 1998 s.29
Triable either way – see Mode of Trial Guidelines
Penalty: Level 5 and/or 6 months

CONSIDER THE SERIOUSNESS OF THE OFFENCE
(INCLUDING THE LEVEL OF RACIAL AGGRAVATION AND THE IMPACT ON THE VICTIM)

IS DISCHARGE OR FINE APPROPRIATE?
IS IT SERIOUS ENOUGH FOR A COMMUNITY PENALTY?
IS IT SO SERIOUS THAT ONLY CUSTODY IS APPROPRIATE?

GUIDELINE: → **ARE MAGISTRATES' SENTENCING POWERS APPROPRIATE?**

+ **CONSIDER AGGRAVATING AND MITIGATING FACTORS** **!**

for example
Deliberate kicking/biting
Extensive injuries
Group action
Offender in position of authority
On hospital/medical premises
Premeditated
Victim particularly vulnerable
Victim serving the public
Weapon
This list is not exhaustive

for example
Single blow
Minor wound
Provocation
This list is not exhaustive

If offender is on bail, this offence is more serious

If offender has previous convictions, their relevance and any failure to respond to previous sentences must be considered – they may increase the seriousness

TAKE A PRELIMINARY VIEW OF SERIOUSNESS, THEN CONSIDER WHETHER THE CASE SHOULD BE COMMITTED FOR SENTENCE, THEN CONSIDER OFFENDER MITIGATION

for example
Age, health (physical or mental)
Co-operation with police
Voluntary compensation
Evidence of genuine remorse

CONSIDER COMMITTAL OR YOUR SENTENCE

Compare it with the suggested guideline level of sentence and reconsider your reasons carefully if you have chosen a sentence at a different level.
Consider a discount for a timely guilty plea.

DECIDE YOUR SENTENCE

NB. COMPENSATION – Give reasons if not awarding compensation

Remember: These are GUIDELINES only

Social Security – false representation to obtain benefit

Social Security Act 1992 s.112
Triable only summarily
Penalty: Level 5 and/or 3 months

CONSIDER THE SERIOUSNESS OF THE OFFENCE
(INCLUDING THE IMPACT ON THE VICTIM)

IS DISCHARGE OR FINE APPROPRIATE?

GUIDELINE: → *IS IT SERIOUS ENOUGH FOR A COMMUNITY PENALTY?*
IS IT SO SERIOUS THAT ONLY CUSTODY IS APPROPRIATE?

➕ CONSIDER AGGRAVATING AND MITIGATING FACTORS ➖

for example
Fraudulent claims over a long period
Large amount
Organised group offence
Planned deception
This list is not exhaustive

for example
Misunderstanding of regulations
Pressurised by others
Small amount
This list is not exhaustive

*If offender is on bail, this offence is more serious
If offender has previous convictions, their relevance and any failure to respond to previous
sentences must be considered – they may increase the seriousness*

TAKE A PRELIMINARY VIEW OF SERIOUSNESS, THEN
CONSIDER OFFENDER MITIGATION

for example
Age, health (physical or mental)
Co-operation with police
Voluntary compensation
Evidence of genuine remorse

CONSIDER YOUR SENTENCE

*Compare it with the suggested guideline level of sentence and reconsider
your reasons carefully if you have chosen a sentence at a different level.
Consider a discount for a timely guilty plea.*

DECIDE YOUR SENTENCE
NB. COMPENSATION – *Give reasons if not awarding compensation*

Remember: These are GUIDELINES only

Taking Vehicle without Consent

Theft Act 1968 s.12
Triable only summarily
Penalty: Level 5 and/or 6 months
May disqualify

CONSIDER THE SERIOUSNESS OF THE OFFENCE
(INCLUDING THE IMPACT ON THE VICTIM)

IS DISCHARGE OR FINE APPROPRIATE?

GUIDELINE: → *IS IT SERIOUS ENOUGH FOR A COMMUNITY PENALTY?*
IS IT SO SERIOUS THAT ONLY CUSTODY IS APPROPRIATE?

➕ CONSIDER AGGRAVATING AND MITIGATING FACTORS ➖

for example
Group action
Premeditated
Related damage
Professional hallmarks
Vulnerable victim
This list is not exhaustive

for example
Misunderstanding with owner
Soon returned
Vehicle belonged to family or friend
This list is not exhaustive

*If offender is on bail, this offence is more serious
If offender has previous convictions, their relevance and any failure to respond to previous
sentences must be considered – they may increase the seriousness*

TAKE A PRELIMINARY VIEW OF SERIOUSNESS, THEN
CONSIDER OFFENDER MITIGATION

for example
Health (physical or mental)
Co-operation with police
Voluntary compensation
Evidence of genuine remorse

CONSIDER YOUR SENTENCE

*Compare it with the suggested guideline level of sentence and reconsider
your reasons carefully if you have chosen a sentence at a different level.
Consider a discount for a timely guilty plea.*

DECIDE YOUR SENTENCE
NB. COMPENSATION – *Give reasons if not awarding compensation*

Remember: These are GUIDELINES only

Theft in Breach of Trust

Theft Act 1968 s.1
Triable either way – see Mode of Trial Guidelines
Penalty: Level 5 and/or 6 months

CONSIDER THE SERIOUSNESS OF THE OFFENCE
(INCLUDING THE IMPACT ON THE VICTIM)

IS IT SERIOUS ENOUGH FOR A COMMUNITY PENALTY?

IS IT SO SERIOUS THAT ONLY CUSTODY IS APPROPRIATE?

GUIDELINE: → *ARE MAGISTRATES' SENTENCING POWERS APPROPRIATE?*

⊕ CONSIDER AGGRAVATING AND MITIGATING FACTORS ⊖

for example
Casting suspicion on others
Committed over a period
High value
Organised team
Planned
Senior employee
Sophisticated
Vulnerable victim
This list is not exhaustive

for example
Impulsive action
Low value
Previous inconsistent attitude by employer
Single item
Unsupported junior
This list is not exhaustive

If racially aggravated, or offender is on bail, this offence is more serious
If offender has previous convictions, their relevance and any failure to respond to previous
sentences must be considered – they may increase the seriousness

TAKE A PRELIMINARY VIEW OF SERIOUSNESS, THEN CONSIDER WHETHER THE CASE SHOULD BE COMMITTED FOR SENTENCE, THEN CONSIDER OFFENDER MITIGATION

for example
Age, health (physical or mental)
Co-operation with police
Voluntary compensation
Evidence of genuine remorse

CONSIDER COMMITTAL OR YOUR SENTENCE

Compare it with the suggested guideline level of sentence and reconsider
your reasons carefully if you have chosen a sentence at a different level.
Consider a discount for a timely guilty plea.

DECIDE YOUR SENTENCE
NB. COMPENSATION – Give reasons if not awarding compensation

Remember: These are GUIDELINES only

Theft

Theft Act 1968 s.1
Triable either way – see Mode of Trial Guidelines
Penalty: Level 5 and/or 6 months
May disqualify where committed with reference
to the theft or taking of the vehicle

CONSIDER THE SERIOUSNESS OF THE OFFENCE
(INCLUDING THE IMPACT ON THE VICTIM)

IS DISCHARGE OR FINE APPROPRIATE?

GUIDELINE: → *IS IT SERIOUS ENOUGH FOR A COMMUNITY PENALTY?*

IS IT SO SERIOUS THAT ONLY CUSTODY IS APPROPRIATE?

ARE MAGISTRATES' SENTENCING POWERS APPROPRIATE?

⊕ CONSIDER AGGRAVATING AND MITIGATING FACTORS ⊖

for example
High value
Planned
Sophisticated
Adult involving children
Organised team
Related damage
Vulnerable victim
This list is not exhaustive

for example
Impulsive action
Low value
This list is not exhaustive

If racially aggravated, or offender is on bail, this offence is more serious
If offender has previous convictions, their relevance and any failure to respond to previous
sentences must be considered – they may increase the seriousness

TAKE A PRELIMINARY VIEW OF SERIOUSNESS, THEN CONSIDER OFFENDER MITIGATION

for example
Age, health (physical or mental)
Co-operation with police
Voluntary compensation
Evidence of genuine remorse

CONSIDER YOUR SENTENCE

Compare it with the suggested guideline level of sentence and reconsider
your reasons carefully if you have chosen a sentence at a different level.
Consider a discount for a timely guilty plea.

DECIDE YOUR SENTENCE
NB. COMPENSATION – Give reasons if not awarding compensation

Remember: These are GUIDELINES only

Threatening Behaviour

Public Order Act 1986 s.4
Triable only summarily
Penalty: Level 5 and/or 6 months

CONSIDER THE SERIOUSNESS OF THE OFFENCE
(INCLUDING THE IMPACT ON THE VICTIM)

IS DISCHARGE OR FINE APPROPRIATE?
GUIDELINE: → *IS IT SERIOUS ENOUGH FOR A COMMUNITY PENALTY?*
IS IT SO SERIOUS THAT ONLY CUSTODY IS APPROPRIATE?

CONSIDER AGGRAVATING AND MITIGATING FACTORS

for example	for example
Group action	Minor matter
On hospital/medical premises	Short duration
People put in fear	*This list is not exhaustive*
Victim serving the public	
Vulnerable victim	
This list is not exhaustive	

If offender is on bail, this offence is more serious
If offender has previous convictions, their relevance and any failure to respond to previous sentences must be considered – they may increase the seriousness

TAKE A PRELIMINARY VIEW OF SERIOUSNESS, THEN CONSIDER OFFENDER MITIGATION

for example
Age, health (physical or mental)
Co-operation with police
Voluntary compensation
Evidence of genuine remorse

CONSIDER YOUR SENTENCE

Compare it with the suggested guideline level of sentence and reconsider
your reasons carefully if you have chosen a sentence at a different level.
Consider a discount for a timely guilty plea.

DECIDE YOUR SENTENCE
NB. COMPENSATION – Give reasons if not awarding compensation

Remember: These are GUIDELINES only

TV Licence Payment Evasion

Wireless Telegraphy Act 1949 s.1
Triable only summarily
Penalty: Level 3

CONSIDER THE SERIOUSNESS OF THE OFFENCE

IS DISCHARGE OR FINE APPROPRIATE?
GUIDELINE: → *IS IT SERIOUS ENOUGH FOR A COMMUNITY PENALTY?*
(PROBATION AND CURFEW ORDERS ARE THE ONLY AVAILABLE COMMUNITY PENALTIES FOR THIS OFFENCE)

GUIDELINE FINE — STARTING POINT A

CONSIDER AGGRAVATING AND MITIGATING FACTORS

	for example
Failure to respond to payment opportunities	Accidental oversight
This list is not exhaustive	Confusion of responsibility
	Licence immediately obtained
	Very short unlicensed use
	This list is not exhaustive

If offender is on bail, this offence is more serious
If offender has previous convictions, their relevance and any failure to respond to previous sentences must be considered – they may increase the seriousness

TAKE A PRELIMINARY VIEW OF SERIOUSNESS, THEN CONSIDER OFFENDER MITIGATION

for example
Age, health (physical or mental)

CONSIDER YOUR SENTENCE

Compare it with the suggested guideline level of sentence and reconsider
your reasons carefully if you have chosen a sentence at a different level.
Consider a discount for a timely guilty plea.

DECIDE YOUR SENTENCE

Remember: These are GUIDELINES only

Vehicle Interference

Criminal Attempts Act 1981 s.9
Triable only summarily
Penalty: Level 4 and/or 3 months

CONSIDER THE SERIOUSNESS OF THE OFFENCE
(INCLUDING THE IMPACT ON THE VICTIM)

IS DISCHARGE OR FINE APPROPRIATE?

GUIDELINE: → IS IT SERIOUS ENOUGH FOR A COMMUNITY PENALTY?

IS IT SO SERIOUS THAT ONLY CUSTODY IS APPROPRIATE?

➕ CONSIDER AGGRAVATING AND MITIGATING FACTORS ➖

for example
Disabled passenger vehicle
Emergency service vehicle
Group action
Planned
Related damage
This list is not exhaustive

for example
Impulsive action
This list is not exhaustive

If racially aggravated, or offender is on bail, this offence is more serious
If offender has previous convictions, their relevance and any failure to respond to previous
sentences must be considered – they may increase the seriousness

TAKE A PRELIMINARY VIEW OF SERIOUSNESS, THEN CONSIDER OFFENDER MITIGATION

for example
Age, health (physical or mental)
Co-operation with police
Voluntary compensation
Evidence of genuine remorse

CONSIDER YOUR SENTENCE

Compare it with the suggested guideline level of sentence and reconsider
your reasons carefully if you have chosen a sentence at a different level.
Consider a discount for a timely guilty plea.

DECIDE YOUR SENTENCE
NB. COMPENSATION – Give reasons if not awarding compensation

Remember: These are GUIDELINES only

Violent Disorder

Public Order Act 1986 s.2
Triable either way – see Mode of Trial Guidelines
Penalty: Level 5 and/or 6 months

CONSIDER THE SERIOUSNESS OF THE OFFENCE
(INCLUDING THE IMPACT ON THE VICTIM)

IS DISCHARGE OR FINE APPROPRIATE?

IS IT SERIOUS ENOUGH FOR A COMMUNITY PENALTY?
IS IT SO SERIOUS THAT ONLY CUSTODY IS APPROPRIATE?

GUIDELINE: → ARE MAGISTRATES' SENTENCING POWERS APPROPRIATE?

➕ CONSIDER AGGRAVATING AND MITIGATING FACTORS ➖

for example
Busy public place
Fighting between rival groups
Large group
People actually put in fear
Planned
Vulnerable victims
Weapon
This list is not exhaustive

for example
Impulsive
Nobody actually afraid
Provocation
This list is not exhaustive

If racially aggravated, or offender is on bail, this offence is more serious
If offender has previous convictions, their relevance and any failure to respond to previous
sentences must be considered – they may increase the seriousness

TAKE A PRELIMINARY VIEW OF SERIOUSNESS, THEN CONSIDER WHETHER THE CASE SHOULD BE COMMITTED FOR SENTENCE, THEN CONSIDER OFFENDER MITIGATION

for example
Age, health (physical or mental)
Co-operation with police
Voluntary compensation
Evidence of genuine remorse

CONSIDER COMMITTAL OR YOUR SENTENCE

Compare it with the suggested guideline level of sentence and reconsider
your reasons carefully if you have chosen a sentence at a different level.
Consider a discount for a timely guilty plea.

DECIDE YOUR SENTENCE
NB. COMPENSATION – Give reasons if not awarding compensation

Remember: These are GUIDELINES only

Wounding – Grievous Bodily Harm

Offences Against the Person Act 1861 s.20
Triable either way - see Mode of Trial Guidelines
Penalty: Level 5 and/or 6 months

CONSIDER THE SERIOUSNESS OF THE OFFENCE
(INCLUDING THE IMPACT ON THE VICTIM)

IS DISCHARGE OR FINE APPROPRIATE?
IS IT SO SERIOUS THAT ONLY CUSTODY IS APPROPRIATE?

GUIDELINE: → *ARE MAGISTRATES' SENTENCING POWERS APPROPRIATE?*

 CONSIDER AGGRAVATING AND MITIGATING FACTORS

for example	for example
Deliberate kicking/biting	Single blow
Extensive injuries	Minor wound
Group action	Provocation
Offender in position of authority	*This list is not exhaustive*
On hospital/medical premises	
Premeditated	
Victim particularly vulnerable	
Victim serving the public	
Weapon	
This list is not exhaustive	

If offender is on bail, this offence is more serious
If offender has previous convictions, their relevance and any failure to respond to previous sentences must be considered – they may increase the seriousness

TAKE A PRELIMINARY VIEW OF SERIOUSNESS, THEN CONSIDER WHETHER THE CASE SHOULD BE COMMITTED FOR SENTENCE, THEN CONSIDER OFFENDER MITIGATION

CONSIDER COMMITTAL OR YOUR SENTENCE

for example
Age, health (physical or mental)
Co-operation with police
Voluntary compensation
Evidence of genuine remorse

Compare it with the suggested guideline level of sentence and reconsider your reasons carefully if you have chosen a sentence at a different level.
Consider a discount for a timely guilty plea.

DECIDE YOUR SENTENCE
NB. COMPENSATION – *Give reasons if not awarding compensation*

Remember: These are GUIDELINES only

Careless Driving

Road Traffic Act 1988 s.3
Triable only summarily
Penalty: Level 4
Must endorse (3-9 points OR may disqualify)

CONSIDER THE SERIOUSNESS OF THE OFFENCE

GUIDELINE: → *IS DISCHARGE OR FINE APPROPRIATE?*
IS IT SERIOUS ENOUGH FOR A COMMUNITY PENALTY?

(PROBATION AND CURFEW ORDERS ARE THE ONLY AVAILABLE COMMUNITY PENALTIES FOR THIS OFFENCE)

GUIDELINE — STARTING POINT B

 CONSIDER AGGRAVATING AND MITIGATING FACTORS

for example	for example
Excessive speed	Sudden change in weather conditions
High degree of carelessness	Minor risk
Serious risk	Momentary lapse
Using a hand-held mobile telephone	Negligible/parking damage
This list is not exhaustive	*This list is not exhaustive*

Death, serious injury or damage is capable of being aggravation

If offender is on bail, this offence is more serious
If offender has previous convictions, their relevance and any failure to respond to previous sentences must be considered – they may increase the seriousness

TAKE A PRELIMINARY VIEW OF SERIOUSNESS, THEN CONSIDER OFFENDER MITIGATION

CONSIDER YOUR SENTENCE

for example
Co-operation with police
Voluntary compensation
Evidence of genuine remorse

Endorse (3-9 points OR period of disqualification)
Consider other measures (including disqualification until test passed if appropriate – for example, age, infirmity or medical condition).
Compare it with the suggested guideline level of sentence and reconsider your reasons carefully if you have chosen a sentence at a different level.
Consider a discount for a timely guilty plea.

DECIDE YOUR SENTENCE

Remember: These are GUIDELINES only

Dangerous Driving

Road Traffic Act 1988 s.2
Triable either way – see Mode of Trial Guidelines
Penalty: Level 5 and/or 6 months
Must endorse and disqualify at least 12 months
Must endorse (3-11 points) if not disqualified
Must order EXTENDED re-test

CONSIDER THE SERIOUSNESS OF THE OFFENCE
(INCLUDING THE IMPACT ON THE VICTIM)

IS DISCHARGE OR FINE APPROPRIATE?

IS IT SERIOUS ENOUGH FOR A COMMUNITY PENALTY?

IS IT SO SERIOUS THAT ONLY CUSTODY IS APPROPRIATE?

GUIDELINE: → *ARE MAGISTRATES' SENTENCING POWERS APPROPRIATE?*

➕ CONSIDER AGGRAVATING AND MITIGATING FACTORS

for example
- Avoiding detection or apprehension
- Competitive driving, racing, showing off
- Disregard of warnings eg. from passengers or others in vicinity
- Evidence of alcohol or drugs
- Excessive speed
- Prolonged, persistent, deliberate bad driving
- Serious risk
- Using a hand-held mobile telephone
This list is not exhaustive

for example
- Emergency
- Single incident
- Speed not excessive
This list is not exhaustive

Serious injury or damage is capable of being aggravation

If offender is on bail, this offence is more serious

If offender has previous convictions, their relevance and any failure to respond to previous sentences must be considered – they may increase the seriousness

TAKE A PRELIMINARY VIEW OF SERIOUSNESS, THEN CONSIDER WHETHER THE CASE SHOULD BE COMMITTED FOR SENTENCE, THEN CONSIDER OFFENDER MITIGATION

for example
- Co-operation with police
- Voluntary compensation
- Evidence of genuine remorse

CONSIDER COMMITTAL OR YOUR SENTENCE

Endorse licence and disqualify at least 12 months unless special reasons apply. Order EXTENDED re-test.

Compare it with the suggested guideline level of sentence and reconsider your reasons carefully if you have chosen a sentence at a different level.
Consider a discount for a timely guilty plea.

DECIDE YOUR SENTENCE

Remember: These are GUIDELINES only

Driving while Disqualified by Court Order

Road Traffic Act 1988 s.103
Triable only summarily
Penalty: Level 5 and/or 6 months
Must endorse: (6 points OR may disqualify again)

CONSIDER THE SERIOUSNESS OF THE OFFENCE

IS DISCHARGE OR FINE APPROPRIATE?

IS IT SERIOUS ENOUGH FOR A COMMUNITY PENALTY?

GUIDELINE: → *IS IT SO SERIOUS THAT ONLY CUSTODY IS APPROPRIATE?*

➕ CONSIDER AGGRAVATING AND MITIGATING FACTORS

for example
- Efforts to avoid detection
- Long distance drive
- Planned, long term evasion
- Recent disqualification
This list is not exhaustive

for example
- Emergency established
- Full period expired but test not re-taken
- Short distance driven
This list is not exhaustive

If offender is on bail, this offence is more serious

The nature of previous conviction or convictions, their relevance and any failure to respond to previous sentences must be considered – they may increase the seriousness

TAKE A PRELIMINARY VIEW OF SERIOUSNESS, THEN CONSIDER OFFENDER MITIGATION

for example
- Co-operation with police
- Evidence of genuine remorse

CONSIDER YOUR SENTENCE

Endorse (6 points OR period of disqualification)
Compare it with the suggested guideline level of sentence and reconsider your reasons carefully if you have chosen a sentence at a different level.
Consider a discount for a timely guilty plea.

DECIDE YOUR SENTENCE

Remember: These are GUIDELINES only

Excess Alcohol
(Drive or attempt to drive)

s.5(1)(a) Road Traffic Act 1988
Penalty: Level 5 and/or 6 months
Triable only summarily
Must endorse and disqualify at least 12 months;
disqualify at least 36 months for a further
offence within 10 years

CONSIDER THE SERIOUSNESS OF THE OFFENCE

THE LEVEL OF SERIOUSNESS AND GUIDELINE SENTENCE ARE RELATED TO THE BREATH/BLOOD/URINE LEVEL

✚ CONSIDER AGGRAVATING AND MITIGATING FACTORS ➊

for example	**for example**
Ability to drive seriously impaired	Emergency
Caused injury/fear/damage	Moving a vehicle a very short distance
Police chase	*This list is not exhaustive*
Evidence of nature of the driving	
Type of vehicle, eg. carrying passengers for reward/large goods vehicle	
High reading (and in combination with above)	
This list is not exhaustive	

If offender has previous convictions, their relevance and any failure to respond to previous sentences must be considered – they may increase the seriousness

TAKE A PRELIMINARY VIEW OF SERIOUSNESS, THEN CONSIDER OFFENDER MITIGATION

for example
Co-operation with police

If offender is on bail, this offence is more serious

CONSIDER YOUR SENTENCE

Offer a rehabilitation course.
Compare your decision with the suggested guideline level of sentence and reconsider your reasons carefully if you have chosen a sentence at a different level.
Consider a discount for a timely guilty plea.

DECIDE YOUR SENTENCE

BREATH	BLOOD	URINE	DISQUALIFY NOT LESS THAN	GUIDELINE
36-55	80-125	107-170	12 months	B
56-70	126-160	171-214	18 months	C
71-85	161-195	215-260	24 months	C
86-100	196-229	261-308	24 months	CONSIDER COMMUNITY PENALTY
101-115	230-264	309-354	30 months	
116-130	265-300	355-400	30 months	CONSIDER CUSTODY
131+	301+	401+	36 months	

Remember: These are GUIDELINES only

Failing to Stop
Failing to Report

Road Traffic Act 1988 s. 170 (4)
Penalty: Level 5 and/or 6 months
Triable only summarily
Must endorse: (5 – 10 points OR disqualify)

CONSIDER THE SERIOUSNESS OF THE OFFENCE

GUIDELINE: →

IS IT SERIOUS ENOUGH FOR A COMMUNITY PENALTY?
IS IT SO SERIOUS THAT ONLY CUSTODY IS APPROPRIATE?

IS DISCHARGE OR FINE APPROPRIATE?

GUIDELINE FINE — STARTING POINT B

✚ CONSIDER AGGRAVATING AND MITIGATING FACTORS ➊

for example	**for example**
Evidence of drinking or drugs	Believed identity to be known
Serious injury	Failed to stop but reported
Serious damage	Genuine fear of retaliation
This list is not exhaustive	Negligible damage
	No one at scene but failed to report
	Stayed at scene but failed to give/left before giving full particulars
	This list is not exhaustive

If offender has previous convictions, their relevance and any failure to respond to previous sentences must be considered – they may increase the seriousness

TAKE A PRELIMINARY VIEW OF SERIOUSNESS, THEN CONSIDER OFFENDER MITIGATION

for example
Co-operation with police
Voluntary compensation
Evidence of genuine remorse

If offender is on bail, this offence is more serious

CONSIDER YOUR SENTENCE

Endorse (5-10 points OR period of disqualification)
Compare it with the suggested guideline level of sentence and reconsider your reasons carefully if you have chosen a sentence at a different level.
Consider a discount for a timely guilty plea.

DECIDE YOUR SENTENCE

Remember: These are GUIDELINES only

No insurance

Road Traffic Act 1988 s.143
Triable only summarily
Penalty: Level 5
Must endorse (6-8 points OR may disqualify)

CONSIDER THE SERIOUSNESS OF THE OFFENCE

GUIDELINE: →   **IS IT DISCHARGE OR FINE APPROPRIATE?**
IS IT SERIOUS ENOUGH FOR A COMMUNITY PENALTY?

(PROBATION AND CURFEW ORDERS ARE THE ONLY AVAILABLE COMMUNITY PENALTIES FOR THIS OFFENCE)

GUIDELINE FINE — STARTING POINT B

➊ CONSIDER AGGRAVATING AND MITIGATING FACTORS

for example
Deliberate driving without insurance
Gave false details
LGV, HGV, PCV, PSV or minicabs
No reference to insurance ever having
    been held
This list is not exhaustive

for example
Accidental oversight
Genuine mistake
Responsibility for providing insurance
    resting with another – the parent/
    owner/lender/hirer
Smaller vehicle, eg. moped
This list is not exhaustive

If offender is on bail, this offence is more serious
If offender has previous convictions, their relevance and any failure to respond to previous
sentences must be considered – they may increase the seriousness

TAKE A PRELIMINARY VIEW OF SERIOUSNESS, THEN CONSIDER OFFENDER MITIGATION

for example
Difficult domestic circumstances
Evidence of genuine remorse

CONSIDER YOUR SENTENCE

Endorse licence.
Carefully consider the option of disqualification, suggested starting point
    – two months.
Compare your decision with the suggested guideline level of sentence and reconsider
    your reasons carefully if you have chosen a sentence at a different level.
    Consider a discount for a timely guilty plea.

DECIDE YOUR SENTENCE

Remember: These are GUIDELINES only

© The Magistrates' Association   57   *Issue September 2000*

Fraudulent use etc. Vehicle Excise Licence etc.

Vehicle Excise and Registration Act 1994 s.44
Triable either way – see Mode of Trial Guidelines
Penalty: Level 5

CONSIDER THE SERIOUSNESS OF THE OFFENCE

GUIDELINE: →   **IS IT DISCHARGE OR FINE APPROPRIATE?**
IS IT SERIOUS ENOUGH FOR A COMMUNITY PENALTY?

(PROBATION AND CURFEW ORDERS ARE THE ONLY AVAILABLE COMMUNITY PENALTIES FOR THIS OFFENCE)

GUIDELINE FINE — STARTING POINT B

➊ CONSIDER AGGRAVATING AND MITIGATING FACTORS

for example
Deliberately planned
Disc forged or altered
Long term defrauding
LGV, HGV, PCV, PSV, taxi or private hire
    vehicle
This list is not exhaustive

for example

If offender is on bail, this offence is more serious
If offender has previous convictions, their relevance and any failure to respond to previous
sentences must be considered – they may increase the seriousness

TAKE A PRELIMINARY VIEW OF SERIOUSNESS, THEN CONSIDER OFFENDER MITIGATION

for example
Co-operation with police
Evidence of genuine remorse

CONSIDER YOUR SENTENCE

Compare it with the suggested guideline level of sentence and reconsider
    your reasons carefully if you have chosen a sentence at a different level.
    Consider a discount for a timely guilty plea.

DECIDE YOUR SENTENCE

Remember: These are GUIDELINES only

© The Magistrates' Association   56   *Issue September 2000*

Refuse evidential specimen (Drive or attempt to drive)

s.7(6) Road Traffic Act 1988
Penalty: Level 5 and/or 6 months:
Triable only summarily.
Must endorse and disqualify at least 12 months:
disqualify at least 36 months for a further
offence within 10 years

CONSIDER THE SERIOUSNESS OF THE OFFENCE

GUIDELINE: →
IS DISCHARGE OR FINE APPROPRIATE?
IS IT SERIOUS ENOUGH FOR A COMMUNITY PENALTY?
IS IT SO SERIOUS THAT ONLY CUSTODY IS APPROPRIATE?

GUIDELINE FINE — STARTING POINT C

CONSIDER AGGRAVATING AND MITIGATING FACTORS

for example   for example
Police chase
Caused injury/fear/damage
Type of vehicle, eg, carrying passengers for
  reward/large goods vehicle
Evidence of nature of the driving
Ability to drive seriously impaired
This list is not exhaustive

If offender is on bail, this offence is more serious
If offender has previous convictions, their relevance and any failure to respond to previous sentences must be considered – they may increase the seriousness

TAKE A PRELIMINARY VIEW OF SERIOUSNESS, THEN CONSIDER OFFENDER MITIGATION

for example
Voluntary completion of alcohol impaired driver course (if available)
Evidence of genuine remorse

CONSIDER YOUR SENTENCE

Offer a rehabilitation course.
Examine carefully aggravating/mitigating factors disclosed – do these justify any variation in period of disqualification suggested? If substantial aggravating factors, consider higher fine/community penalty/custody
Endorse licence. DISQUALIFY – a minimum period of 18 months is suggested.
Compare it with the suggested guideline level of sentence and reconsider your reasons carefully if you have chosen a sentence at a different level.
Consider a discount for a timely guilty plea.

DECIDE YOUR SENTENCE
Remember: These are GUIDELINES only

Speeding

Road Traffic Act 1984 s.89(10)
Penalty: Level 3 (Level 4 if motorway)
Triable only summarily
Must endorse (3-5 points OR may disqualify)

CONSIDER THE SERIOUSNESS OF THE OFFENCE

GUIDELINE: →
IS DISCHARGE OR FINE APPROPRIATE?
(PROBATION AND CURFEW ORDERS ARE THE ONLY AVAILABLE COMMUNITY PENALTIES FOR THIS OFFENCE)

CONSIDER AGGRAVATING AND MITIGATING FACTORS

for example
Emergency established
Limit change (eg, 40 to 30 mph)
This list is not exhaustive

If offender is on bail, this offence is more serious
If offender has previous convictions, their relevance and any failure to respond to previous sentences must be considered – they may increase the seriousness

GUIDELINE PENALTY POINTS	LEGAL SPEED LIMITS	EXCESS SPEED - MPH	FINE
3	20-30 mph	Up to 10 mph	A
	40-50 mph	Up to 15 mph	
	60-70 mph	Up to 20 mph	
4 or 5	20-30 mph	From 11-20 mph	B
	40-50 mph	From 16-25 mph	
	60-70 mph	From 21-30 mph	
6 OR disqualify up to 42 days	20-30 mph	From 21-30 mph	B
	40-50 mph	From 26-35 mph	
	60-70 mph	From 31-40 mph	
6 OR disqualify up to 56 days			

TAKE A PRELIMINARY VIEW OF SERIOUSNESS, THEN CONSIDER OFFENDER MITIGATION

for example
Co-operation with police
Fixed penalty not taken up for valid reason

CONSIDER YOUR SENTENCE

Endorse (3-6 points OR period of disqualification; new drivers 6 points)
Consider other measure (including disqualification until test passed if appropriate).
Compare it with the suggested guideline level of sentence and reconsider your reasons carefully if you have chosen a sentence at a different level.
Consider a discount for a timely guilty plea.

DECIDE YOUR SENTENCE
Remember: These are GUIDELINES only

Offences considered appropriate for guideline of discharge or fine, other than in exceptional circumstances

	PENALTY POINTS	MAXIMUM PENALTY	FINE
ALCOHOL/DRUGS			
In charge whilst unfit through drink/drugs or refusing evidential specimen	10*	Level 4 and/or 3 months E	B
Consider disqualification if evidence of driving or other aggravating factor. Offer a rehabilitation course if disqualifying for 12 months or more.			
Refusing roadside breath test	4	Level 3 E	A
DRIVER			
Not supplying details *If company-owned, use higher fine when unable to apply endorsement as a minimum*	3*	Level 3 E	B
LICENCE OFFENCES			
† No driving licence, where could be covered, eg. if licence not renewed, but would have covered class of vehicle driven, or holder of full licence has lost or misplaced it.	–	Level 3	A
† Driving not in accordance with provisional licence (includes where no licence ever held)	3-6	Level 3 E	A
† No excise licence	–	Level 3 or 5 times annual duty (whichever greater)	Actual duty lost plus penalty of Guideline Fine – Starting Point A (1-4 months unpaid duty), Aα2 (4-6 months), Aα3 (6-12 months) subject to a maximum of twice the duty
LIGHTS – Driving without	–	Level 3	A
OWNERSHIP – Not notifying DVLA of change etc.	–	Level 3	A
PARKING OFFENCES			
† Dangerous position	3	Level 3 E	A
† Pelican/zebra crossing	3	Level 3 E	A
TEST CERTIFICATE – Not held	–	Level 3	A
TRAFFIC DIRECTION OFFENCES			
† Fail to comply with height restriction	3	Level 3 E	A
† Fail to comply with red traffic light	3	Level 3 E	A
† Fail to comply with stop sign/double white lines	3	Level 3 E	A
† Fail to give precedence – pelican/zebra crossing	3	Level 3 E	A
TRAFFIC OR POLICE SIGNS (non endorsable)			
† Fail to comply	–	3	A

† *All these items are eligible for fixed penalty offer. If fixed penalty was offered, consider any reasons for not taking up and, if valid, fine amount of appropriate fixed penalty and endorse if required, considering whether costs be waived and allow a maximum of 28 days to pay. Or, if fixed penalty refused or not offered, consider whether known circumstances merit any discount for a guilty plea (but never go below the fixed penalty amount) or if there are aggravating factors which merit increasing the fine. In all cases, consider the safety factor, damage to roads, commercial gain and, if driver is not the owner, with whom prime responsibility should lie.*

E: Must ENDORSE (unless special reasons) and may disqualify

Remember: These are GUIDELINES only

Offences considered appropriate for guideline of discharge or fine, other than in exceptional circumstances – contd.

	PENALTY POINTS	MAXIMUM PENALTY	FINE
VEHICLE DEFECTS UP TO AND INCLUDING 3.5 TONNES GROSS VEHICLE WEIGHT			
Defects			
† Brakes/Steering/Tyres (each)	3	Level 4 E	A
† Loss of wheel	3	Level 4 E	A
† Exhaust emission	–	Level 3	A
† Other offences	–	Level 3	A
Loads, danger of injury by:			
† Condition of vehicle/accessories/equipment	3	Level 4 E	A
† Purpose of use/passenger numbers/how carried	3	Level 4 E	A
† Weight, position or distribution of load	3	Level 4 E	A
† Insecure load	3	Level 4 E	A
† Overloading or exceeding maximum axle weight	–	Level 5	A* Plus increase in proportion to percentage of overloading

* Examine carefully evidence of responsibility for overload and, if commercial gain relates to owner, increase the fine.

† *All these items are eligible for fixed penalty offer. If fixed penalty was offered, consider any reasons for not taking up and, if valid, fine amount of appropriate fixed penalty and endorse if required, considering whether costs be waived and allow a maximum of 28 days to pay. Or, if fixed penalty refused or not offered, consider whether known circumstances merit any discount for a guilty plea (but never go below the fixed penalty amount) or if there are aggravating factors which merit increasing the fine. In all cases, consider the safety factor, damage to roads, commercial gain and, if driver is not the owner, with whom prime responsibility should lie.*

E: Must ENDORSE (unless special reasons) and may disqualify

Remember: These are GUIDELINES only

Motorway Offences

	PENALTY POINTS	MAXIMUM PENALTY	FINE
DRIVING			
† Driving in reverse on motorway	3	Level 4 E	B
† Driving in reverse on sliproad	3	Level 4 E	A
† Driving in wrong direction on motorway * Consider disqualification	3*	Level 4 E	B
† Driving in wrong direction on sliproad	3	Level 4 E	A
† Driving off carriageway – central reservation	3	Level 4 E	A
† Driving off carriageway – hard shoulder	3	Level 4 E	A
† Driving on sliproad against no entry sign	3	Level 4 E	A
† Making U-Turn * Consider disqualification	3*	Level 4 E	A
LEARNERS			
† Learner driver or excluded vehicle	3	Level 4 E	A
STOPPING			
† Stopping on hard shoulder of motorway	-	Level 4	A
† Stopping on hard shoulder of sliproad	-	Level 4	A
THIRD LANE			
† Vehicle over 7.5 tonnes or drawing trailer in third lane	3	Level 4 E	A
WALKING			
† Walking on motorway or sliproad	-	Level 4	A
† Walking on hard shoulder or verge	-	Level 4	A

† All these items are eligible for fixed penalty offer. If fixed penalty was offered, consider any reasons for not taking up and, if valid, fine amount of appropriate fixed penalty and endorse if required, considering whether costs be waived and allow a maximum of 28 days to pay. Or, if fixed penalty refused or not offered, consider whether known circumstances merit any discount for a guilty plea (but never go below the fixed penalty amount) or if there are aggravating factors which merit increasing the fine.

In all cases, consider the safety factor, damage to roads, commercial gain and, if driver is not the owner, with whom prime responsibility should lie.

Remember: These are GUIDELINES only

Offences relating to buses and goods vehicles over 3.5 tonnes gross vehicle weight (GVW)

	PENALTY POINTS	MAXIMUM PENALTY	OWNER/ OPERATOR	DRIVER OR OWNER/DRIVER**
DEFECTS				
Brakes	3	Level 5 E	C	B
Steering	3	Level 5 E	C	B
Tyres (per tyre)	3	Level 5 E	C	B
Loss of wheel	3	Level 5 E	C	B
Exhaust emission	-	Level 4	C	B
Other offences	-	Level 4	C	B
LOADS				
Condition of vehicle/accessories/ equipment	3	Level 5 E	C	B
Purpose of use/number of passengers/ how carried	3	Level 5 E	C	B
Weight, position or distribution of load	3	Level 5 E	C	B
Insecure load	3	Level 5 E	C	B
Overloading or exceeding maximum axle weight	-	Level 5	C* *Plus increase in proportion to percentage of overloading	B*
OPERATORS LICENCE				
Not held	-	Level 4	C	B
TACHOGRAPH				
Not properly used	-	Level 5	C	B
Falsification/fraudulent use	-	Level 5	C	B
SPEED LIMITERS – WHERE APPLICABLE				
Not being used or incorrectly calibrated	-	Level 5	C	B

** For an owner/driver, take net turnover into account as appropriate

E: Must ENDORSE (unless special reasons) and may disqualify

Remember: These are GUIDELINES only

Seriousness

Establishing the Seriousness of the Offence

In establishing the seriousness of the case before them, courts should:

- make sure that all factors which aggravate or mitigate the offence are considered. The lists in the *Guidelines* are neither exhaustive nor a substitute for the personal judgment of magistrates. Factors which do not appear in the *Guidelines* may be important in individual cases;
- consider the various seriousness indicators, remembering that some will carry more weight than others;
- note that, by statute, racial aggravation increases the seriousness of any offence – s.82 *Crime and Disorder Act 1998* – but see the note on specific racially aggravated offences created under ss.29-32 of the same Act;
- always bear in mind that, by statute, the commission of an offence on bail aggravates its seriousness;
- consider the effect of using previous convictions, or any failure to respond to previous sentences, in assessing seriousness. Courts should identify any convictions relevant for this purpose and then consider to what extent they affect the seriousness of the present offence;
- note that, when there are several offences to be sentenced, the court must have regard to the totality principle;

When the court has formed an initial assessment of the seriousness of the offence(s), consider any offender mitigation.

Impact on the victim

The impact of the offence upon the victim should be taken into account as a seriousness factor.

Reduction in sentence for guilty pleas

(Section 48 Criminal Justice and Public Order Act 1994)

In deciding what sentence to pass on a person who has pleaded guilty the court has to take into account the stage in the proceedings at which that plea was indicated and the circumstances in which the indication was given. If the court imposes a less severe penalty than it would have given, it must state this in open court.

The principles of 'discount' apply as much to magistrates' courts as they do to Crown Courts. A timely guilty plea may attract a sentencing discount of up to a third but the precise amount of discount will depend on the facts of each case. A change of plea on the day set down for trial may attract only a minimal reduction in sentence; the court must still consider whether discount should be given.

Discounts apply to fines, periods of community sentences and custody. Mandatory periods of disqualification and mandatory penalty points cannot be reduced for a guilty plea. Reasons should be given for decisions.

Pre Sentence and Specific Sentence Reports

The purpose of a Pre-Sentence report (PSR) is to provide information to the sentencing court about the offender and the offences charged so that the court has sufficient relevant information to enable it to decide a suitable sentence.

The revised National Standards require a PSR to contain:

- an assessment of the offending behaviour
- an assessment of the risk to the public
- a clear and realistic indication of the action which can be taken by the court to reduce re-offending

When adjourning a case for receipt of a PSR the court should indicate to the officer preparing the report (preferably in writing)

- the court's preliminary view of the level of seriousness
- the aim of the sentence
- any particular issues to be addressed in the report

The court must make it clear to all that the sentencing bench is not bound by the preliminary indication of seriousness.

A PSR must be provided within a maximum of 15 working days of the court's request or any shorter time agreed. Any delay must be explained in writing.

The Specific Sentence Report (SSR) has a similar purpose to the PSR but, while still in writing, is in an expedited form. The SSR is intended for the more straightforward cases where the required information is readily available from the probation officer in court. The SSR is designed to be available on the same day on which the court's request is made, unless there are exceptional circumstances or the probation officer preparing the report considers further investigation and a full PSR to be necessary.

Giving reasons

Magistrates should normally give reasons for their findings and decisions; this is obligatory under the Human Rights Act.

- The offender should be told the reasons for the decision.
- The victim will want to know the reasons for the decision.
- The public are entitled to know what is going on in the criminal justice system, and to have confidence in it.
- If a sentence is unusual the case for reasons is doubly important.
- Ill-informed criticism in the media may be reduced if reasons have been given in public and recorded.
- In preparing an SSR or a PSR, or in implementing a community sentence, the probation service must know what the magistrates had in mind.
- If a case has to be adjourned, and a differently constituted bench sits next time, the later bench must know the reasons for the decisions of the earlier bench.

And:

- The reasons will be necessary if there is an appeal by way of case stated.

There are now many instances where the giving of reasons is required by law:

- Why bail is refused.
- Why the offence is so serious as to justify prison.
- Why a defaulter is being sent to prison.
- If a compensation order is not awarded.
- If a sentence discount is given.
- If the court does not disqualify the driver or endorse his licence for 'special reasons'.

Having reached their findings and reasons, it is perfectly proper for the magistrates to seek the advice and assistance of the legal adviser in how best to formulate and articulate those reasons for the purpose of the pronouncement.

Financial penalties

Fining

Fines are suitable as punishment for cases which are not serious enough to merit a community penalty, nor so serious that a custodial sentence must be considered.

The aim should be for the fine to have equal impact on rich or poor and before fixing the amount of a fine, the court must enquire into the offender's financial circumstances, preferably using a standard means form.

A fine must not exceed the upper statutory limit. Where this is expressed in terms of a 'level' the maxima are:

Level 1	£200
Level 2	£500
Level 3	£1,000
Level 4	£2,500
Level 5	£5,000

The fine must reflect the seriousness of the offence and must be proportionate both to the offence and the offender.

A reduction must be considered for a guilty plea – up to a third if the plea was timely (see page 66), and the appropriate announcement made.

Where compensation is awarded this must take priority over fines or costs (see pages 75-77).

The suggested fines in these Guidelines are given as either A, B or C and some example fines are given on page 85. This guidance should not be used as a tariff and every offender's means must be individually considered.

Where a defendant is to be fined for several offences and his means are limited it may be better to fix the relevant fine level for the most serious offence and order 'no separate penalty' on the lesser matters.

It is useful if the defendant can be given a document which sets out the total fines, rate of payment, date of first payment and place of payment before leaving the court.

Assessing means

Before fixing the amount of any fine the Criminal Justice Act 1991 s.18 requires the court to inquire into the financial circumstances of the offender so far as they are known.

The means form is the starting point, then any necessary further questioning about income and expenditure can be done by the clerk and/or the magistrates.

The first figure needed is net income – the guideline fines on the chart on page 85 are based on income net of tax and national insurance contributions. An assessment should then be made of the

disposable or spare income left to the offender after unavoidable ordinary living expenses, such as food, housing, clothing, council tax and essential services have been deducted.

The court should discover whether the offender has savings or other disposable or realisable capital assets.

The financial circumstances of third parties, eg. other members of the family, are irrelevant, save insofar as the offender derives income or benefit from such persons.

Before the actual fine has been announced, enquiry should be made to establish the extent of any outstanding fines and consideration as to the appropriate course of action, which may be to transfer the fine to be collected by the local court.

If for any reason the magistrates are not satisfied with the information they have received, and they feel they cannot sentence until they have such information, they may adjourn the case for further information to be supplied, and they may make a financial circumstances order requiring a statement of means to be provided, Criminal Justice Act 1991 s.20.

The fine is payable in full on the day and the defendant should always be asked for immediate payment. If periodic payments are allowed, the fine should normally be payable within a maximum of twelve months. It should be remembered however, that for those on very low incomes it is often unrealistic to expect them to maintain weekly payments for as long as a year.

The fine should be a hardship, depriving the offender of the capacity to spend the money on 'luxuries', but care should be taken not to force him or her below a reasonable 'subsistence' level.

Fining in the defendant's absence

If, having been given a reasonable opportunity to inform the court of his means, the offender refuses or fails to do so, the magistrates may draw such inference as to means as they think just in the circumstances. It is inappropriate simply to fine the maximum level.

Costs

The following guidance was given by the Court of Appeal in R. v. Northallerton Magistrates' Court ex parte Dove:

1. An order for costs to the prosecutor should never exceed the sum which, having regard to the defendant's means and any other financial order imposed upon him, he is able to pay and which it is reasonable to order him to pay.

2. Such an order should never exceed the sum which the prosecutor had actually and reasonably incurred.

3. The purpose of the order is to compensate the prosecutor and not to punish the defendant.

4. The costs ordered to be paid should not in the ordinary way be grossly disproportionate to the fine imposed for the offence. If the total of the proposed fine and the costs sought by the prosecutor exceeds the sum which the defendant could reasonably be ordered to pay, it was preferable to achieve an acceptable total by reducing the sum of costs ordered than by reducing the fine.

5. It is for the defendant to provide the justices with such data relevant to his financial position as would enable them to assess what he could reasonably afford to pay, and if he fails to do so the justices are entitled to draw reasonable inferences as to his means from all the circumstances of the case.

6. It is incumbent on any court which proposed to make any financial order against a defendant to give him a fair opportunity to adduce any relevant financial information and to make any appropriate submissions.

Community penalties

The purpose of a community penalty is to provide a rigorous and effective punishment for an offender whose offence requires more than a financial penalty but is not so serious as to necessitate imprisonment. A community penalty has three principal elements: restriction of liberty, reparation and prevention of re-offending.

Community sentences include:

- attendance centre orders
- probation orders with or without special requirements
- community service orders
- combination orders
- curfew orders

The restrictions on liberty imposed by the sentence must be commensurate with the seriousness of the offence and the order must be the one most suitable for the offender.

It is generally good practice to require a Pre Sentence or Specific Sentence Report when considering whether to impose a community penalty. In ordering such a report the court should indicate its view of the level of seriousness and the aim of the sentence. In pronouncing sentence the court should stress the need of the offender to co-operate and the consequences of breach.

Penalties for breach of a community sentence are:

- a fine of up to £1,000, the order to continue
- community service of up to 60 hours, the order to continue
- revocation and re-sentencing for the original offence (in which case the probable sentence will be custody)
- attendance centre order

See the revised National Standards and the new inter-agency publication *Towards Good Practice – Community Sentences and the Courts.*

The court may ask to be kept informed of the offender's progress under the order.

Electronic monitoring of curfew orders

Curfew orders enforced by electronic monitoring are available for offenders aged sixteen and over.

The curfew order is a community sentence requiring an offender to remain at a specified place from two to twelve hours a day on from one to seven days a week, for a maximum period of six months. The court must obtain and consider information about the proposed curfew address including the attitude of others affected by the order. The order must take account of religious beliefs, employment, education and the requirements of other community orders.

The offender's consent is not required.

The aims of the order are:

- to restrict liberty in a systematic controlled way
- to make it harder for the offender to commit crimes
- to interrupt the pattern of offending by removing the offender from the circumstances of his/her offending
- provide clear evidence of curfew compliance

The order can be used as a stand alone order, in combination with any other community order, or can be added to a pre-existing community order.

When considering whether to impose an order the offence must be assessed by the court to be 'serious enough' – and the level of punishment appropriate. When ordering a Pre-Sentence Report the court must specifically ask the probation service to carry out a curfew assessment even if an 'all options open' report is specified.

Breach of court orders

The breach of court orders should never be treated lightly. They should be rigorously enforced. In making any pronouncement on sentence the breach should be given special mention.

A failure by the court to respond effectively to a breach can:

- erode public confidence in the courts
- undermine the work of the agency supervising the order
- allow the offender to feel he has 'got away with it'

The offender should be clearly told of the seriousness of the offence and, if the court decides to allow an order to continue, be told what is expected of him/her and the likely consequence of any further breach.

In the case of community sentences there are National Standards revised in April 2000 which lay down strict enforcement requirements for the probation service.

The seriousness of any offence should be matched not just by the severity of the sentence but also by the intensity of the enforcement.

Compensation Orders

The Legal Framework

Having assessed the seriousness of the offence, including the impact on the victim, and any aggravating and mitigating factors affecting the offender, the court is under a duty to consider compensation in every case involving death, personal injury, loss or damage (Powers of the Criminal Courts Act 1973 s.35), whether or not an application has been made.

Priorities

If the sentence is to be financial, then the order of priorities is compensation, fine, costs. Compensating the victim is more important than paying money to the state. If the sentence is to be a community penalty, the court should consider carefully the overall burdens placed on the offender if a compensation order is to be made too. If the sentence is to be custody, then a compensation order will be unlikely unless the offender has financial resources available with which to pay.

Giving Reasons

If, having considered making a compensation order, the court decides that it is not appropriate to make one, it has a statutory duty to give its reasons for not ordering compensation.

Limitations on Powers

Magistrates have the power to award compensation for personal injury, loss or damage up to a total of £5,000 for each offence. An exception is where the injury, loss or damage arises from a road accident: a compensation order may not be made in such a case unless there is conviction of an offence under the Theft Act or if the offender is uninsured and the Motor Insurers' Bureau will not cover the loss. If in doubt, seek advice from the clerk. Compensation should only be awarded in fairly clear, uncomplicated cases: if there are disputes and complications, the matter should be left to the civil courts.

No Double Compensation

Any victim may bring a civil action for damages against the offender: if that action is successful, the civil court will deduct the amount paid by the offender under a compensation order. In this way, there should be no double compensation. The same applies where the victim receives a payment under the Criminal Injuries Compensation Scheme. The magistrates' court should therefore take no account of these other possibilities.

Criminal Injuries Compensation Board

The Criminal Injuries Compensation Scheme provides state compensation for the victims of crimes of violence, particularly those who are seriously injured. The minimum award is currently £1,000. Courts are encouraged to make compensation orders, whether or not the case falls within the Criminal Injuries Compensation Scheme, in order to bring home to offenders themselves the consequences of their actions.

The Purpose of Compensation Orders

The purpose of making a compensation order is to compensate the victim for his or her losses. The compensation may relate to offences taken into consideration, subject to a maximum of £5,000 per charge. Compensation for personal injury may include compensation for terror, shock or distress caused by the offence. The court must have regard to the means of the offender when calculating the amount of the order. Up to three years can be allowed for the compensation to be paid in certain cases.

The Approach to Compensation

In calculating the gross amount of compensation, courts should consider compensating the victim for two types of loss. The first, sometimes called "special damages", includes compensation for financial loss sustained as a result of the offence – e.g. the cost of repairing damage, or in cases of injury, any loss of earnings or dental expenses. If these costs are not agreed, the court should ask for evidence of them. The second type of loss, sometimes called "general damages", covers compensation for the pain and suffering of the injury itself and for any loss of facility.

Calculating the Compensation

The amount of compensation should be determined in the light of medical evidence, the victim's sex and age, and any other factors which appear to the court to be relevant in the particular case. If the court does not have sufficient information, then the matter should be adjourned to obtain more facts.

The Table on the next page gives some general guidance on appropriate starting points for general damages.

Once the court has made a preliminary calculation of the appropriate compensation, it is required to have regard to the means of the offender before making an order. Where the offender has little money, the order may have to be scaled down significantly. However, even a compensation order for a fairly small sum may be important to the victim.

Type of injury	Description	Starting point
Graze	Depending on size	Up to £75
Bruise	Depending on size	Up to £100
Black eye		£125
Cut: no permanent scar	Depending on size and whether stitched	£100-£500
Sprain	Depending on loss of mobility	£100-£1,000
Finger	Fractured little finger, recovery within month	£1,000
Loss of non-front tooth / Loss of front tooth	Depending on cosmetic effect	£500-£1,000 / £1,500
Eye	Blurred or double vision	£1,000
Nose	Undisplaced fractured of nasal bone	£1,000
Nose	Displaced fracture of bone requiring manipulation	£1,500
Nose	Not causing fracture but displaced septum requiring sub-mucous resection	£2,000
Facial scar	However small, resulting in permanent disfigurement	£1,500
Wrist	Simple fracture, recovery within month	£3,000
Wrist	Displaced fracture, limb in plaster, recovery in 6 months	£3,500
Leg or arm	Simple fracture of tibia, fibula, ulna or radius, recovery within month	£3,500
Laparotomy	Stomach scar 6-8 inches (resulting from operation)	£3,500

Environmental Protection Act 1990

Health and Safety at Work Act 1974

Legislation

The main environmental protection and drinking water offences are:

- Section 23 Environmental Protection Act 1990 – carrying on a prescribed process without, or in breach of, authorisation in integrated pollution control and local authority air pollution control.
- Section 33 Environmental Protection Act 1990 – deposition, recovering or disposing of waste without a site licence or in breach of its conditions.
- Sections 33 and 34 Environmental Protection Act 1990 – fly-tipping (offence is aggravated by dangerous or offensive material, tipping near housing etc., escape of waste, intention to avoid paying landfill tax.
- Section 85 Water Resources Act 1991 – polluting controlled waters.
- Section 70 Water Industry Act 1991 – supplying water unfit for human consumption.

The main health and safety offences are :

- Section 33 Health and Safety at Work Act 1974, sub-sections (1) (g) and (o) – failing to comply with an improvement or prohibition notice, or a court remedy order.
- Section 33(1) (a) – breaching general duties in sections 2 to 6 Health and Safety at Work Act.
- Section 33(1) (c) – breach of health and safety regulations or licensing conditions.

It is important to seek guidance from the clerk in all these serious cases. The Court of Appeal, in R v F. Howe and Son (Engineers) Ltd (CA 6.11.98 [1997] Crim LR 238, gave guidance on health and safety sentencing.

Seriousness

Offences under these Acts are serious, especially where the maximum penalty in the magistrates' court is £20,000. Imprisonment is available for some offences. It is important to be careful when accepting jurisdiction as to whether the cases ought properly to be heard in the Crown Court. This is especially so when dealing with large companies. In R v How, the Court of Appeal said that a fine needs to be large enough to bring home to those who manage a company, and their shareholders, the need to protect the health and safety of workers and the public. If a guilty plea is made, again a committal for sentence under section 38 would seem more appropriate. Simple cases can, of course, be dealt with. Matters to consider when assessing seriousness include:

- Offence deliberate breach of the law rather than carelessness
- Financial motive – profit or cost-saving or neglecting to put in place preventative measures or avoiding payment for relevant licence
- Considerable potential for harm to workers or public
- Regular or continuing breach, not isolated lapse
- Failure to respond to advice, cautions or warning from regulatory authority
- Death or serious injury or ill-health has been a consequence of the offence
- Ignoring concerns raised by employees or others
- Having knowledge of risks, but ignoring them
- Previous offences
- Extent of damage and cost of rectifying it
- Attitude to the enforcing authorities
- Offending pattern

Costs: follow event. Consider fine first and then costs.

Computing penalties for a company: Look at net turnover.

Racially Aggravated Offences

The present position on sentencing for racial harassment and racially aggravated offences has been substantially clarified by the Crime and Disorder Act 1998. As previously stated, the new offences have been created by s.29-s.32 which carry increased maximum sentences when compared with the basic offences from which they are derived. The increase in maximum sentence must lead sentencers to reach a provisional sentence in excess of the appropriate one for the basic offence. Parliament has given a specific message to sentencers that it expects those who have been convicted of offences which are defined as having a racial element to receive higher tariff penalties. Conversely, as indicated, if there is a conviction for one of the non-aggravated offences, the sentence must be on the basis that the offence was not racially aggravated otherwise the decision would amount to sentencing for a more serious offence than the one for which the offender has been convicted.

Fine enforcement

Unless an offender is appearing at the fine enforcement court because a review date was fixed when the fine was imposed, he will be either answering to a summons or on a warrant following a summons; in both instances he will probably have also had a reminder (court practices differ in this respect).

The court should first receive a history of the case(s): the offence, the original means form, the date of the sentence, the order of the court regarding payment and the record of payment to date.

Then, an up-to-date means form should be considered, followed by questioning by the clerk and/or the magistrates to establish any change of circumstances since the fine was imposed and the reason given for the failure to pay as ordered.

The court can remit fines after a means enquiry and may order it if the court 'thinks it just to do so having regard to a change of circumstances' which may reasonably be found where:

- The defaulter's means have changed
- Information available to the court on a means enquiry was not before the sentencing court
- Arrears have accumulated by the imposition of additional fines to a level which makes repayment of the total amount within a reasonable time unlikely

- Defaulters are serving a term of imprisonment, remission may be a more practical alternative than the lodging of concurrent warrants of imprisonment
- Compensation and costs cannot be remitted but in circumstances where payment is unlikely or impractical due to the defaulter's means or circumstances then victims and claimants should be consulted about enforcement

The Magistrates' Courts Act 1980 section 82 requires that before a court may issue a warrant of commitment for non-payment of fines it must have: 'considered or tried all other methods of enforcing payment of the sum and it appears to the court that they are inappropriate or unsuccessful'. The court must record the reasons for not trying each of the methods.

The options are:

- **Money Payment Supervision Order:** for those under 21 years of age the court must place the defaulter under such an order (before making any decision to submit to detention) unless satisfied it is undesirable or impracticable so to do.
- **Attendance Centre Order:** for under 25 year olds only. It requires a defaulter to attend for two or three hours on a Saturday at a local attendance centre. The total number of hours must not exceed 24 if the defaulter is under 16, or 36 when he/she is 16 or over.
- **Deduction from Benefit:** the maximum the DSS will deduct is currently £2.60 per week and only if there is no more than one current deduction already in existence.
- **Attachment of Earnings Order:** the order requires an employer to make periodical payments from the defaulter's earnings to the court so this method is only suitable where the defaulter is

---

Road Traffic Offences

Disqualification

Some offences carry mandatory disqualification. This mandatory disqualification period may be automatically lengthened by the existence of certain previous convictions and disqualifications.

Sentencers should not disqualify in the absence of the defendant but should take steps to ensure the defendant attends the court.

Penalty points and disqualification

All penalty points offences carry also as an alternative discretionary power to disqualify for a selected period and also discretionary power to disqualify until a test is passed.

The number of variable penalty points or the period of disqualification is targeted strictly at the seriousness of the offence and in either case must not be reduced below the statutory minimum, where applicable.

Penalty points and (non-totting) disqualification cannot be awarded for the same offence, or even for offences being convictions on the same occasion.

Disqualifications for less than 56 days

A disqualification for less than 56 days is also more lenient in that it does not revoke the licence and cannot increase subsequent mandatory periods unless it is imposed under the points provisions.

Discount for guilty plea

The precise amount of discount for a timely guilty plea will depend on the facts of each case. It should be given in respect of the fine or periods of community penalty or custody, but does not apply to mandatory periods of disqualification.

The multiple offender

Where an offender is convicted of several offences committed on one occasion, it is suggested that the court should concentrate on the most serious offence, carrying the greatest number of penalty points or period of disqualification.

The application of the totality principle may then result in less than the total of the suggested amounts of fines for the remaining individual offences, or the court may decide to impose no separate penalty for the lesser offences.

Totting

Repeat offenders who reach 12 points or more within a period of three years become liable to a minimum disqualification for 6 months, and in some instances 12 months or 2 years – but must be given an opportunity to address the court and/or bring evidence to show why such disqualification should not be ordered or should be reduced. Totting disqualifications, unlike other disqualifications, erase all penalty points.

Totting disqualifications can be reduced or avoided for exceptional hardship or other circumstances. No account is to be taken of non-exceptional hardship or circumstances alleged to make the offence(s) not serious. No such ground can be used again to mitigate totting, if previously taken into account in totting mitigation within the three years preceding the conviction.

Driver – not supplying details

This offence is now prevalent and must be regarded more seriously.

New drivers

From June 1997, newly qualified drivers who tot up 6 points or more during a two year probationary period from the date of passing the driving test will automatically have their licence revoked and will have to apply for a provisional licence until they pass a repeat test. The totting must also include any points imposed prior to passing the test provided they are within three years.

Goods Vehicles over 3.5 tonnes, buses and coaches

Owners and drivers of such vehicles are often in the average or high income scale. If, exceptionally, low income is applicable, seek documentary evidence and reduce the fine as appropriate.

Fixed penalties

If a fixed penalty was offered, consider any reasons for not taking up and, if valid, fine the amount of the appropriate fixed penalty and endorse if required, considering whether costs should be waived.

in settled employment. A protected earnings rate needs to be fixed together with a normal deduction rate, after enquiring into the defendant's means and needs and obligations.

- **Distress Warrant:** authorises the bailiffs to seize goods belonging to the defaulter and sell them in order to pay the fine, together with the bailiff's costs. Its issue may be postponed on terms.

- **Imprisonment:** the court must conduct a means enquiry before finding culpable neglect or wilful refusal to pay. An opportunity must be provided for legal representation. The aim in fixing a period of commitment should be to identify the shortest period which is likely to succeed in obtaining payment and the periods prescribed in schedule 4 of the Magistrates' Courts Act 1980 (set out below) should be regarded as maxima rather than the norm. The period of imprisonment may be suspended pending regular payments.

Maximum periods of imprisonment in default of payment

An amount not exceeding £200	7 days
An amount exceeding £200 but not exceeding £500	14 days
An amount exceeding £200 but not exceeding £1,000	28 days
An amount exceeding £1,000 but not exceeding £2,500	45 days
An amount exceeding £2,500 but not exceeding £5,000	3 months
An amount exceeding £5,000 but not exceeding £10,000	6 months
An amount exceeding £10,000	12 months

Notes

Warrants of overnight detention: the defaulter can be held overnight in the police station. He must be released at eight o'clock the following morning or the same morning if arrested after midnight.

Search: magistrates can order the defaulter to be searched and any money found on him/her to be used to pay the fine.

EXAMPLE GUIDELINE FINES

Based on weekly income net of Tax and National Insurance

Decrease/ increase according to income	NET WEEKLY INCOME – £s								
	100	130	160	190	220	250	300	350	400
FINE A	50	65	80	95	110	125	150	175	200
FINE B	100	130	160	190	220	250	300	350	400
FINE C	150	195	240	285	330	375	450	525	600

If the offence is aggravated, but not serious enough for a community penalty, INCREASE the fine.
If there are mitigating elements, REDUCE the fine

REDUCE IF GIVING SOME DISCOUNT FOR A TIMELY GUILTY PLEA – SEE PAGE 66

IF THERE IS INSUFFICIENT INCOME TO PAY A FINE AND COMPENSATION,
CONSIDER ORDERING ONLY THE COMPENSATION – SEE PAGE 75

Stating the reasons for sentence

1. We are dealing with an offence of:

   ....

2. We have considered the impact on the victim which was ....

   ....

3. We have taken into account the following aggravating features of the offence:

   ....

   ....

4. And the following mitigating features of the offence:

   ....

   ....

5. (where relevant) We have taken into account that the offence was:

   racially aggravated

   committed on bail

6. We have taken into account your previous record, specifically the offences of ....

   and your failure to respond to the sentences imposed.

7. We have taken into account the following matters in mitigation:

   ....

   ....

8. We have taken into account the fact that you pleaded guilty [at an early stage] [but not

   until ....] and we have reduced the sentence accordingly.

9. And, as a result, we have decided that the most appropriate sentence for you is:

   ....

10. (where relevant) We have decided not to award compensation in this case because:

   ....

Issue September 2000

Appendix D: Penalty Points and Disqualification

OFFENCE CODES—ENDORSEMENTS AND DISQUALIFICATION   Revised 2003

Where a court orders a driving licence to be endorsed and/or an offender to be disqualified, the details of the offences are coded. The codes appear on driving licences and DVLA printouts: see, generally, *The Sentence of the Court, Chapter 8.* The codes are often abbreviations of the names of offences, e.g.: SP = speeding, CD = careless driving. The offence codes are as follows (March 2003):

CODE	OFFENCE	POINTS

Offences in Relation to Accidents

AC10	Failing to stop after an accident	5 - 10
AC20	Failing to give particulars or to report an accident within 24 hours	5 - 10
AC30	Undefined accident offence	4 - 9

Driving Whilst Disqualified

BA10	Driving whilst disqualified by order of a court	6
BA30	Attempting to drive whilst disqualified by order of a court	6

Careless Driving Offences

CD10	Driving without due care and attention	3 - 9
CD20	Driving without reasonable consideration for other road users	3 - 9
CD30	Driving without due care and attention or without reasonable consideration for other road users	3 - 9
		(mainly Scottish courts)
CD40	Causing death by careless driving when unfit through drink	3 - 11*
CD50	Causing death by careless driving when unfit through drugs	3 - 11*
CD60	Causing death by careless driving with alcohol level above the limit	3 - 11*
CD70	Causing death by careless driving and then failing to provide specimen for analysis	3 - 11*

Dangerous (Formerly Reckless) Driving Offences

DD30	Reckless driving	Replaced by DD40 from 1 July 1992
DD40	Dangerous driving	3 - 11*
DD60	Manslaughter or, in Scotland, culpable homicide while driving a motor vehicle	3 - 11*
DD70	Causing death by reckless driving	Replaced by DD80 from 1 July 1992
DD80	Causing death by dangerous driving	3 - 11*

Drink or Drugs Offences

DR10	Driving or attempting to drive with alcohol concentration above limit	3 - 11*
DR20	Driving or attempting to drive when unfit through drink	3 - 11*
DR30	Driving or attempting to drive and then refusing to provide specimen for analysis	3 - 11*
DR40	In charge of a vehicle with alcohol concentration above limit	10
DR50	In charge of a vehicle when unfit through drink	10
DR60	Failure to provide a specimen for analysis in circumstances other than driving or attempting to drive	10
DR70	Failing to provide specimen for a breath test	4
DR80	Driving or attempting to drive when unfit through drugs	3 - 11*
DR90	In charge of a vehicle when unfit through drugs	10

Insurance Offence

IN10	Using a vehicle uninsured against third party risks	6 - 8

Licence Offences

LC20	Driving otherwise than in accordance with a licence	3 - 6
LC30	Driving after making a false declaration about fitness when applying for a licence	3 - 6
LC40	Driving a vehicle having failed to notify a disability	3 - 6
LC50	Driving after a licence has been revoked or refused on medical grounds	3 - 6

Construction and Use Offences (Vehicles or Parts)

CU10	Using a vehicle with defective brakes	3
CU20	Causing or likely to cause danger by reason of use of unsuitable vehicle or using a vehicle with parts or accessories (excluding brakes, steering or tyres) in dangerous condition	3
CU30	Using a vehicle with defective tyres	3
CU40	Using a vehicle with defective steering	3
CU50	Causing or likely to cause danger by reason of load or passengers	3

Miscellaneous Offences

MS10	Leaving vehicle in a dangerous position	3
MS20	Unlawful pillion riding	3
MS30	Play street offence	2
MS40	Driving with uncorrected defective eyesight or refusing to submit to a test of eyesight	3
		(See also MS70 and MS80)

Miscellaneous Offences (continued)

MS50	Motor racing on the highway	3 - 11*
MS60	Offences not covered by other codes	As appropriate
MS70	Driving with uncorrected defective eyesight	3
MS80	Refusing to submit to an eyesight test	3
MS90	Failure to give information as to identity of driver etc.	

Motorway Offence

MW10	Contravention of special roads regulations (excluding speed limits)	3

Pedestrian Crossing Offences

PC10	Undefined contravention of pedestrian crossing regulations	3 (mainly Scottish courts)
PC20	Contravention of pedestrian crossing regulations with moving vehicles	3
PC30	Contravention of pedestrian crossing regulations with stationary vehicle	3

Speed Limit Offences

SP10	Exceeding goods vehicle speed limit	3 - 6
SP20	Exceeding speed limit for type of vehicle (excluding goods/passenger vehicles)	3 - 6
SP30	Exceeding statutory speed limit on a public road	3 - 6
SP40	Exceeding passenger vehicle speed limit	3 - 6
SP50	Exceeding speed limit on a motorway	3 - 6
SP60	Undefined speed limit offence	3 - 6

Traffic Directions and Signs Offences

TS10	Failing to comply with traffic light signals	3
TS20	Failing to comply with double white lines	3
TS30	Failing to comply with a 'stop' sign	3
TS40	Failing to comply with directions of a constable or traffic warden	3
TS50	Failing to comply with a traffic sign (except 'stop' signs, traffic lights or double white lines)	3
TS60	Failing to comply with school crossing patrol sign	3
TS70	Undefined failure to comply with a traffic direction or sign	3

Aggravated Vehicle Taking

UT50	Aggravated taking of a vehicle	3 - 11*

Special Codes

TT99 *Only* used for disqualification under totting-up procedures.

NE99 Used where points or disqualification are still relevant but endorsement no longer applicable.

AIDING, ABETTING, COUNSELLING, PROCURING These are coded as per the main list of codes above but with zero changed to 2, e.g. UT10 becomes UT12.

CAUSING OR PERMITTING These are coded as per the main list of codes above but with zero changed to 4.

INCITING These are coded as per the main list of codes above but with zero changed to 6 e.g. DD30 becomes DD36.

Periods of Time

These are signified as follows: D = Days, M = Months, Y = Years.

* These offences involve mandatory disqualification except where special reasons are found by a court. The offences then carry 'notional points'—on a range from 3 to 11—i.e. which are imposed if special reasons are found: see, generally, *Chapter 8*.

Appendix E: Fairness, Equal Treatment and Human Rights[1]   Revised 2003

The following notes seek to provide a broad reminder of items that magistrates need to be aware of in order to reinforce their judicial oath and to ensure that no-one leaves court feeling that he or she has been unfairly treated because of his or her gender, race, religion, disability (or for any other reason):

- **listen carefully** to what witnesses/defendants call themselves. To many people their name and whether they are addressed as 'Miss', 'Mrs', 'Dr' etc. may be important. If in doubt, ask the individual how they would like to be addressed, or how they pronounce their name.
- **don't make assumptions** about people based, e.g. on their gender, race, disability, religion or occupation.
- avoid using **inappropriate expressions** such as 'My dear', or describing someone as 'half-caste' or 'coloured';
- avoid making jokes particularly at the expense of someone appearing before the court, or 'humorous' remarks based upon someone's gender, racial origin, physical characteristics etc.
- be prepared to **'remind'** colleagues should they make inappropriate remarks.

Points to Remember

- Generally speaking, people appreciate being addressed accurately and appropriately.
- It is through words and behaviour that we express how we think and feel.
- The inadvertent use of inappropriate words or behaviour may cause offence.
- Some words or phrases once commonplace are no longer acceptable today.
- A fair environment can help to avoid contempt situations (see *Reference Sheet 5*).

Some Further Considerations

Magistrates have a general duty to act fairly, impartially and without bias—in accordance with 'natural justice' and Articles 6 and 14 of the European Convention On Human Rights (below). The Macpherson Inquiry into the death of the black teenager Stephen Lawrence has served to emphasise the nature and prevalence of 'institutional racism'. Indeed, research and experience indicate that through lack of understanding people can give the impression of being discriminatory despite their best efforts. Some years ago, a Crown Court judge said:

You are four coloured men. I do not want you to think for one moment that *if you were four white men* standing here you would be getting a moment less *by way of sentence* than you in fact will get. You are being sentenced for robbery not for the colour of your skin.

On appeal (and leaving aside that 'coloured' is nowadays unacceptable), Lord Justice Roch said:

No doubt this was well intentioned but [the judge] should not have said it. The colour, race, or religion of defendants was wholly irrelevant because all were equal in the eyes of the law, the only exception being made in the case of a public order offence which was racially motivated.

---

[1] Based on information and opinions supplied from a number of sources. In particular the advice of Terry Moore, Richard Powell and Nicholas Stevens is gratefully acknowledged and the text incorporates passages based substantially on their copyright work.

Section 95 Criminal Justice Act 1991

Section 95 reinforces common law principles by requiring the Home Secretary to publish each year such information as he considers expedient for the purposes of facilitating the performance by persons engaged in the administration of criminal justice of their duty to avoid discriminating against any person on the ground of race, sex or any other improper ground. Publications stemming from this provision are usually available through local court offices. Knowledge of such matters and an awareness of their implications are of considerable importance to sentencers and deserve a high priority.

Human Rights

As explained in *Chapter 2*, the European Convention On Human Rights and Fundamental Freedoms provides, in Article 6, for the right to a fair trial and makes clear that the rights and freedoms set out in the Convention must be enjoyed equally by all people. Article 14 states:

The enjoyment of the rights and freedoms set forth in this Convention shall be secured without discrimination on any ground such as sex, race, colour, language, religion, political or other opinion, national or social origin, association with a national minority, property, birth or other status.

This is broader than many statutes on discrimination, covering as it does people of 'other status', Article 14 does not stand alone, but in effect should be related to each of the rights in the Convention and read in conjunction with them.

Reasons for decisions

One way of ensuring fair and proper decisions is to use decision-making structures such as those issued by the Judicial Studies Board. Reasons also serve to demonstrate and reinforce fairness in accordance with both domestic law and European obligations.

Principles governing the giving of reasons in the magistrates' court
In summary, giving reasons has two purposes:

- to ensure that justice is both done and seen to be done by the person to whom the decision is addressed and by the community at large; and
- to enable an aggrieved party to consider whether to exercise any right of appeal.

Basically speaking, magistrates must be able to show that they have properly considered each case on its individual facts and merits. They must identify the facts, issues and submissions in the case; reach a decision in accordance with the law based on their findings; and announce and explain their findings and their decision based on those findings.

Fairness, pronouncements and reasons
Provided that any standard form of words (such as contained in the *Pronouncements*, and *Verdict and Sentence* forms in *Section 5*) is made sufficiently personal to the individual defendant and his or her case, the use of a standardised or general approach is to be encouraged and the outcome unlikely to render proceedings unfair. Such an approach must never take the place of legal advice given (or repeated) in open court by a legal adviser which allows comment by the defendant or his or her representative (see *Chapter 12, Judicial Advice*).

One way of looking at the situation is for magistrates, at appropriate stages in their decision, to ask themselves 'Why are we doing this?' and, when addressing the defendant and other people in court, to translate this into 'We consider/are taking this course *because* ...'. Other points to note are:

- reasons may be given orally but should always be recorded in writing at the time
- in all but the most straightforward cases it would be quite impractical for a chairman not to make use of some written note
- judgement, including reasons, should be given as soon as practicable
- reasons should explain *and not merely seek to justify* what has already been decided
- there is no requirement to deal with each and every argument raised, but reasons should allow an aggrieved party to know what the court considered important and how it dealt with submissions made.

The nature and extent of reasons

This depends on the kind of decision and the circumstances of the case. Given the nature of the magistrates' summary jurisdiction, it is suggested that reasons need not be extensive, at least not in the way comprehensive judgments of the higher courts are on appeal. But they must be proper (i.e. relevant and clear), adequate (i.e. sufficiently detailed) and intelligible (i.e. in language which can be understood by the person to whom the reasons are addressed and other people). They must also deal with the facts, relevant law and any substantial points raised before the court so as to enable the parties to know what conclusion the magistrates reached on the controversial issues. The following approach can be suggested:

- once the court has reached its determination the reasons for it might be reviewed against a threefold test:
  - would a reasonable man or woman with notice of all the facts and representations made to the court be able to understand the decision itself, the basis of that decision, and why any conclusions were reached on disputed facts or contentious submissions?
  - would he or she (with notice of all the facts and representations made to the court) be able to properly consider whether to exercise his or her right of appeal in respect any finding and/or order made by the court?
  - will the individual defendant in the case understand these matters, given his or her individual capacity to comprehend things?

The legal adviser's role in the decision-making and reason-giving process should be in accordance with relevant *Practice Directions* (see *Chapter 12*). Subject to this, it is thus suggested that he or she should:

- facilitate the decision-making process as appropriate by tendering relevant advice including e.g. pointing out any apparent deficiency in the reasoning process, for instance that legally irrelevant considerations appear to have been taken into account or that the conclusion may not be legally supportable; and
- record, in consultation with the magistrates, the reasons for their decision and the main findings of fact and law.

It is also appropriate for the legal adviser to remind the justices of the structured approach to decision-making and relevant guidelines as noted at various points in this handbook. He or she is able to take the justices through such guidance and remind them of evidence and of submissions that may be relevant to the heading under which the court is considering its decision. However, the legal adviser must never become involved in the decision-making process itself. Both the decision and the reasons must always remain those of the magistrates alone.

Where it is impracticable to expect either the legal adviser or the justices to properly conduct the decision-making process in the presence of the accused and his or her representatives, this process may be conducted in private, subject to the adviser's overriding duty to explain any advice he or she gave in open court so as to allow further representations or comments to be made by the parties.

Example of a sentence decision

As noted, decisions must relate to each individual case. Stereotype explanations serve to defeat the object of reaching a fair decision based on the facts and law applicable in individual circumstances. Before announcing sentence,[2] this might be achieved—after the court has gone through the full decision-making process—by the chairman summarising the court's reasons thus:

'XY', you were at an earlier hearing found guilty of assault occasioning actual bodily harm.

The court which found you guilty did, in giving its findings and reasons, stress that this was an unprovoked attack on an innocent passer-by involving a number of punches to his face and ribs. You were also found, by your own admission, to have consumed a considerable amount of alcohol.

The earlier court expressly rejected your contention you had been taunted by the victim or that you were justified in acting in self-defence.

Our usual approach to offences of assault occasioning actual bodily harm is to start by considering a custodial sentence.

The facts of your case do, in fact, make it more serious than the average. We have nevertheless taken full notice of the pre-sentence report prepared by the National Probation Service and what your solicitor has said on your behalf (including your good work record, etc. ...). However, your offence was, itself, clearly so serious that it calls for a custodial sentence and nothing we have heard justifies a lesser sentence.

The chairman would then make the formal pronouncement of sentence, dealing with all statutory and good practice requirements.

---

2 Some courts prefer to give such reasons after pronouncing sentence: seek advice locally.

Appendix F: Offenders Below 18 Years of Age

Revised 2003

The Sentence of the Court deals only with *adult* offenders, i.e. people aged 18 and over. People below that age ('juveniles' or 'youths') are either:

- children: 10 to 13 years of age inclusive; or
- young persons: 14 to 17 years of age inclusive

all of whom normally appear in the youth court not the adult magistrates' court. They may, however, sometimes appear in the magistrates' court, most frequently:

- for remand (often a 'first remand' if no youth court is sitting)
- when jointly charged with someone aged 18 or over
- when charged with aiding, abetting, counselling, procuring, allowing or permitting an offence alleged against a person aged 18 or over (or vice versa, i.e. the adult may be the abettor)
- when charged with an offence arising out of circumstances which are the same as or connected with those giving rise to an offence with which a person aged 18 years or over is charged.

If convicted, the magistrates' court must normally remit a juvenile offender to the youth court for sentence but in certain circumstances it may decide to retain jurisdiction when its sentencing powers are restricted to:

- an absolute discharge or a conditional discharge
- a fine (subject to special maxima 🕮✪)
- binding over the parent or guardian
- a referral order to a youth offending panel to devise an intervention plan (this is now the only option in relation to 'first time offenders' unless a discharge (or in the case of the youth court a custodial sentence) is appropriate 🕮✪.
- any appropriate ancillary orders, e.g. compensation, endorsement, forfeiture.

There is, more often than not, merit in remitting a case to the youth court after conviction unless the outcome is clearly straightforward except where a referral order is the only option and referral to the youth court could thus serve no real or obvious purpose.' Among other considerations:

- youth court magistrates receive special training
- the sentencing powers of the youth court
  —are more flexible and
  —specifically designed for a younger age group
- the statutory guiding principles of the youth court make preventing offending a primary consideration, whilst the 'welfare principle' in the Children and Young Persons Act 1933—to which youth courts are attuned—must be reconciled with the underlying standard of 'just deserts' approach to sentencing. *All courts* are required to have regard to the 1933 Act which states:

> Every court in dealing with a child or young person who is brought before it, either as an offender or otherwise, shall have regard to the welfare of the child or young person, and shall in a proper case take steps for removing him from undesirable surroundings, and for securing that the proper provision is made for his education and training.

- the rules for pre-sentence reports (PSRs) are stricter in relation to youths—meaning that in practice a PSR will *have to be* obtained and there will thus often need to be an adjournment anyway

¹ There may be exceptions, e.g. to link up with other matters in that court, but always nowadays 🕮✪

- a wider range of orders is available in the youth court
- there is a more specific and direct duty to address reparation issues and, in practice, to pursue principles of restorative justice.

A note on publicity
The press is severely restricted concerning what can be reported from the *youth court*. Similarly, when a youth appears in the *adult court* (in whatever capacity) that court may wish to consider using a discretionary power to impose restrictions 🕮✪.

Human Rights Act 1998

As a result of the European Court of Human Rights decision in *T v United Kingdom* (Application 24724/94) and *V v United Kingdom* (Application 24888/94), *The Times*, 17 December 1999 ('the Bulger case'), the then Lord Chief Justice issued a *Practice Direction* to Crown Courts. The principles equally apply to joint trials of adults and juveniles in the magistrates' court.

> Account must be taken of the age, maturity and development (intellectual and emotional) of a juvenile and all aspects of the case. He or she should be exposed to avoidable intimidation, humiliation or distress. The proceedings should thus be adapted and regard had to the welfare of any juvenile.
>
> Accordingly, it can be suggested that a joint trial with an adult should be avoided if at all possible unless, e.g. such a trial would be in the interests of the youth.
>
> When a juvenile does appear in the adult magistrates courts, the procedures should be modified where practicable to follow the spirit of the direction. Hence, a youth should normally be free to sit with his/her family or others in a place permitting informal communication with his/her lawyer and others with whom he or she wants or needs to communicate; any trial should be held in a courtroom in which all the participants are on the same, or almost the same level; and the timetable for any trial must take into account the inability of some youths to concentrate over long periods.
>
> The proceedings should be explained in simple terms, and any trial conducted in terms the young defendant can understand.
>
> Whenever a youth appears before the adult court for trial, those attending should be restricted to a small number: generally, *seek advice* 🕮✪.

Reprimands and Warnings

The statutory system of reprimands and warnings (sometimes called 'final warnings') for people under 18 years of age allows the police to take a graded response to what would, for adults, amount to a caution (i.e. as opposed to prosecution). The chief significance for the adult court is that a juvenile who receives a police warning cannot ordinarily be given a conditional discharge for an offence committed within the following two years—i.e. unless the court is 'of the opinion that there are exceptional circumstances relating to the offence or the offender'. If it does give a conditional discharge it must state that it is of this opinion and why.

Grave Crimes

A youth court can—*at the outset of a case*—and in respect of certain serious (what are termed 'grave') crimes, such as rape, wounding, aggravated burglary or sexual assault, decline altogether to deal with the matter and commit the accused to the Crown Court for trial. The nature of the individual offence, the age of the offender and other relevant considerations are weighed by the youth court to determine whether it should exercise this power pursuant to section 53 Children and Young Persons Act 1933. Certain cases *must* be sent to the Crown Court under this provision, i.e. where homicide is involved.

Index

Overview of the Main Sentencing Disposals Always take advice on the full requirements 📖✋
Always consider **COMPENSATION** at all appropriate points: *Chapter 5*

DISPOSAL	AGE	CRITERIA	MINIMUM (Adults)	MAXIMUM (Adults)	NOTES
DEFERMENT OF SENTENCE	10 yrs upwards	Interests of justice to defer	None	6 months	Consent needed. Defer once only
ABSOLUTE DISCHARGE	10 yrs upwards	'Punishment Inexpedient'			
CONDITIONAL DISCHARGE	10 yrs upwards	'Punishment Inexpedient'	None specified	3 years	
FINE	10 yrs upwards	Punishment Appropriate – but any Compensation will take Priority	None specified	Level 1 £200 Level 2 £500 Level 3 £1,000 Level 4 £2,500 Level 5 £5,000 (Possibly higher)	Based on seriousness of offence *and* offender's 'financial circumstances'
COMMUNITY REHABILITATION ORDER (CRO)	16 yrs upwards	'Serious Enough' **and** Rehabilitation **or** Protecting Public **or** Preventing Re-offending	6 months	3 years	PSR/SSR unless 'unnecessary'. Suitability test. Accredited programmes + added requirements. May need agreement
COMMUNITY PUNISHMENT ORDER (CPO)	16 yrs upwards	Offence Imprisonable **and** 'Serious Enough'	40 hours	240 hours	PSR/SSR unless 'unnecessary'. Suitability test. CPO assessment. Work available.

COMMUNITY PUNISHMENT AND REHABILITATION ORDER (CPRO)	16 yrs upwards	As for both CRO and CPO re these respective parts	40 hours CPO 12 months CRO	100 hours CPO 3 years CRO	As for both CRO and CPO as above
CURFEW ORDER (plus Electronic Monitoring)	16 yrs upwards	'Serious Enough'	2 hours per day / No minimum number of days specified	12 hours per day / Up to 7 days a week for up to 6 months	Information about address and attitude of others affected. Often PSR/SSR
ATTENDANCE CENTRE ORDER (as sentence not as for fine default)	10-20 yrs (24 for default of fine etc.)	Offence Imprisonable **and** 'Serious Enough'	12 hours	36 hours	Centre to be reasonably accessible. PSR not essential
DRUG TREATMENT AND TESTING ORDER (DTTO)	16 yrs upwards	'Serious Enough' **and** Dependent on or propensity to misuse drugs	6 months	3 years	PSR/SSR unless 'unnecessary'. Arrangements to be available. Review hearings
DRUG ABSTINENCE ORDER (DAO)	18 yrs upwards	'Serious Enough'	6 months	3 years	Not yet generally available
EXCLUSION ORDER	10 years upwards	'Serious Enough'	No lower limit specified	2 years	Not yet generally available
IMPRISONMENT	21 yrs upward	Imprisonable **and** 'So Serious' **or** Public Protection (sex/violence)	5 days (or short local detention)	Possibly up to 6 months (12 months if 2 or more either way offences)	PSR/SSR unless 'unnecessary'. May suspend 1-2 yrs if 'exceptional circumstances'
YOUNG OFFENDER INSTITUTION	18-20 yrs	As above	21 days	As above	As above but cannot suspend

AN OPEN INVITATION

The Waterside A to Z of Criminal Justice and Penal Affairs is scheduled for publication towards the end of 2003.

The work—which is currently in progress—already contains over 15,000 entries comprising words, phrases, acronyms, abbreviations, explanations and items of interest about criminal justice and penal affairs.

The entries are both current and historical covering important landmarks, key developments, trials, cases, events, issues, publications and people who have made a significant contribution to the system as it is today.

Each entry consists of one or more paragraphs (entries are sometimes longer depending on the subject matter). The work is cross-referenced so that connections can be made between related (and sometimes not so obviously-related) subjects.

The work builds on experience of writing, editing and publishing in this field over many years—including some 200 Waterside Press projects alone since 1989. The aim is for the *A to Z* to be a comprehensive, interesting, useful and functional collection of concise explanations.

No matter how extensive the research, there is always 'yet another' area to explore. If you think that you have a topic, issue or information which might be included—perhaps something that you felt could, or should, have been explained to you at some point, or which still puzzles or perplexes you—you are invited to email a brief note to editorial@watersidepress.co.uk (or you can write to Bryan Gibson at Waterside Press, Domum Road, Winchester SO23 9NN) when an item will be considered for inclusion (if too late for the first edition, then in subsequent ones).

For further details of *The Waterside A to Z of Criminal Justice and Penal Affairs* (and other publications from the growing Waterside Press list) please visit **www.watersidepress.co.uk** or contact us on 01962 855567 or at the address given above.